Studies of the New Testament and Its World

EDITED BY JOHN RICHES

The Second and Third Epistles of John

The Second and Third Epistles of John: History and Background

by

JUDITH LIEU

edited by

JOHN RICHES

T. & T. CLARK
59 GEORGE STREET
EDINBURGH

Typeset by C. R. Barber & Partners, Fort William,
printed by Billing & Sons, Worcester,
bound by Hunter & Foulis Ltd, Edinburgh

for

T. & T. CLARK LTD, EDINBURGH
First printed 1986

British Library Cataloguing in Publication Data

Lieu, Judith
The Second and Third Epistles of John:
history and background.——(Studies of the
New Testament and its world)
1. Bible. N.T. Epistles of John, 2nd——
Criticism, interpretation, etc. 2. Bible.
N.T. Epistles of John, 3rd——Criticism,
interpretation, etc.
I. Title   II. Series
227′.9506   BS2805.2
ISBN 0-567-09443-X

Contents

Preface   ix
Introduction   1

Chapter One: Acceptance into the Canon   5
  'The letter' of John   6
  Doubts about 2 and 3 John   10
  1 and 2 John   18
  Acceptance of Three Letters of John   30

Chapter Two: Letters or Epistles?   37

Chapter Three: The Letters of the 'Presbyter'   52
  The 'Presbyter'   52
  2 John   64
  3 John   101

Chapter Four: 'If anyone comes . . .'   125
  The Early Church Background   125
  The Johannine Background   135
  The Outcome in 2 and 3 John   148

Chapter Five: The Johannine 'Gospel'?   166
  Tradition and Spirit   171
  The Community in History and the World   180
  The Believer and the Community   190
  The Role of Jesus   198
  Conclusion   205

Appendix I: Tables   217
Appendix II: Text and Parallels   223

Bibliography:
1. Texts and Sources   230
2. Secondary Works   230

Indexes:
Biblical References   248
Ancient Authors and Sources   256
Modern Authors   258
Subjects   262

Preface

During my post-graduate research my confession that I was working on 2 and 3 John often brought the surprised question, 'Why 2 and 3 John?' My only answer was to turn the question back to the questioner – 'Why 2 and 3 John? What are they doing in the New Testament? How did they get there? What are they and why were they written? For what are they evidence?' This study asks and seeks to answer those questions, and the answers become windows through which we can gain a new perspective on wider issues of the New Testament, and particuarly the Johannine, literature and world.

The book began life as a doctoral dissertation for the University of Birmingham completed in 1980. I owe a special debt to my supervisor, Dr. Frances M. Young, who was not only an unfailing source of advice and criticism but who also acted as a sounding board against which I could develop my own ideas and understanding. Professor C.K. Barrett first encouraged me to compensate for some of the neglect 2 and 3 John have often suffered and to approach the Johannine tradition through their detailed study; his continued active interest in my work has been an invaluable help and stimulus. I would also like to thank Professor J.N. Birdsall for specific points of advice and information.

The task of revision was begun while I was teaching at The Queen's College, Birmingham. I am deeply grateful to the staff and students there in that what I lacked in time to proceed very fast was more than compensated for by the continual provocation to relate the rigours of Biblical study to the needs and questions of the modern church; to my colleagues at King's College I owe thanks for the time to complete the task.

John Riches's encouragement to me to revise the original thesis for inclusion in this series acted as a very necessary incentive; I am grateful for that and for his long patience in awaiting the finished product. It is due in no small part to my husband, Samuel's, confidence in my research, to his loving care and much practical help that the book is now finished. It is to my parents, whose support and interest has never flagged, that I would like to dedicate this study.

Abbreviations

Abbreviations of periodicals and series etc. follow those of *Theologische Realenzyklopädie: Abkürzungsverzeichnis*, ed. S. Schwertner, Berlin & New York 1976.

Introduction

Our first chapter begins with some words of Bede that although some considered 2 and 3 John not to be the work of the Apostle John, 'the general consensus of the church' had now decided in favour of apostolic authorship; it ends with Cosmas Indicopleustes's perfunctory dismissal of 2 and 3 John as unnecessary for the perfect Christian who can find all his needs met by the 'commonly accepted' books. Herein lies the problem of 2 and 3 John within the New Testament—what are they about, from where did they come, why were they accepted and what has been or still is the use of such short and apparently inconsequential letters?

The primary purpose of this study is to answer these questions, and this will mean examining 2 and 3 John in their own right and not, as is so often the case, in the shadow of, and along lines determined by, the Gospel and First Epistle. From different perspectives they can be viewed within the canon of the New Testament, as letters, against the background in the life of the early church which provides a context for the situation they reflect, and finally within the theology of the Johannine literature. Yet when we do this we find ourselves not in a minor backwater of the New Testament but facing some of the most central issues in its study, issues which are not only of historical reconstruction and methodology, but which are fundamentally theological.

Easily passed over and rarely cited to establish the great doctrines or spiritual insights of the church, 2 and 3 John confront us with some of the basic questions as to what forces led the early church, by exclusion or by affirmation, to draw boundaries and to achieve what has been called 'normative self-definition'.[1] The traditional answer has been to describe the

[1] For the term and for the issue see *Jewish and Christian Self-definition* (3 vols.), ed. E.P. Sanders et. al., London 1980–82, especially vol. 1.

development of canon, creed and church ministry—each of which is germane to 2 and 3 John; yet it has become increasingly clear that this account itself gives rise to innumerable questions as to how these particular 'fences' came to take the form they do.

A presupposition of much current research into the New Testament and early church is that the answers to our questions will not only appeal to overtly theological factors but that there are also social—in the widest possible sense—elements or perspectives. Yet such 'sociological' factors are rarely explicitly discussed by our sources, for their avowed purpose lies elsewhere, and we are left with the necessity of reconstruction and hypothesis. All this is true of 2 and 3 John both in their origins and in their history in the church.

We start to explore their origins and use by following their path to acceptance within the New Testament canon. Here in particular they illustrate the hesitancy with which some parts of the New Testament achieved that status. They reveal too that the process towards acceptance was not a linear one but was made up of many strands; more importantly, they show that the question whether some parts of the New Testament are more central than others has been a consistently recurring one—a question which invites not only a historical but also a theological answer. The question of apostolic authorship is no longer a leading issue in modern discussion of the canon. Instead this centres on content or message—how far each book contains the essential 'gospel', however that be defined—or on how the recognised diversity within the New Testament can be held together and interpreted.[2] Yet when the issue is posed in these

[2] See the various approaches represented in *Das Neue Testament als Kanon*, ed. E. Käsemann, Göttingen 1970; also K. Aland, *The Problem of the New Testament Canon*, London 1962, and E. Best, 'Scripture, Tradition and the Canon of the New Testament', *JRLB* 61 (1978/9) 258–89. Characteristic of one approach today are the words of E. Käsemann, *The Testament of Jesus*, London 1968, 76, 'The authority of the canon is never greater than the authority of the Gospel which should be heard from it'.

terms 2 and 3 John still invite judgement; we may follow Bede
and accept the decision of the church and then have to make
sense of the place of 2 and 3 John in the canon; an alternative
may be to ask how clearly the proclamation of the gospel is
heard in them and whether with Cosmas we must acknowledge
their peripheral character and practical disuse.[3]

When we go on to examine the content and significance of 2
and 3 John we soon recognise that both talk about the exclusion
of other 'Christians'—in one it is advocated against discredited
claimants to the status, in the other it has been experienced by
the author and his supporters. Here too we meet the church
drawing boundaries, deciding who is 'in' or 'out', not without
contention. Matters of faith ('creed') and church leadership are
undoubtedly involved but the origins and status of both are
unclear. Exploring these will take us into questions of the
development of authority structures, of the social tensions and
conflict between different types of lifestyle and leadership, of the
role of the household-church, and of patterns of control
including not only the more obvious 'creeds' but also the use of
letters themselves. All these are areas which have been the object
of enthusiastic attention in recent New Testament scholarship,
in recognition of the interaction between theological
perspectives and social factors in the origins and growth of the
Christian church—although that enthusiastic attention has
often been directed elsewhere in the New Testament than to 2
and 3 John.

Yet in the end, these two letters will make little sense if it is
forgotten that they are 'Johannine'. Although their relationship
with the Gospel and First Epistle of John is a less contentious
issue than once it was, its importance is that it demonstrates that
the discovery of social factors cannot become an alternative to
the recognition of theological factors; theological climate is part

[3] See ch. 1, p. 36 and n. 112.

of the social world in the New Testament. How far does our knowledge of John and 1 John help us understand the two minor Epistles; how far do the latter throw light on the Gospel and First Epistle? If we decide that they are 'Johannine' is this only a literary and historical statement or is it also a theological judgement in the same way as a discussion of the 'Pauline' nature of the Pastorals can so easily become?

The central focus of our exploration of the 'problem of 2 and 3 John' must be the detailed study and exegesis of the two Epistles. Much else of the argument, inevitably based as it is on inference and comparison, depends for its conviction on the foundation of that exegesis. The picture which results of 2 and 3 John within the New Testament and Johannine literature will be important for our understanding of the history of one part of the Christian church. But in any study of the Johannine literature theological questions are never very far away. If it is *possible* to describe the historical process, even the history of a theology, while refraining from theological judgement,[4] is it always *proper* to do so? Or does such a description within the framework of New Testament theology lead to theological insights and invite judgement?[5] This too is a current issue in New Testament study, and perhaps it always has been; we met it here first through Bede and Cosmas, and we shall meet it at the end where historical and theological exploration lead to the asking of new questions.

---

[4] See R. Brown, *The Community of the Beloved Disciple*, London 1979, 106f. who refuses to say whether the position of either the author of 1 John or his opponents was truly derived from the 'proclamation of Christianity available to us through the fourth Gospel' or was a distortion of its meaning; instead he accepts the church's judgement in including 1 John in the canon.

[5] See how Käsemann, *Testament*, starts (3) by declaring that his ultimate aim is not the theological interpretation of the Gospel but the discovery of its historical situation, but ends (77–8) by a clear affirmation of the theological proclamation of the Gospel and its validity.

Chapter One

ACCEPTANCE INTO THE CANON

'Some think that this and the following letter are not of John the Apostle but of a certain John the Presbyter, whose tomb has been pointed out in Ephesus up to the present day. Indeed, Papias, a hearer of the Apostles and bishop in Hierapolis, frequently mentions him in his works. But now the general consensus of the church is that John the Apostle also wrote these letters.'[1]

The tradition reported here by Bede in the eighth century goes back long before him and has found its advocates periodically up to the present; it provides a starting point for our exploration of the place of 2 and 3 John in the New Testament canon. How was this 'general consensus' achieved and why had some suggested alternative theories of the Epistles' origin? Similar questions could well be asked of some of the other books of the New Testament and the variety of routes towards recognition which 2 and 3 John followed provides a good illustration of what sometimes seems a haphazard and erratic course in the development of the canon. These are, of course, historical questions about that development and yet, as we shall see, they are inseparable from the particular questions about the background of 2 and 3 John as well as from the wider ones about the nature and also the origins of the New Testament canon.

In tracing that 'erratic course' of these two members of the canon we must proceed with some caution. In view of their brevity and apparent lack of intrinsic interest few modern readers would be surprised that 2 and 3 John are rarely quoted

---

[1] Bede, *Expositio in II Epistolam Iohannis* (CChr.SL 121, 329). See below pp. 13-14.

by the Church fathers; failure to quote need not imply ignorance or rejection of the authority of 2 and 3 John. On the other hand, particularly in the early period, echoes of the language may point to a common tradition rather than literary knowledge, while even proven knowledge need not entail the ascription of any particular authority. Yet despite such caution a picture of the roles of 2 and 3 John in the early church can be sketched and it is a coherent, albeit surprisingly complex, picture.

'The letter' of John

That 1 John should have been mentioned and used before there is any reference to a second or third Epistle is hardly surprising for it is longer and has much more theological content. Whether this may on occasion mean that 2 and 3 John were either not known or not accorded authority is difficult to determine.

Our earliest witnesses come from Asia Minor and their testimony will only leave us with uncertainties. According to Eusebius, Papias, bishop of Hierapolis in the first part of the second century, 'used testimonies from the former letter of John and also that of Peter'.[2] 'Former' is Eusebius's word, not Papias's, and need not suggest Papias knew another Johannine letter.[3] Although Papias has often been linked with the 'Johannine school' via the 'Presbyter John' of Bede's comment, we know nothing of the context or purpose of Papias's 'testimonies' from 1 John.[4] As for his contemporary, Polycarp

[2] Eusebius, *Historia Ecclesiastica* (*HE*) III.39.17 (GCS 9, 292).

[3] Contrast B.F. Westcott, *A General Survey of the History of the Canon of the New Testament*, 7th ed., London 1896, 78 n. 1. Eusebius uses 'former' in his own list in *HE* III.25.2 (GCS 9, 252).

[4] On the 'Presbyter John' see below pp. 55-62. Papias's description of the commandments as 'reaching us from the truth itself' in Eusebius, *HE* III.39.3 (GCS 9, 286) need not show knowledge of 3 Jn 12.

of Smyrna (d. *c.* 156), it has often been remarked that he, although also a disciple of John according to Irenaeus, in his extant letter to the Philippians does not refer to that John or quote from the Gospel ascribed to him. However, in that letter, when warning his readers against heresy, he does echo the language of the Epistles: 'For everyone who *does not* confess *that* Jesus Christ *has come* in the flesh is an antichrist'.[5] This recalls both 1 Jn 4.2, 'Every spirit which confesses Jesus Christ *having come* in flesh is of God', and 2 Jn 7, 'For many deceivers . . . who *do not* confess Jesus Christ *coming* in flesh'; most significantly all three passages link a similar false confession with the 'antichrist', a term which is first found in 1 and 2 John. The wording of these confessions will occupy us at length later; 1 John gives only the positive, 'true' form, while the negative formulation in 2 John is distinguished by its use of the present tense 'coming'. Polycarp shares with 1 John the singular 'he (who)' and the perfect 'has come'—although in using the infinitive (cf. 'that') where 1 John uses a participle, the attack against heresy is made more explicit.[6] Since the negative form is determined by the definition of heresy any allusion need only be to the passage in 1 John without any conscious echo of 2 John. Even so there is nothing to suggest that Polycarp is consciously quoting an authoritative document of the church and this might be nothing more than the use of traditional language against heresy.[7]

During the course of the second century 1 John did become widely known and recognised as 'the letter' of John. We shall return to Irenaeus, Clement of Alexandria and the Muratorian Canon below; in the last named 1 Jn 1:1f. is used in defence of the Fourth Gospel which suggests that it was the more secure of

[5] Polycarp, *Epistle to the Philippians* 7.1, Πᾶς γάρ, ὃς ἂν μὴ ὁμολογῇ Ἰησοῦν Χριστὸν ἐν σαρκὶ ἐληλυθέναι, ἀντίχριστός ἐστιν.

[6] See below pp. 81.

[7] So H. v. Campenhausen, *Polycarp von Smyrna und die Pastoralbriefe*, SHAW, Heidelberg 1951, 41. See also E.C. Hoskyns, *The Fourth Gospel*, ed. F.N. Davey, 2nd ed., London 1947, 99f.

the two. About this time the Alogi rejected the Gospel and Apocalypse of John but did not debate the First Epistle; far from meaning that this was because it was not then given apostolic authority, it may imply it was beyond dispute and created no theological problems for the Alogi.[8] In this context it is appropriate for us to begin to look for evidence of 2 and 3 John.

By the beginning of the third century in Africa 1 John is clearly known, apparently without 2 or 3 John. Tertullian quotes from 1 John as from 'the letter' of the Apostle John to whom he also ascribed the Gospel and the Apocalypse. He explicitly uses the Epistle against heresy and to this end quotes 1 Jn 4.2 in a negative form; of 2 and 3 John as part of the Apostle's work he shows no knowledge.[9] A similar 'negative' use of 1 Jn 4.2 is also found in Cyprian who likewise accepts 1 John as by the Apostle, often introducing it by the formula 'in his letter' (in epistula sua). The failure to specify 'first' could be taken to prove that he only knew of one letter were it not for the fact that later writers who undoubtedly knew 2 and 3 John also used the formula of 1 John.[10] We find a similar situation in references to 1 Peter and, indeed, the phrase is later used of 2 Peter and cannot imply ignorance of the First Epistle.[11] Nonetheless, the phrase may have originated when only one

[8] Epiphanius, *Panarion* LI.34 (GCS 31, 308). P. Corssen, *Monarchianische Prologe zu den vier Evangelien*, TU 15, Leipzig 1896, 50f. suggests that the Alogi did not explicitly reject 1 John because it was not widely given apostolic authority at the time; contrast A. Ehrhardt, 'The Gospels in the Muratorian Fragment', in *The Framework of the New Testament Stories*, Cambridge 1964, 11–36, who argues that 1 John was widely accepted even by the Alogi (p. 32).

[9] e.g. Tertullian, *De Pud.* XIX.10; *Scorp.* XII.4; *De Idol.* II.3 (CChr.SL 2, 1321, 1092, 1102). On the problem of deciding whether quotations are from 1 Jn 4.2 or 2 Jn 7 see below pp. 31-2.

[10] Clement of Alexandria, *Strom.* III.4.32 (GCS 52, 210); Ambrose, *De Fide* I.117 (CSEL 78, 50); Augustine, *De Civ. Dei* XX.8.87 (CChr.SL 48, 714); Cassiodorus, *Expositio in Psal.* 36.25 (CChr.SL 97, 335).

[11] Ambrose, *Explanatio Psal.* XXXVI.2 (CSEL 64, 71) refers to 1 Peter as 'in epistula sua' while *De Inc. Dom.* 82 (CSEL 79, 265) refers to 2 Peter in the same way.

letter ascribed to Peter and to John was known and it is notable that with one exception (see below) the phrase is never used when referring to 2 or to 3 John. However, Cyprian himself makes no use of 2 or 3 John and that silence is most eloquent when in his *Testimonies* he collects proof-texts to establish that 'one should not speak with heretics' yet fails to include 2 Jn 10–11—verses which would make the point rather more forcefully than those he does use.[12]

Even so, even within one province opinions could vary considerably and Cyprian himself must have come to know 2 John even if he never acknowledged its authority by using it himself. At the Council of Carthage held under him in AD 256 to discuss the rebaptism of schismatics, one of the bishops, Aurelius of Chullabi, quoted 2 Jn 10–11 as the work of the Apostle in support of the necessity of rebaptism for admission into the church. It is he who cites it as if from the First Epistle, 'John the Apostle laid down in his letter (in epistola sua) . . .'.[13] The use of these verses then became a recurring theme in the controversies of the area and a source of much debate.[14] The fluidity regarding the writings ascribed to John the Apostle at this time is further underlined by a quotation in Ps. Cyprian, *De*

---

[12] Cyprian, *Testimonia (ad Quirinium)* III.78 (CChr.SL 3, 161f.) is a collection of proof-texts against speaking with heretics (Cum hereticis non loquendum) citing Tit 3.10–11 (identified as Colossians); 1 Jn 2.19; 2 Tim 2.17. However, Cyprian may be working over earlier sources; see R.P.C. Hanson, *Tradition in the Early Church*, London 1962, 261–4. P. Schepens, ' "Iohannes in epistula sua" (Saint Cyprien, *passim*)', *RSR* 11 (1921) 87–9 notes that Cyprian can quote from Romans as 'epistula sua' while knowing other Pauline letters but he does not discuss the evidence of the *Testimonia*.

[13] *Sententiae LXXXVII episcoporum*, 81 (ed. H.F. v. Soden, *Nachrichten von der königlichen Gesellschaft der Wissenschaften zu Göttingen, Phil.-hist. Klasse* 3 (1909) 247–307, 275f.). H.F. v. Soden, *Das Lateinische Neue Testament in Afrika zur Zeit Cyprians*, TU 33, Leipzig 1909, 13 sees Cyprian's failure to refer to 2 John despite its use by Aurelius and Firmilian (see below p. 33 and n. 102) as evidence of the lack of uniformity in respect to the NT canon even within one province.

[14] See below pp. 33-4 and nn. 100–102.

Montibus Sina et Sion, which is often dated before AD 240. In a work most of whose citations are identifiable Scripture it is intriguing to find a quotation from 'John his disciple *ad populum*'; neither the quotation nor the letter can be further identified![15]

Elsewhere in the church we may point to the fact that 2 and 3 John were not translated into Syriac at the same time as 1 John, which no doubt reflects a time and place when they were not known or were rejected, a pattern which continued to characterise the eastern church.[16] The Gnostic writings from Nag Hammadi make use of 1 John but not of the other two letters, but, as is so often the case, these are not settings where we would expect to find 2 or 3 John.[17]

Doubts about 2 and 3 John

The first clear references we do have to a further *pair* of 'Johannine' letters are those which imply some hesitation about their authenticity, no doubt because of their later advent into wide circulation. The first such witness—and therefore our first

[15] Ps. Cyprian, *De Montibus Sina et Sion* 13 (CSEL 3.3, 117), 'in epistula Iohannis discipuli sui ad populum. ita me in vobis videte, quomodo quis vestrum se videt in aquam aut in speculum'. On this see J.E. Bruns, 'Biblical Citations and the Agraphon in Pseudo-Cyprian's Liber De Montibus Sina et Sion', *VigChr* 26 (1972) 112–16. There may be some connection with the *Acts of John* 95–96. See also T. Zahn, *Geschichte des Neutestamentlichen Kanons* (2 vols.), Erlangen 1888–92, I, 217–18, who attributes the growth of doubts about 2 and 3 John in Africa to the appearance of such apocrypha.

[16] See below pp. 15–17.

[17] 1 John seems to be alluded to, for example, in the *Gospel of Philip* (N.H. II.3) and in the *Gospel of Truth* (N.H. I.3) 30.27–31; 36.14–17; 43.14. (English translation in ed. J.M. Robinson, *The Nag Hammadi Library in English*, Leiden 1977, 131–151; 37–49). See R.McL. Wilson, 'The New Testament in the Nag Hammadi Gospel of Philip', *NTS* 9 (1962/3) 291–4. On supposed echoes of 1 John elsewhere in the early church see A.E. Brooke, *A Critical and Exegetical Commentary on the Johannine Epistles*, ICC, Edinburgh 1912, lii–lv.

witness to 3 John—is Origen (d. *c.* 254) who is reported by Eusebius as saying 'he (the Apostle John, author of the Gospel and Apocalypse) also left a letter of very few lines and it may be also a second and a third; but not everyone says these are genuine. However, together they do not come to a hundred lines'.[18] Origen may well have shared these doubts for neither 2 nor 3 John are quoted in his extant works and 1 John is referred to as 'his' or 'the' letter.[19] Origen's wide travels mean we cannot know whether this approach had an Alexandrian origin but certainly it does seem to have had wider influence after him.[20] Only a little later Dionysius of Alexandria confirms that 2 and 3 John were known there although he uses them hesitantly. By a contrast of language and thought he sought to demonstrate that the John of the Apocalypse could not be identified with the Apostle, the accepted author of the Gospel; he points out that neither in the Gospel nor in the Catholic Epistle does the Apostle name himself 'John' (contrast Rev 1.1, 4) and 'not even in the second and third extant letters of John, despite their brevity, is John prefixed by name'.[21] The comment comes as a parenthesis

[18] Origen in Eusebius, *HE* VI.25.10 (GCS 9, 578). M. Müller, 'Die Überlieferung des Eusebius in seiner Kirchengeschichte über die Schriften des NT und deren Verfasser', *ThStKr* 105 (1933) 425–55 suggests that 'ἔστω' (it may be) implies that Origen had only heard of 2 and 3 John.

[19] In *Hom. in Jos.* VII.1 (SC 71, 196) the list of apostolic 'trumpets' implies seven Catholic epistles, including three of John. This is only extant in Rufinus's Latin translation and the question remains open whether the full canon is to be atttributed to Rufinus's editing. See M. Stenzel, 'Der Bibelkanon des Rufin von Aquileja', *Bib.* 23 (1942) 43–61, 52–3. J. Ruwet, 'Les "Antilegomena" dans les oeuvres d'Origène', *Bib.* 23 (1942) 18–42 argues without proof that Origen did not share the doubts he knew concerning Hebrews, James, 2 and 3 John and Jude.

[20] Zahn, *Geschichte*, I, 215 believes that Origen's position reflects his travels rather than that of Alexandria. However, that 3 John is first mentioned in Alexandria has been used as evidence of the Epistles' Alexandrian origin; see J.J. Gunther, 'The Alexandrian Gospel and Letters of John', *CBQ* 41 (1979) 581–603, 602.

[21] Dionysius of Alexandria in Eusebius, *HE* VII.25.7ff. (GCS 9, 692ff.).

in an argument otherwise entirely dependent on the Gospel and 1 John and the strange use of 'extant' (φερομένη) and of passive verbs (as 'is prefixed') may suggest some doubt in their use.[22]

Eusebius's adoption of this position, possibly influenced by Origen, is explicit. In his *Ecclesiastical History* (*c.* 300) 1 John and 1 Peter are included among the 'recognised' books, accepted in the past and the present without opposition, while 2 and 3 John with the remaining Catholic Epistles belong to those which are 'disputed' (ἀντιλεγόμενοι) but 'known' (γνωρίμοι). His description of them as 'the so-called second and third of John, whether they are of the Evangelist or some other of the same name' shows that despite the anonymity of the text their attribution to 'John' was accepted but that silence by earlier writers had led to the questioning of its reference and also of the status of the letters in the church.[23]

Jerome (342–420) witnesses to the continuation of this tradition in the West, now with a suggestion as to the true identity of the author. In his account *Of Illustrious Men* 18, after quoting a famous passage of Papias which refers to a John the Elder (also found in Eusebius, *HE* III.39.3–4),[24] he says 'From this catalogue of names it appears that the John who is placed among the apostles is other than the John the Elder whom he lists after Aristion. I say this because of the opinion mentioned above which we reported as handed down by many that the two later Epistles of John are not of the Apostle but of the Presbyter'. The reference is to his earlier (ch. 9) ascription of the

---

[22] The reference to 2 and 3 John reads (ibid. VII.25.11), 'ἀλλ' οὐδὲ ἐν τῇ δευτέρᾳ φερομένῃ καὶ τρίτῃ, καίτοι βραχείαις οὔσαις ἐπιστολαῖς, ὁ Ἰωάννης ὀνομαστὶ πρόκειται, 'ἀλλὰ ἀνωνύμως "ὁ πρεσβύτερος" γέγραπται'.

[23] Eusebius, *HE* III.25.2f. (GCS 9, 250). Rufinus's translation omits 'so-called' ὀνομαζομένη; see Stenzel, 'Bibelkanon', 56. In *HE* III.24.17 (ibid.) Eusebius says 1 John has been acknowledged without dispute by those of the present and of the past.

[24] See below ch. 3, p. 55 and n. 11.

Gospel to John the Apostle of whom he said 'he also wrote one Epistle whose opening is "What was from the beginning ... concerning the word of Life", which is acknowledged by learned men of the church everywhere. As for the other two whose openings are "The elder to the elect lady and her children", and, of the next, "The elder to the beloved Gaius whom I love in truth", these are said to be of John the Presbyter. For to this very day the other tomb at Ephesus is pointed out as his; however, some think that both the memorials are of the same person, John the Evangelist'.[25] That Jerome elsewhere quotes 2 and 3 John as by the Apostle suggests he did not share the doubts he reports.[26]

The development of the tradition of two Johns is an interesting one. Dionysius of Alexandria found in the report of two 'memorials' of John in Ephesus a possible answer to his search for a second John to whom to attribute Revelation. Eusebius combined this report, known perhaps only from Dionysius, with the reference to 'John the Elder' in the ambiguous passage from Papias and assigned both the second memorial and, tentatively, Revelation to this John.[27] The further step of identifying the 'Elder' of 2 Jn 1 and 3 Jn 1 with this same John is then taken or reported by Jerome, although he in turn may have been dependent on Eusebius for knowledge both of his existence in the excerpt from Papias and of his

[25] Jerome *De Viris Illustribus* 18; 9 (ed. G. Herding, Leipzig 1924, 22, 15). On the translation of 'Elder' by 'senior' see below p. 31.

[26] For Jerome's use of 2 and 3 John see *Epist.* 123.11; 146.1 (CSEL 56, 84, 310); *Comm. in Ep. ad Titum* I.8–9 (PL 26:602–3). This did not stop later writers appealing to him for the ascripton of 2 and 3 John to 'the Presbyter John'; see below pp. 35-6 and n. 110.

[27] Eusebius's own reference to the two 'memorials' in *HE* III.39.6 repeats almost word for word the account by Dionysius of Alexandria which he reports in VII.25.16 (GCS 9, 288, 696). B. Kötting, *Peregrinatio Religiosa*, Münster 1950, 173–4 suggests that there were two 'memorials' to John—a tomb outside the city walls and the house where he lived.

tomb.[28] He then became the source for the continuation of the tradition in later commentators, including Isidore of Seville, Bede and Oecumenius, and, with increasing confidence, for its revival at the Reformation and so to the present day.[29] Thus legend and hypothesis became 'fact'—but it is a markedly tenuous tradition and one which, as we shall see, does not bear much scrutiny.[30]

Doubts about 2 and 3 John had made their home in the West; in a Roman list probably emanating from a council held under Pope Damasus in AD 382 one epistle among the 'epistulae canonicae' is attributed to John the Apostle and two to John the Presbyter, a distinction removed in the later editing of the text.[31] Whether or not Jerome's influence is to be seen, the canonical status of the letters does not seem to be effected. However, in the fourth century 'Cheltenham List' (*Canon Mommsensiensis*), where three Epistles of John and two of Peter are listed, the scribe has written under each 'one only', presumably in rejection of 2 and 3 John and of 2 Peter.[32]

---

[28] See above. On Jerome's dependence on Eusebius in the *De Viris Illustribus* see J.N.D. Kelly, *Jerome*, London 1975, 174–8.

[29] Isidore of Seville, *De Eccl. Officiis* I.12.12 (PL 83:750); on Bede see p. 1 and n. 1; 'Oecumenius', *Comm. in Epist. I, II, III Joannis* (PG 119:686). On the revival of the tradition at the time of the Reformation see below p. 36. Grotius in his 'Preface to the so-called second letter of John' (quoted in W.G. Kummel, *The New Testament, The History of the Investigation of its Problems*, London 1973, 328) even claims that Jerome saw the tombs!

[30] See below ch. 3, pp. 61–2.

[31] 'Iohannis apostoli epistula una/alterius Iohannis presbyteri epistulae duae'. See C.H. Turner, 'Latin Lists of the Canonical Books. I. The Roman Council under Damasus, AD 382', *JThS* I (1900) 554–60, who argues for the originality of the *Decretum Damasi* despite its later editing under Gelasius and Hormisdas.

[32] Text in W. Sanday, 'The Cheltenham List of the Canonical Books of the Old and New Testament and of the Writings of Cyprian', *Studia Biblica* III, Oxford 1891, 216–325, 222–5. Harnack suggested that the 'una sola' might refer to Jude and James, but this would hardly explain the force of the 'sola' (ibid., 243).

However, although we have reported more doubts than confidence in 2 and 3 John's apostolic authority, by the end of the fourth century it was the confidence which was winning. In c. AD 312 Alexander of Alexandria had used 2 Jn 10–11 against the Arians and although those who use 2 and especially 3 John are few and far between, by the end of the fourth century three letters of John the Apostle are regularly included in New Testament lists.[33]

In the East uncertainty persisted somewhat longer and the picture is a confused one. Although Gregory of Nazianzus (329–389) accepted seven Catholic Epistles, neither he nor the other Cappadocians use 2 and 3 John, while his contemporary, Amphilocius of Iconium, records doubts about these two together with 2 Peter and Jude.[34] Among writers of the Antiochene school, Severian of Gabala refers to the rejection of 2 and 3 John by the 'fathers',[35] and they are not used in the surviving works of John Chrysostom despite the statement in *Suidas* that he accepted three letters of John as well as Revelation; significantly, the *Synopsis of Sacred Scripture* attributed to him lists only three Catholic Epistles (James,

---

[33] Cyril of Jerusalem, *Catech.* IV.33–6; Athanasius, *Festal Letter* (AD 367); Filastrius, *Div. Heres. Liber.* 88.5; Rufinus, *Comm. in Symb. apost.* 337; Gregory of Nazianzus, *Carm.* XII.3 etc. For the text of these lists see Zahn, *Geschichte* II, 1–318 and Westcott, *Canon*, 548–590. However, neither Filastrius nor Gregory use 2 or 3 John. One of the first not merely to list 2 and 3 John but to use them without question is 'Ambrosiaster', *Comm. in Ep. ad Rom.* 12.18; 16.23 (CSEL 81.1, 413, 491).

[34] Amphilocius of Iconium, *Iambi ad Seleucum* II.310–5 (ed. E. Oberg, Patristische Texte und Studien 9, Berlin 1969, 39), '... καθολικῶν ἐπιστολῶν τινὲς μὲν ἑπτὰ φάσιν, οἱ δὲ τρεῖς μόνας χρῆναι δέχεσθαι ...'.

[35] Ps. Chrysostom, *De qua Potestate (Mt 21.23)* (PG 56:424) emphasises that 1 John is among the 'ἐκκλησιαζομένων' while the fathers 'ἀποκανονίζουσι' 2 and 3 John. According to G. Bardy, 'Séverien', *Dictionnaire de Theologie Catholique* 14, 2 (1941) 2003, n. 8 this may not be the work of Severian. Cosmas (see n. 45) does report that Severian had doubts about 2 and 3 John.

1 Peter and 1 John).[36]

Some were even more cautious about the Catholic Epistles; none of them are used in the surviving works of Diodore of Tarsus, Chrysostom's teacher, (d. *c.* 390), although in *Suidas* he is credited with a commentary on 1 John.[37] His disciple, Theodore of Mopsuestia, was charged by an opponent, Leontius of Byzantium, with rejecting James and the following Catholic Epistles; if Leontius placed James at the head of the Catholic Epistles then Theodore rejected them all, and indeed none are used in his surviving writings while Isho'dad of Merv (*c.* 850) is silent about the minor Epistles and explicitly claims that Theodore never used James, 1 Peter or 1 John.[38] On the other hand Theodore may have accepted 1 Peter and 1 John, Leontius putting James in third place, and in line with this Junilius Africanus, who often reflects Theodore's thought, ascribed 1 Peter and 1 John to the books of 'perfect authority'

[36] *Suidae Lexicon* §461 (ed. A. Adler, Leipzig 1928–38, II.647), 'δέχεται δὲ ὁ Χρυσόστομος καὶ τὰς ἐπιστολὰς αὐτοῦ τὰς τρεῖς καὶ τὴν Ἀποκάλυψιν'; *Synopsis Scripturae Sacrae* (PG 56:317), 'καὶ τῶν καθολικῶν ἐπιστολαὶ τρεῖς'. A catena on 3 Jn 8 is ascribed to Chrysostom in K. Staab, 'Die griechischen Katencommentare zu den katholischen Briefen', *Bib.* 5 (1924) 296–353, 321. In ed. J.A. Cramer, *Catenae Graecorum Patrum in Novum Testamentum* vol. 8 *In Epistolas Catholicas et Apocalypsin*, Oxford 1884, it is anonymous. Ps. Chrysostom, *De Pseudoprophetis* (PG 59:554, 556, 557) cites 2 John while Palladius in his biography of Chrysostom uses 3 John (PG 47:73). Isidore of Pelusium who followed Chrysostom's exegesis quotes 2 Jn 8 in his letters, II.300; V.144 (PG 78:727, 1409).

[37] *Suidae Lexicon* §1149 (ed. cit., II.103). See Jerome, *De Vir. Illus.* 119 (ed. cit., 62), 'Extant eius in Apostolum commentarii'. See E. Schweizer, 'Diodor von Tarsus als Exeget', *ZNW* 40 (1941) 33–75, who accepts that Diodore used none of the Catholic Epistles or Revelation, although in a footnote he raises a query about 1 John and 1 Peter (51).

[38] Leontius of Byzantium, *C. Nestorianos et Eutychianos* III.14 (PG 86:1365) 'τοῦ μεγάλου Ἰακώβου τὴν ἐπιστολήν, καὶ τὰς ἑξῆς τῶν ἄλλων ἀποκηρύττει καθολικάς'. Isho'dad of Merv (ed. M. Gibson, *The Commentaries of Isho'dad of Merv* vol. IV *Acts of the Apostles and Three Catholic Epistles in Syriac and English*, Horae Semiticae X, Cambridge 1913) comments on James, 1 Peter and 1 John but finds them inferior and appeals to Theodore who never mentions them or uses illustrations from them (ed. cit. 36, 49).

but James, 2 Peter, Jude and 2 and 3 John with Revelation to those of 'secondary authority' (media auctoritas).[39] Yet Theodoret of Cyr (d. *c.* 466), who defended both Diodore and Theodore, did accept three Catholic Epistles.[40] In the midst of a complex picture the obscurity surrounding 2 and 3 John is at least one constant theme!

As for the Syriac speaking church, although the oldest translation probably contained no Catholic Epistles, James, 1 Peter and 1 John were included in the Peshitto (mid fifth century).[41] The remaining ones were added in the sixth century Philoxenian recension used only among the Monophysites.[42] 1 Peter and 1 John are the only Catholic Epistles in the Syriac writings of Ephraem, although all seven are used in the Greek writings ascribed to him.[43] This uncertain position is one which was to continue in the East.[44]

---

[39] Junilius Africanus, *Instituta Regularia* I.6–7 (H. Kihn, *Theodor von Mopsuestia und Junilius Africanus als Exegeten*, Freiburg 1880, 478–80). Kihn believes that Theodore did accept 1 Peter and 1 John, while T. Zahn, 'Das Neue Testament Theodors von Mopsuestia und der ursprungliche Kanons der Syrer', *NKZ* 11 (1900) 788–806 and J. Leipoldt, *Geschichte des neutestamentlichen Kanons* (2 vols.), Leipzig 1907–8, I, 247 follow Isho'dad in arguing that Theodore accepted none of the Catholic Epistles.

[40] Theodoret of Cyr, *Eranistes* (ed. G. Ettlinger, Oxford 1975, 91, 1.6); he refers to 1 Peter and 1 John each as 'the letter'. He also quotes from Revelation as by 'John' (ed. cit. 102, l.19f.). Jas 5.13 is quoted in *In Psal.* XXVI.6 (PG 80:1053A).

[41] That the earliest Syriac Canon contained no Catholic Epistles is implied by Aphraat, the Doctrine of Addai and the Syriac stichometry in A.S. Lewis, *Catalogue of the Syriac MSS in the Convent of S. Catherine on Mount Sinai*, Studia Sinaitica I, London 1894, 8–16. See Zahn, 'Das NT Theodors' and *Geschichte*, I, 373ff. On the Peshitto see B.M. Metzger, *The Early Versions of the New Testament,* Oxford 1977, 48–63.

[42] See J. Gwynn, *Remnants of the Later Syriac Versions of the Bible*, London and Oxford 1909; Metzger, *Early Versions*, 63–8.

[43] Ed. J.S. Assemani, *Opera Omnia Ephraemi*, Rome 1732–46, I.76 cites 3 Jn 4 and III.52 cites 2 Jn 9 but these are only in Greek.

[44] There are no Catholic Epistles in the East Syrian Lectionary (ed. A.J. Maclean, London 1894); on Isho'dad of Merv see above n. 38. See further Leipoldt, *Geschichte* I, 245ff.

The general picture we have explored is well summarised in the sixth century by Cosmas Indicopleustes—some have doubted all the Catholic Epistles, some accept 1 Peter and 1 John, while 'among the Syrians only James, 1 Peter and 1 John are found'. Although some accept three Epistles of John, for himself he feels that the perfect Christian can get all he needs from the books which are universally recognised.[45]

1 and 2 John

However, Cosmas's account does not tell the whole story, for it appears that even while 2 and 3 John were moving through obscurity, questioning and eventual acceptance in some parts of the church, elsewhere the Second Epistle was being acknowledged alongside the First with no hint of its having another partner.

(a) Irenaeus and Clement of Alexandria

Irenaeus, bishop of Lyons at the end of the second century, had heard Polycarp in his youth and believed him to have been a disciple of John—a claim which has been the inspiration of much scholarly debate.[46] Eusebius reports that he used many testimonies from the first (πρώτης) letter of John and also the former letter of Peter;[47] in fact he quotes from both 1 and 2 John, but in such a manner as to imply his quotations are from one letter. On one occasion 2 Jn 11 is quoted in condemnation of heretics as the words of 'John the disciple of the Lord', Irenaeus's usual epithet for the author of the Fourth Gospel whom he

---

[45] Cosmas Indicopleustes, *Topographia Christiana* VII.68–70 (SC 197, 129–133). See below p. 36.

[46] See C.K. Barrett, *The Gospel according to St. John*, 2nd ed., London 1978, 100–105.

[47] Eusebius, *HE* V.8.7 (GCS 9, 446).

undoubtedly held to be the Apostle.[48] Later, admidst a row of references to the Gospel and First Epistle, 2 Jn 7–8 is cited with the introduction 'and his disciple John urges us to avoid them (i.e. heretics) in the Epistle mentioned above saying . . .'; the reference can only be back to his earlier use of 1 John, which is in fact cited in the next sentence with the words 'And again in the letter he says'.[49] Irenaeus clearly knew 1 and 2 John but possibly as a single letter, while he gives no hint of 3 John.

For the second of those two passages we are unfortunately dependent on a Latin translation of Irenaeus's work; the same is true of the crucial evidence for Clement of Alexandria's position (c. 150–215). Among his many works Clement wrote a commentary on some of the biblical books, apparently including some later to be excluded from the canon. For its precise contents we have only the conflicting reports of others together with a Latin translation (usually known as the *Adumbrationes*) of the commentary on 1 Peter, 1 and 2 John and Jude. Cassiodorus senator (c. 480–580) claimed ultimate responsibility for this translation, which also involved appropriate censorship, although surprisingly his list of the 'canonical epistles' on which Clement commented reads 1 Peter, 1 and 2 John and James—the last surely a mistake for Jude.[50] Yet this conflicts with Eusebius's report that Clement covered 'the whole of the canonical Scriptures without omitting the disputed books, namely Jude and the rest of the Catholic Epistles, Barnabas and the so-called Apocalypse of Peter', and also with Photius's much later (ninth century) account which refers only to Genesis, Exodus, the Psalms, the

[48] Irenaeus, *Adversus Haereses* I.16.3 (SC 264, 262). On the problem of Irenaeus's identification of 'John the disciple of the Lord' with the Apostle see J.J. Gunther, 'Early Identifications of the Authorship of the Johannine Writings', *JEH* 31 (1980) 407–27, 417ff., 426.

[49] *AH* III.16.8 (SC 211, 318–20). See below p. 32 on the text of 2 Jn 7 here.

[50] Cassiodorus, *Institutiones divinarum Litterarum* VIII.4 (ed. R.A.B. Mynors, *Cassiodori Senatoris Institutiones*, Oxford 1937, 29).

19

Epistles of Paul, the Catholic Epistles and Ecclesiasticus.[51] The discrepancies between the reports and the unusual phrasing of the earliest, Eusebius, puts none of them above suspicion; moreover Rufinus's translation of Eusebius implies that he already had no direct knowledge of the books or their contents while Photius is generally dismissive of the many blasphemies contained in them and only says 'certain passages' in the books covered were commented on.[52] There is no internal evidence from the *Adumbrationes* themselves and elsewhere Clement quotes only from 1 Peter, Jude and 1 John, which he calls the 'greater' letter of John.[53] It does seem possible to accept Cassiodorus's list with the correction to Jude, and still to explain the other reports—otherwise the disappearance of a commentary on 3 John from those on 1 and 2 John would be hard to explain. Thus it appears Clement chose to comment on—and perhaps knew—only 1 and 2 John.[54]

(b) *Muratorian Canon*

The so-called Muratorian Canon is a discussion of the books we might think of as the New Testament extant only in an eighth century Latin manuscript. On internal grounds it is usually dated to the end of the second century,[55] which, if correct,

---

[51] Eusebius, *HE* VI.14.1 (GCS 9, 548); Photius, *Biblioteca* Cod. 109 (ed. R. Henry, *Photius Bibliothèque* 8 vols., Paris 1959–77, II, 79f.).

[52] Rufinus, *HE* VI.13.2 (GCS 9, 547) refers to the eight books of the 'Ὑποτυπώσεων' about which he is unable to give any information—an addition to the text of Eusebius. At VI.14.1 (GCS 9, 549) he omits the summary of contents. Photius, loc. cit.

[53] For the *Adumbrationes* see GCS 17, 203–15. At *Strom.* II.15.66 (GCS 52 (15), 148) 1 John is called 'greater' (μείζονι) but in the Greek of this period this need not mean 'of two'.

[54] This is the view taken by Sanday, 'Cheltenham List', 248–9 and Leipoldt, *Geschichte* I, 232–3; contrast J. Ruwet, 'Clément d'Alexandrie: Canon des Écritures et Apocryphes', *Bib.* 29 (1948) 77–99, 240–68, 391–408.

[55] For text and comments see Westcott, *Canon*, Appendix C; ed. S.P. Tregelles, *Canon Muratorianus*, Oxford 1867; E.S. Buchanan, 'The Codex

would make it the oldest discussion of books acknowledged by the church. Yet it is a notoriously difficult text to interpret with confidence; it is clearly incomplete starting as it does with the end of a sentence and continuing with a reference to Luke as the third Gospel. Even within the text appeal to scribal miscopying and omission seems unavoidable, an appeal which is justified by the discrepancies between two versions of part of Ambrose's *De Abrahamo* which follow in the manuscript.[56] Arguably a translation from Greek, the Latin itself is marked by mistakes in spelling and grammar. Most problematically, the document does not read as a unity and may be made up of fragments from a longer work or works with different purposes. Hence it is hazardous to argue from the author's silences and difficult to know for whom he speaks. Certainly it would seem wrong to think of this as in any sense an official list.[57]

After the reference to Luke's Gospel an explanation of the origin of the Fourth Gospel is given which is clearly apologetic in origin—it was at the instigation of Andrew and the other disciples that John wrote his Gospel. A further guarantee is given by quoting John's claim to be an eye- and ear-witness 'in his letter' (1 Jn 1.1f.).[58]

After discussing Acts, the letters of Paul to seven churches (signifying universality after the pattern of the Apocalypse) and also those to individuals, the list refers to the spurious ('finctae')

Muratorianus', *JThS* 8 (1907) 537–45. A dating at the end of the second century is favoured by the reference to *Hermas* as written 'very recently (nuperrime) and in our own times by Hermas while his brother, bishop Pius, was presiding over the church at Rome'; Pius is dated *c*. AD 142–55. However, A.C. Sundberg, 'Canon Muratori: A Fourth Century List', *HThR* 66 (1973) 1–41, has argued for a later date and Eastern origin; his arguments while not conclusive raise important issues.

[56] See Westcott, *Canon*, 538ff.

[57] See Sundberg, 'Canon Muratori', 4ff.

[58] 'in epistulis suis' (10a, l.28) but in this period the plural could be used of a single letter. On the force of the appeal to 1 John in support of the Gospel see Ehrhardt, 'The Gospels in the Muratorian Fragment', 28–29, 34.

epistles of Paul to the Laodicaeans and Alexandrians 'which cannot be accepted into the catholic church' ('quae in chatholicam eclesiam recepi non potest'). The tone has now changed from an interest in the origins of the books to the question of their reception into the church, reflecting either the diverse origins of the material or the move from the books Eusebius later describes as 'acknowledged' to those that were disputed. It is in this context that there follow the words 'Certainly the letter of Jude and two with the title of (?) John are held in the catholic (?) and Wisdom written by the friends of Solomon in his honour' ('epistola sane iude (*read* Iudae) et superscrictio (*read* superscriptio) iohannis duas (*vulgar Latin nominative or read* duae) in catholica habentur et sapientia ab amicis salomonis in honore ipsius scripta').[59]

'Superscrip(c)tio' makes little sense; the translation given assumes reading 'superscriptae', 'with the title', presumably referring to the absence of any name in the initial greeting, unlike the letters of Paul and Jude. This fits normal use and the probable Greek original better than the alternative of reading 'superscripti' and translating 'of the above mentioned John' or 'of the John in the title'.[60] 'In catholica' is best understood as 'in catholica ecclesia', 'in the catholic church', the absence of 'ecclesia' being a scribal omission, although Tertullian does use the adjective on its own of the church.[61] Again this seems preferable to translating 'of John two together with the Catholic

---

[59] 11a, ll.6–9.

[60] 'Superscriptae' (implying an underlying Greek, if such there was, ἐπιγεγραμμέναι as in Eusebius *HE* VII.25.7 of the Gospel 'entitled according to John') is read by Zahn, *Geschichte* II, 88ff. and by Westcott, *Canon*, 546. Earlier, in the 2nd edition (1866) Westcott had read 'superscripti' (genitive agreeing with 'iohannis') 'of the above mentioned John' as does Tregelles, *Canon Muratorianus*, 49. F. Hesse, *Das Muratori'sche Fragment*, Giessen 1873, read 'superscripti', meaning 'of the John in the title'.

[61] Tertullian, *De Praes. Haer.* 269, 302 (CChr.SL 1, 208, 210) without 'ecclesia' provided.

one' (i.e. 1 John), since the designation of 1 John as 'the Catholic Epistle,' only came later into currency.[62]

Although 1 John had been cited earlier in conjunction with the Gospel this would no more obviate reference to it in its proper place than does comparison of the Apocalypse with Paul's sevenfold address prevent its later mention after the, admittedly awkward, comment on Wisdom. Although the surprising absence of 1 Peter provides a timely warning against undue confidence in interpretation,[63] to assume that both it and 1 John have been lost in the history of the text's composition is to retreat behind unproveable supposition. As the text stands it knows only two letters of John, 1 John and surely 2 John, which 'are held' in the church.[64] Although 3 John would hardly fit in with the author's scheme of universality of intention, he can cope with Paul's letters to individuals, and so the Muratorian Canon is a further witness to confident acceptance of 1 and 2 John, accompanied by ignorance of the Third Epistle.

(c) *The Latin Tradition*

Although translation did not necessarily imply the ascription of

---

[62] P. Katz, 'The Johannine Epistles in the Muratorian Canon', *JThS* NS 8 (1957) 273–4 argues for 'dua(e) sin catholica', 'sin' being a transliteration for the Greek 'σύν' (with); C.F.D. Moule, *The Birth of the New Testament*, London 1962, 206, n. 1 proposed an original Greek 'πρὸς τὴν καθολικήν' since 'πρός' could mean 'in addition to' and yet be translated by 'in'; this was partially anticipated by Dr. W. Fitzgerald in 1860 who suggested an original Greek 'πρὸς τῇ καθολικῇ' (Tregelles, *Canon Muratorianus*, 50). The first clear reference to the 'catholic epistle' is by Apollonius (*c.* AD 197) in Eusebius *HE* V.18.5 (GCS 9, 474). K. Stendahl, 'The Apocalypse of John and the Epistles of Paul in the Muratorian Fragment', in *Current Essays in New Testament Interpretation*, ed. W. Klassen & G. Snyder, London 1962, 239–45 rejects Katz's interpretation as involving too technical a use of 'catholica'.

[63] M.-J. Lagrange, 'Le Canon d'Hippolyte et le Fragment de Muratori', *RB* 42 (1933) 161–86 reads 'Peter' for 'John' here.

[64] Some hesitation may be implied by 'habentur' instead of 'recipiuntur' (as in 11a, ll.4,10). Westcott, *Canon* (2nd ed.), 192 suggested the use of 'sane' implied some hesitation. See also Zahn, *Geschichte* II, 88f.

particular authority, it might be expected that the history of the versions will reflect something of the history of the canon. Already we have seen this to be the case with the Syriac version;[65] on the other hand, although the varying quality of the Greek text of the Catholic Epistles, even within a single manuscript, may be attributed to reliance on manuscripts of different origins when the Catholic Epistles were first brought together as a group, it is often very difficult to relate such textual variations to the history of the canon.[66] This warns against overconfidence when evidence as clear as the stages of the Syriac translation is missing.

This warning holds true of the Latin translation of the New Testament; its origins are surrounded with obscurity, and although it has been argued that nothing disproves the theory of an original single translation of the Catholic Epistles,[67] this remains at best an hypothesis. The multiformity of the Latin translation in the period before the Vulgate is witnessed to by manuscripts and patristic citations reflecting an Old Latin text. To some extent it is possible to isolate from within this multiformity recognisable 'text-types' represented by particular manuscripts and authors, sometimes associated with particular geographical areas within a given period.[68] The

[65] See above p. 17.

[66] See K. Aland, *Der Text des Neuen Testaments*, Stuttgart 1982, 58ff. However, W.L. Richards, *The Classification of the Greek Manuscripts of the Johannine Epistles*, SBLDS 35, Montana 1977, 72–75, 196–8, stresses the problems of interpretation—there are examples where within a single manuscript 1 and 3 John reflect a different text from 2 John.

[67] That the Catholic Epistles were translated at the same time is argued by W. Thiele, *Epistulae Catholicae: Vetus Latina: Die Reste der altlateinischen Bibel* 26/1, Freiburg 1956–69, 97*.

[68] Thiele distinguishes the following text-types:

African: K   The text of Carthage to the time of Cyprian.

                 C   A younger text in Donatists, Optatus, early Augustine.

European: S   'Spanish'; Ps. Augustine, *Speculum*, some Priscillian.

attempt has further been made to trace a development through these text-types from the earliest 'African' witnesses to the increased use of vocabulary favoured by European authors and the forms to be found in the Vulgate; thus vocabulary is used to help 'plot' manuscripts and citations on the line of development.[69] This can only be done tentatively and the evidence defies precision, while the results are often difficult to interpret.[70] The resulting pattern of development varies from Epistle to Epistle which in part, but only in part, may reflect their history in the canon: with books given less authority and less frequently cited there would be less tendency to refine the translation or to bring it into conformity with the Greek text, but at the same time, and perhaps working in the opposite direction, less concern about accuracy and care of translation and less opposition to changes.[71]

In the case of the Johannine Epistles, it is not surprising that 2 John does not share the same translation history as 1 John but shows signs of a slower development.[72] Rather more surprising

	T	Some MSS including 67=1 (Codex Pal. Legionensis/Leon Palimpsest), Cassiodorus, Didymus the Blind, Jerome, *Comm. in Ep. ad Titum* for 3 Jn 5.
	V	Vulgate.
Others:	R	Lucifer of Calaris—a mixed text.
	Aug.	Augustine's own text.

See W. Thiele, *Wortschatzuntersuchungen zu den lateinischen Texten der Johannesbriefe*, Freiburg 1958, 10.

[69] See the introduction to Thiele, *Epistulae Catholicae*; also B. Fischer, 'Das Neue Testament in lateinischer Sprache', in *Die Alten Übersetzungen des Neuen Testaments, die Kirchenväterzitate und Lektionare*, ed. K. Aland, Berlin/New York 1972, 1–92, 9ff.

[70] Some Patristic authors represent more than one text-type. See the reviews by H.F.D. Sparks and G. Willis in *JThS* NS 17 (1966) 451–3 and 453–6.

[71] For this in the case of the Greek manuscript tradition see Richards, *Classification*, 74–5.

[72] See Thiele, *Wortschatzuntersuchungen*, 42. For example 'ἵνα μή' is rendered by 'ne', an African form, in Lucifer and in V in 2 Jn 8, but by 'ne' in T and by 'ut non' in V in 1 John.

is the somewhat greater gap between 3 John and 2 or 1 John even within a single manuscript. Thus in the important Leon Palimpsest (MS 67 = l)[73] ἀγάπη (love) is rendered by the older 'African' 'dilectio' in 3 John, but by 'caritas' in 1 and 2 John, a translation which only comes into 3 John in the Vulgate; so also in the same manuscript πονηρός (evil) is translated by the older 'malus' in 3 John, but by 'malignus' in 1 and 2 John, that translation again coming into 3 John in the Vulgate. In each case the 'older' translation—i.e. the form found in 3 John—had been used at an earlier stage in the development of the Latin text of 1 and 2 John.[74] Even where comparison is not possible with the other two Epistles, 3 John reveals the continuance of old forms of translation to a later stage both in choice of vocabulary and in its greater freedom of translation.[75] It is because 3 John had 'lagged behind' in this way that the difference between the Vulgate and the text represented by MS 67 is much more marked in 3 John than in 1 and 2 John.[76] The presence of such 'old' forms suggests that 3 John was not translated substantially

[73] On this manuscript see B. Fischer, 'Ein neuer Zeuge zum westlichen Text der Apostelgeschichte', in *Biblical and Patristic Studies*, ed. J.N. Birdsall & R.W. Thomson, Freiburg 1963, 33–64.

[74] As well as 'ἀγάπη' (1 John *passim*; 2 Jn 3, 6; 3 Jn 6), 'ἀγαπήτος' (3 Jn 1, 2, 5) is rendered by 'dilectissimus' or 'dilectus' in T and by 'carissimus' in V in 3 John while in 1 John 'carissimus' is used in both T and V (there are no examples in 2 John); Thiele, *Wortschatzuntersuchungen*, 26f., 30 identifies 'dilectus/issimus' and 'malus' as older forms common in African text-types. The translation of 'μαρτυρεῖν' by 'testimonium' and a verb in V in 3 Jn 3, 6, 12 is also said to be 'African' by Thiele (ibid.); it survives in only one place in the Vulgate in 1 John (5.7–8), 'testari' or 'testificare' being used elsewhere. This example is also given by T.W. Manson, 'Entry into Membership of the Early Church', *JThS* 48 (1947) 25–33, 32–3. Manson's other examples are vitiated by referring only to the Vulgate.

[75] Thiele, *Epistulae Catholicae*, 90* gives examples.

[76] Examples have already been given where T and V differ in 3 John; however, the Vulgate of 3 John remains freer in relation to the Greek than is the case in 1 and 2 John; see A. v. Harnack, *Zur Revision der Prinzipien der neutestamentlichen Textkritik*, Leipzig 1916, 57–74.

later than the other Epistles despite the absence of any representatives of the earliest stages of the development. On the other hand, the same manuscript contains ways of translation which would normally be seen as signs of a later stage such as 'protinus' for εὐθέως (immediately) and 'eicere' for ἐκβάλλειν (cast out), both retained in the Vulgate.[77]

This evidence has been given with considerable caution both because of our uncertainties about how the text developed and because of the frequent variation both in the quality of the Latin translation even within one manuscript and in forms of citation even by one author.[78] At most it suggests that the Johannine Epistles, which we might expect to be treated as a unity, do not share the same translation history and that 3 John is most distinctively the 'odd man out'. This may mean that there were in circulation and use copies of 1 and 2 John without 3 John, which thus underwent less revision. In the Greek manuscript tradition P 72, which contains 1 and 2 Peter and Jude amidst a curious collection of texts, warns us against assuming that the Catholic Epistles would necessarily have been treated as a complete and separate corpus.[79]

Our conclusion that 1 and 2 John may have been known where 3 John was not does receive support from some of the Latin Fathers. Already we have seen the quotation of 2 Jn 10–11 in Africa in the mid-third century, perhaps in close association with 1 Jn, but without mention of a third letter.[80] The following century Lucifer of Calaris (d. c. 371) refers to 1 and 2 John as by the Apostle, 2 John being 'the second epistle', but nowhere

[77] Thiele, *Wortschatzuntersuchungen*, 31; so perhaps also the translation of 'ἐθνικός' (3 Jn 7) by 'gentilis' in T and by 'gens' in V when the African tradition would favour 'ethnicus', although this may reflect the reading 'ἐθνῶν'.

[78] See above n. 70.

[79] For P[72] see. ed. M. Testuz, *Papyrus Bodmer VII–IX*, Cologny-Genève 1959, 8ff. The contents also include *3 Corinthians*, Melito etc.

[80] See above p. 9 and n. 13.

mentions 3 John; similarly Priscillian (d. 385) quotes 1 and 2 John, although not explicitly as separate letters, but has no reference to the Third Epistle, the only one of the Catholic Epistles he does not use.[81] The following century Ps-Augustine *Speculum* quotes all the Catholic Epistles except 3 John, and clearly ascribes 2 John to the Apostle.[82] These writers each represent distinctive forms of the Old Latin text, but there is some relationship between them in 1 and 2 John.[83] Perhaps another indicator of the separate history behind 3 John is the Old Latin reading in 2 Jn 1, 'Iohannes senior . . .' (John the elder . . .), with no parallel in 3 Jn 1, the witnesses to which include MS 67 and Cassiodorus who draws attention to the difference.[84]

Finally we may note the vexed problem of the title 'Ad Parthos' (To the Parthians) which 1 John bears in Augustine and in other Latin Fathers—perhaps under the same influence—, and also (at the end) in MS 67; it is also to be found in many copies of the Vulgate.[85] The origin of the title has not been convincingly established but there are some indications of a link with 2 John. It seems likely it originated in Greek and there is

---

[81] Lucifer, *De non Conveniendo cum Haereticis* XIII–XIV (CSEL 14, 28–30); Lucifer also quotes from 1 Peter and Jude among the Catholic Epistles. Priscillian, *Tractatus* I (*Liber Apologeticus*) (CSEL 18, 31), after a quotation from 1 Jn 4.2, 'sicut et ipse alibi: qui non confitetur Christum Iesum in carne venisse hi sunt seductores et antichristi'.

[82] Ps. Augustine, *Speculum* (*De Div. Scripturis*) 2 (CSEL 12, 315), after a quotation from 1 John, 'Item in eiusdem II. Quonian multi fallaces . . . (2 Jn 7)', and 50 (ibid., 517), 'Item Iohannes apostolus II. Si quis venit . . . (2 Jn 10f.)'.

[83] See Thiele, *Epistulae Catholicae*, 82*, 88*, 384.

[84] Cassiodorus, *Complex. in Epist. Apost.* (PL 70:1373); MSS 67, 54 (see *JThS* 12 (1911) 497–534), C (Codex Cavensis), X (Codex Complutensis 1), and three Spanish manuscripts to which Thiele gives the sigla Σ^{TCO}. Thiele, *Epistulae Catholicae*, 386 also cites Jerome, *Comm. in Agg.* (PL 25:1404B) but this may be a misinterpretation of the punctuation.

[85] Augustine, *Tractatus* X (PL 35:1977ff.) 'in epistolam Ioannis ad Parthos'; for other Patristic references see Brooke, *Epistles*, xxx–xxxii; T. Zahn, *Forschungen zur Geschichte des neutestamentlichen Kanons* III, Erlangen 1884, 99–103.

Greek minuscule witness for the title attached to 2 John;[86] it is also given to 2 John in some manuscripts of Ps-Augustine, *Speculum*, although variants in the tradition there show its meaning was no longer understood.[87] There is some evidence in the Sahidic version for a colophon identifying 2 John as 'to the virgins', implying a Greek 'πρὸς παρθένους'.[88] It is attractive to see a link with Clement of Alexandria's comment on 2 John, extant only in Latin translation, that it was written 'ad virgines' (to virgins) and also that it was written to a certain 'Babylonian', although the link could work in more than one way. The Greek παρθένους ('parthenous': virgins) could have been miscopied or misunderstood as πάρθους ('parthous': Parthians), or Clement may have written the latter, thus agreeing with his reference to the Babylonian Electa (Babylon being held by the Parthians), and have been miscopied or mistranslated.[89] At the very least some sort of link between 1 and 2 John in transmission is implied and it may be that the title was transferred from 2 to 1 John early in the Latin tradition.

Clearly not everyone in the early church thought of 2 and 3 John as the inseparable pair. While some knew only 1 John as apostolic and entertained doubts about the origin and importance of 2 and 3 John, this alternative tradition, witnessed mainly in the West, acknowledged from an early date both 1 and 2 John as apostolic but left 3 John in obscurity—perhaps

---

[86] See Brooke, *Epistles*, xxxi.

[87] Ps. Augustine, *Speculum* 2 where the variants are 'ad partos secunda', 'ad partes', and 'ad pastores scd'a'.

[88] See G. Horner, *The Coptic Version of the New Testament in the Southern Dialect*, Vol. VII, *The Catholic Epistles and the Apocalypse*, Oxford 1924, 175. However in his discussion of the manuscript, (4 = Parchment Vatican 63) he says the description of the letter as 'to the virgins' comes before the Third Epistle in the heading (557).

[89] Clement of Alexandria, *Adumbrationes in Ep.II Joannis* (GCS 17, 215) 'Secunda Iohannis epistola, quae ad virgines scripta est, simplicissima est. Scripta vero est ad quandam Babyloniam, "Electam" nomine'; it is natural to see a link with 1 Pet 5.13 in this comment. (See Zahn, *Forschungen* III, 99–103).

reflecting the introduction of 2 John independently from the Third Epistle.

The Acceptance of Three Letters of John

As Bede reported, the 'general consensus of the church' came to be in favour of all three letters of John as apostolic. Although, as we have seen, listing did not always lead to use, from the second half of the fourth century 2 and 3 John are to be found as part of a canon which, excepting some debate about Revelation, is identical with ours.[90]

The path by which this consensus was reached is, like so much else in the history of the canon, obscure. 2 John may well have played the greater part in bringing the two smaller Epistles to acceptance and would have been helped in this by that tradition which had never doubted it. Yet how these different traditions of use related to each other and how they would have been reflected in manuscripts and in church use remains something of a mystery.[91]

Important in the process of acceptance is the interaction between interpretation and conformity, real or contrived, with the doctrines or the needs of the church or individual writer: such conformity aided acceptance while acceptance led to appropriate interpretation. As we see how 2 and 3, but especially 2, John were interpreted and used in the early church, we can see something of the conditions under which they were accepted.

Surprisingly, discussion of the epithet 'elder' in the first verse

---

[90] See n. 33.

[91] Thiele, *Epistulae Catholicae*, 15* describes a Latin manuscript (65, c. 800) which does not include 3 John or Jude and leaves no room for them, the Apocalypse being on the verso of the sheet containing 2 John; yet at this date it is difficult to know how to interpret this.

of each letter does not focus on the authorship question; it was neither felt to be incompatible with apostolic authorship by either side in the debate nor appealed to by those who ascribed the letters to John the Presbyter. The Latin translation 'senior' rather than 'presbuteros' both reflects and aided this; it encouraged the interpretation of seniority in years and wisdom, although Jerome does use the verse to show that in the New Testament 'presbyter' could be used of a bishop![92]

As for the 'elect lady' of 2 John, the metaphorical interpretation referring to the church proved dominant and probably aided and then was encouraged by the acceptance of the Epistle as 'catholic'.[93] The literal interpretation referring to an individual is witnessed first by Clement of Alexandria, while Oecumenius later has to refute objections to 2 and 3 John based on the inappropriateness of their individual address for 'catholic' Epistles.[94] Philemon among the letters of Paul had encountered similar problems at an earlier date but it is to the Pauline letters addressed to individuals and to there being neither male nor female in Christ that Oecumenius now appeals.

We have already observed both the similarity between 2 Jn 7 and 1 Jn 4.2f. and the differences—notably the negative form and the surprising use of the present participle 'coming' (ἐρχόμενον) in the former. To identify which verse is being

[92] The term is usually explained as 'aetate provectus' although in Euthalius, *Elenchus Sept. Epist. Cath.* (PG 85:665–92) 1 John is introduced as by John who wrote the Gospel, 2 John simply as by 'the presbyter'. For Jerome see *Epist.* 146.1 (CSEL 56, 310) and Kelly, *Jerome*, 147, 212.

[93] Jerome, *Epist.* 123 (CSEL 56, 84); Cassiodorus, *Complex. in Epist. Apost.* (PL 70:1373); Ps. Hilary, *Tract. in Sept. Epist. Can.* (PLS 3:126).

[94] Clement of Alexandria: see n. 89; Oecumenius, *Comm. in Epist. I, II, III Joannis* (PG 119:686–7); Walafridius Strabo, *Glossa Ordinaria in Ep. II B. Joannis* (PL 114:703). See also the *argumentum* to 2 John in U (Codex Ulmensis), 'Usqueado ad sanctam foeminam scribit, ut eandem dominam non dubitet literis appellare' (J. Wordsworth et al. *Novum Testamentum Domini nostri Iesu Christi Latine sec. edit. S. Hieronymi ad codicum manuscriptorum fidem* 3.2, Oxford 1949, 380).

31

quoted is often difficult, especially if a negative form is required by the context—as it often is since the most common context is the description of heretics.[95] The present participle is not noted by any early writer until Oecumenius specifically comments on it referring it to the second coming.[96] Irenaeus's quotation of the verse, only extant in the Latin, in fact uses a perfect infinitive and whether this reflects a perfect participle in his Greek (as in 1 Jn 4.2) or the influence of the Old Latin on the translator is uncertain.[97] The pre-Vulgate Latin translation does use the perfect infinitive 'venisse' (there being no active perfect participle in Latin), and even after the Vulgate introduced the present participle 'venientem' in conformity with the Greek most interpreters assume a past tense.[98] There is also a tendency in the Latin tradition to bring the word order into agreement with that found in 1 Jn 4.2;[99] clearly the verse was understood as, and useful as, a parallel to the passage in 1 John.

However, it is vv. 9–11 which were particularly valuable as a proof-text in a number of contexts. Since here there is no

[95] See above p. 8 on Tertullian and Cyprian. In *The Epistles of St. John*, London 1883, 157 B.F. Westcott saw the influence of 2 John in Tertullian and Cyprian, but in *Canon*, 379–80 he decided that knowledge of 1 John only was implied.

[96] Although he has noted the tense of 'ἐρχόμενον' and referred it to the second coming Oecumenius brings the argument back to the incarnation by saying that anyone who rejects the second coming will also reject the first.

[97] *AH* III.16.8 (SC 211, 318–20); see above p. 19. See A. Souter, 'The New Testament Text of Irenaeus', in *Novum Testamentum Sancti Irenaei Episcopi Lugdunensis*, ed. W. Sanday & C.H. Turner, Oxford 1923, cxii–clxix.

[98] 'Venisse' is read by 'Ambrosiaster' *Comm. in Ep. ad Rom.* 12.18 (see n. 33), Ps. Augustine, *Speculum* 2, Priscillian, *Tract.* I, and Lucifer, *De non Conveniendo* XIII (see nn. 81–2). It is also read by Beatus of Liebana, *Ad Elip. Epist.* I.23 (PL 96:907) who usually follows the Vulgate text. It is implied by the commentaries of Bede, Cassiodorus, Clement of Alexandria and Euthalius that they took the verb as a perfect.

[99] Thus when citing 2 Jn 7 several authors follow the order of 1 John by reading 'in flesh' before the participle (Ambrosiaster, Ps. Augustine, *Speculum*, Cassiodorus, Irenaeus and Priscillian).

parallel in 1 John their usefulness may have helped secure the ascription of apostolic authority to 2 John and hence earned a place for both Epistles among the recognised books of the New Testament, for it is these verses which are the first to be used regularly. Primarily they gave sanction to the refusal of fellowship to heretics and schismatics; Irenaeus uses them against Gnostics while for Aurelius of Chullabi (AD 256) they establish the necessity for schismatics to be rebaptised before reception into the church, an interpretation Augustine later refuted by arguing that the reference was to relationships with heretics in general and not to baptism as such.[100] By this time the verses were already being used to support the expulsion and avoidance of Arians—so already by Alexander of Alexandria in AD 312—and soon became a standard proof-text on 'not having dealings with heretics', to be applied as appropriate.[101] Ironically, they also had to be considered by the recipients of such treatment; Firmilian echoes v. 10 when speaking of Stephen of Rome's refusal to accept the African envoys in the controversy over rebaptism, while Optatus (AD 367) asserts that in denying Christians a brotherly greeting, the Donatists are failing to recognise that the words of the 'Apostle', quoting 1 Cor 5.11; 2 Jn 10; 2 Tim 2.7, were said about heretics and are inappropriate against Christians![102] Textual variants reflect this use; instead of the ambiguous 'Everyone who leads forward' (πᾶς ὁ προάγων) of v. 9, the Greek variant 'Everyone who goes

---

[100] Irenaeus: see p. 18 and n. 48; Aurelius: see p. 9 and n. 13. Augustine, De Baptismo VII.89 (CSEL 51, 365–6).

[101] Alexander in Socrates, HE I.6 (ed. W. Bright, Oxford 1893, 8); Ambrose, Epist. 11.4 (PL 16:986); Lucifer, De non Conveniendo XIII; Ps. Augustine, Speculum 50; Vincent of Lerins, Commonitorium 24(33) (ed. R.S. Moxon, Cambridge 1915, 96–7).

[102] Firmilian in Cyprian, Epist. 75.25 (CSEL 3.2, 826); Optatus, C. Parmenianum IV.5 (CSEL 26, 108); O.R. Vassall-Phillips, The Works of St. Optatus against the Donatists, London 1917, 189 suggests the texts had been used by Parmenian or some other Donatist.

astray' (πᾶς ὁ παραβαίνων), and the Old Latin 'Everyone who goes back' (recedit) defined the heretics much more clearly, and something similar is reflected in the other versions.[103] Again, even after the Vulgate adopted 'goes ahead' (praecedit) in conformity with the Greek text, the Old Latin interpretation continued to be adopted.[104] In a different way the mention of both Father and Son in v. 9 proved a useful weapon in Trinitarian controversy.[105]

Little of this interaction between usefulness, interpretation and acceptance can be found in 3 John. Once accepted 3 John provided the moral that the materially rich should help the poor or those rich only in spiritual goods and demonstrated the virtue of not retaliating when maligned.[106] Only Jerome sees the Epistle as a sad prophecy of his own day when bishops, neglecting their own duty of hospitality, expel the laity who seek to fulfil it.[107]

It would seem that 2 John was frequently interpreted in the light of the First Epistle, often being brought into conformity with it. At the same time it supplemented 1 John by providing a sanction against false teachers. This would have encouraged the acceptance of these two letters as a pair. In comparison 3 John was felt to have little to offer and appears as a 'hanger on', only really coming to be used once it was accepted and had to be interpreted. Thus, in contrast to the case of the Pauline corpus,

[103] See ch. 3 p. 91 and n. 106.

[104] Thus Beatus (see n. 98) reads 'recedit' as do some MSS of Bede, according to Thiele, *Epistulae Catholicae*, 390; Ps. Fulgentius, *Pro Fide Catholica* (De Trinitate) 6 (CChr.SL 90, 245) and Ps. Vigilius, *C. Varimardum* III.31 (CChr.SL 90, 111) omit the verb.

[105] Lucifer, loc. cit. (n. 101); Ps. Fulgentius and Ps. Vigilius, locc. citt. (n. 104). See also Jerome's rendering of 'this teaching' in v. 10 as 'ecclesiasticam fidem' in *Epist.* 89.2 (CSEL 55, 143).

[106] Gregory the Great, *Hom. in Ezek.* I.9.17 (PL 76:877): *Hom. in Evang.* I.20.12 (PL 76:1166). Similarly Bede and Ps. Hilary (see n. 93).

[107] Jerome, *Comm. in Ep. ad Titum* I.8–9 (PL 26:602–3).

34

there is never any question as to the order of the Johannine
letters; historically 2 and 3 John were accepted subsequently and
in relation to the First Epistle, while as a consequence they
(especially 2 John) were interpreted in its light with little
awareness of their particularity.

A possible reconstruction might be that as books of reputed
apostolic authorship were circulated some churches received
1 John alone while others also knew its 'appendix' 2 John which
before long proved to be useful in its own right. In due course
3 John became more widely known and was either
automatically attached to 2 John or, in areas which had
originally only known 1 John, the pair together would be
viewed with some hesitation. It would seem that the claim that
they were written by 'John' was being made from the start of
their public circulation despite their anonymity; certainly, later
alternative proposals of authorship—Papias's 'Presbyter
John'—were based on conjecture and on no independent
historical information.

At this point the questions of authorship and of canonical
status were not always identical; for some, such as Cosmas or
Severian of Gabala, apostolic authorship is essential, but for
others, the *Decretum Damasi* and perhaps the Euthalian material,
attribution to the Presbyter does not deny canonical status.[108]
Neither should we see the inclusion of 2 and 3 John in lists of
recognised books of the New Testament as the end of their
story. Not all those who so include them make actual use of
them, or indeed of the other disputed writings.[109] There is an
ambivalence here which is part of the continuing history of the
canon and which reemerged very clearly during the period of
the Reformation. Then, partly on Jerome's authority(!), 2 and 3

---

[108] Severian: see p. 15 and n. 35; Cosmas: see p. 18, 36 and nn. 45, 112.
Cosmas talks of the Epistles as being of 'certain simple presbyters' (loc. cit.);
Decretum Damasi: see p. 14 and n. 31; Euthalius: see n. 92.

[109] See above n. 33.

John were attributed to the Elder John and therefore accorded less authority, particularly for doctrinal purposes, by Cardinal Cajetan in the Roman Catholic church and also by Erasmus, while a similar conclusion is reached by some of the Reformers—although less authority did not necessarily mean exclusion from the canon.[110] Debate was halted by the Council of Trent for the Roman Catholic church and to some extent by the Articles of Faith for the Reformed churches, and with it acknowledgement of different levels of authority within the canon.[111] Yet the problem of the canon is not a closed one, and Cosmas's words[112] probably echo well what has been felt to be part of that problem, of which 2 and 3 John are only one example: 'The perfect Christian has no need to lean on those which are disputed, because the canonical and commonly accepted writings sufficiently declare everything about the heavens and the earth and their components and the whole Christian doctrine.'

[110] Cardinal Cajetan appeals to Jerome for the distinction between the Apostle as author of 1 John and the Presbyter as author of 2 and 3 John and goes on to say 'Et propterea ambae minoris authoritatis sunt' (Leipoldt, *Geschichte* II, 37). Similarly Erasmus in *In Epist. Ioannis I–III*. Erasmus submitted to the judgement of the church on such questions while Cajetan's critical views were rejected at the Council of Trent (see Kummel, *New Testament*, 19 and n. 7–9). Among the Reformers Karlstadt, *De Canonicis Scripturis Libellus* put James, 2 Peter, 2 and 3 John and Hebrews in 'tertium et infirmum auctoritatis divinae locum'; Calvin does not comment on 2 and 3 John and calls 1 John 'sua canonica epistola'. See H.H. Howorth, 'The Origin and Authority of the Biblical Canon according to the Continental Reformers', *JThS* 8 (1906/7) 321–65: 9 (1908) 188–230.

[111] The *Decretum de libris sacris et de traditionibus recipiendis*, ed. H. Denzinger, *Enchiridion Symbolorum*, 33rd edition, Freiburg 1965, 364–5 rejected any distinction between the classes of canonical books. On the Reformed churches see Westcott, *Canon*, 492, 499–503, 506–7. Article VI of the 39 Articles holds as canonical those books about which there was never any doubt.

[112] Cosmas, *Topog. Christ.* VII.70 (SC 197, 133).

Chapter Two

LETTERS OR EPISTLES?

Amidst all the problems surrounding 2 and 3 John, one thing seems beyond doubt; unlike 1 John they have all the formal characteristics which justify their designation as 'letters'. Indeed, this is more the case with 2 and 3 John than with any of the other New Testament letters, despite the fact that in recent years comparison with the personal letters of the time represented by those surviving on papyrus has usually started with the Pauline letters.[1]

The length of the letters illustrates this well, for brevity was in theory, and usually in practice, a fundamental characteristic of the classical letter. A letter, according to discussions of the art, should be relatively informal, brief and, as it were, 'half a conversation' or 'dialogue'.[2] The personal and official letters of the period preserved on papyrus also demonstrate the brevity of the letter—a brevity largely determined by the size of papyrus

---

[1] J.L. White, 'Introductory Formulae in the Body of the Pauline Letter', *JBL* 90 (1971) 91–7; idem, *The Form and Function of the Body of the Greek Letter*, Montana 1972; C-H. Kim, *Form and Structure of the Familiar Greek Letter of Recommendation*, Montana 1972. W.G. Doty, *Letters in Primitive Christianity*, Philadelphia 1973, is somewhat inconsistent in his discussion of 2 and 3 John while his assumption of the priority of the Pauline letters and of their similarity to the Hellenistic pattern prevents him from doing justice to the other New Testament letters.

[2] Demetrius, *De Elocutione* §223 (ed. W.R. Roberts, *Demetrius on Style*, Cambridge 1902, 172) quoting Artemon, the editor of Aristotle's letters. According to O. Roller, *Das Formular der paulinischen Briefe*, Stuttgart 1933, 360, n. 173 and 366, n. 176 the average length of Cicero's letters is 331 words, of Pliny's 175 words, of Seneca's 956 words and of Fronto's 235 words; however, Seneca was aware of the proper length of a letter even though his, which were primarily a method of teaching, exceeded it, *Epist. Mor.* XLV.13 (ed. R.M. Gummere, London and Cambridge, Mass. 1967, 298).

used.[3] By the standards of the time most of Paul's letters would have been subject to the judgement Demetrius *On Style* made about this time on Plato's letters, that 'they should not really be called letters but books with a greeting prefixed'.[4] 2 and 3 John alone in the New Testament conform to these standards of brevity; each would probably just fill a papyrus sheet.[5]

Then, as now, epistolary conventions were fairly standardised and it is possible to trace the main stages of the development of the letter form. Again, 2 and 3 John, but particularly the latter, show a number of contacts with this tradition. An example will illustrate this:

> Antonios Maximos to Sabina | [2]his sister, very many greetings. | [3]Above all I pray | [4]that you are well, as I myself | [5]am well. While I was mentioning you | [6]before the gods here | [7]I received a letter | [8]from Antoninos, our fellow | [9]citizen. When I learnt | [10]that you are well I rejoiced greatly. | [11]I too do not hesitate at every opportunity | [12]to write to you concerning | [13]my own and my family's welfare. | [14]Give many greetings to Maximos | [15]and to my lord Kopres. | [16-17]My wife Auphidia greets you, as does my son Maximos | [18]—his birthday is the | [19]thirteenth of Epeip according to the Greek | [20]calendar—and so do Elpis and Fortunata. | [21]Give greetings to the lord ... (*6 lines*) [28]I pray that you are well.[6]

Here the standard form of address (A to B) and greeting is

---

[3] Roller, *Das Formular*, 35 and 359, n. 168E. Any collection of papyrus letters will illustrate this.

[4] Demetrius, *De Elocutione* §228 (ed. cit., 174). According to Roller, *Das Formular*, 38 Paul's letters vary in length between 7101 words (Rom) and 335 words (Philem).

[5] Roller, *Das Formular*, 38; 2 John has 245 words and 3 John 185 words. See also R. Schnackenburg, *Die Johannesbriefe*, 6th edition, Freiburg 1979, 295.

[6] *BGU* (*Aegyptische Urkunden aus den koeniglichen Museen zu Berlin: Griechische Urkunden*, Berlin 1895–) II.632 translated from the text of A. Deissmann, *Licht vom Osten*, 4th edition, Tübingen 1923, no. 13, p. 150 where the lacunae are filled in and interpreted in a different way from the original publication—hence the information about the birthday is highly conjectural.

followed by a health wish. An expression of thanks at the reception of good news then leads into the main body of the letter—in this case the promise of further letters. The letter closes with extended greetings to and from mutual friends, which probably filled the missing lines, and with a final health wish. Clearly the letter was important for maintaining contact and an opportunity to send letters afforded by travellers going in the right direction would be made good use of, even if there was little news to send. 3 John follows a similar general outline—a greeting (v. 1) followed by a health wish (v. 2), joy at the receipt of good news (vv. 3f.) and then, after the body of the letter, greetings to and from mutual friends (v. 15). Within this basic pattern 2 John has an extended and distinctive greeting (vv. 1–3) and no health wish, important features to which we shall return.

After the opening formalities the Elder expresses his pleasure at hearing of the 'Christian life' of the children of the elect lady in 2 John and of Gaius, to whom he is writing, in 3 John using the same conventional phrase as does our example, 'I rejoiced greatly' (ἐχάρην λίαν). In his letters Paul also usually follows his characteristic greeting with a thanksgiving, but he addresses this to God using the verb 'I give thanks' (εὐχαριστῶ).[7] Although this verb is to be found in the thanksgivings of non-Christian letters,[8] the Pauline form is sharply distinguished by its long sentences, balanced structure and fundamentally religious content, such as in 1 Cor 1.4–9. In analysing the Pauline letter form in terms of papyrus models many have therefore chosen to compare Paul's thanksgivings not with the secular 'thanks at good news' but with the wish for good health which, as in Antonios Maximos's letter, often takes the form of a prayer and

---

[7] 1 Cor 1.4; Phil 1.3, 'εὐχαριστῶ τῷ Θεῷ'.

[8] *BGU* II.423, l.6 'εὐχαριστῶ τῷ κυρίῳ Σεράπιδι', giving thanks to Serapis for rescue from danger at sea. This letter and *BGU* II.632 are second century letters by the same author.

to which Paul has no more exact parallel.[9] This has then led to the surprising suggestion that the expression of joy in 2 and 3 John should be seen as the 'functional equivalent' of the Pauline thanksgiving and hence, in parallel with the secular health wish, as part of the opening pleasantries.[10] Clearly this is nonsense; 2 and 3 John follow standard letter-writing practice in expressing joy at hearing good news, while Paul opens his letters in a manner which owes more to liturgical practice than to epistolary convention.[11]

Within the body of the letters several details find ready parallels in the papyri; so for example addressing the recipient in the vocative when introducing a new idea ('lady', 2 Jn 5; 'beloved', 3 Jn 2, 5, 11), a reference to an earlier letter (3 Jn 9), a request courteously introduced by 'I ask you' (2 Jn 5) or by 'Please' (καλῶς ποιήσεις 3 Jn 6)—the last a formula which is extremely common in papyri letters but is found only here in the New Testament.[12] The requests in 2 Jn 5f. and 3 Jn 5f. follow the standard petition form of the papyri, a statement of

[9] *BGU* II.632, ll.3–4, 'πρὸ μὲν πάντων εὔχομαί σε ὑγιαίνειν'.

[10] P. Schubert, *The Form and Function of the Pauline Thanksgivings*, BZNW 20, Berlin 1939, 95 sees the absence of 'εὐχαριστῶ' from the Catholic Epistles as indicative of their distance from the Pauline letters; the latter are genuine letters, the former literary essays or sermon copies. This ignores the 'ἐχάρην' in 2 and 3 John and the 'εὐλόγητος' period in 1 Pet 1.3ff. See also F.W. Funk, 'The Form and Structure of II and III John', *JBL* 86 (1967) 424–30 who describes the 'ἐχάρην' periods in 2 and 3 John as the functional equivalents of the Pauline 'εὐχαριστῶ' periods (426). The use of 'ἐχάρην' if Phil 4.10 is interesting in this context.

[11] J.M. Robinson, 'Die Hodaiot-Formel in Gebet und Hymnus des Frühchristentums' in *Apophoreta*, BZNW 30, Berlin 1964, 194–235 who argues for a Jewish liturgical background against Schubert, *Pauline Thanksgivings*, who argues for an epistolary background.

[12] On these see White, 'Introductory Formulae' and *Form and Function*. See *BGU* II.632, ll.13–14 for a reference to a letter (ἐκομισάμην ἓν ἐπιστόλιον) and *BGU* II.423, l.11 for the vocative 'ἐρωτῶ σε οὖν, κύριέ μου, πατήρ,'; for 'please' see *P. Oslo* (*Papyri Osloenses*, Oslo 1925–00) 55, ll.7–9 'καλῶς οὖν ποιήσεις, ἄδελφε, τοῦτον ὑποδεξάμενος'. See H.A. Steen, 'Les clichés épistolaires dans les lettres sur papyrus grecques', *Classica et Mediaevalia* 1 (1938) 119–76, 138–9.

background, the vocative address, a verb of asking and the request itself.[13] The commendation of Demetrius in 3 Jn 12 has frequently been compared with recommendations in secular letters although we shall discover this to be somewhat more debatable.[14]

Any letter between friends will request or promise visits but there seems to be no stereotyped pattern for this in non-Christian letters.[15] Paul's promises of a visit seem to have become more structured and theologically weighted carrying a note of threat proper to the presence of the apostle.[16] Such threat should not be read into 2 and 3 John where the hope of personal meeting seems rather a way of bringing the letters to a close and where the similar but not identical phrasing may point to an author's personal conventions. However, the greater grammatical clumsiness and the addition of the Johannine 'that our joy may be complete' in 2 Jn 12 may suggest a more self-conscious or artificial use of the device there.[17]

The closing exchange of greetings to and from third parties is common in papyrus and other New Testament letters.[18]

[13] See J.L. White, *The Form and Structure of the Official Petition*, Montana 1972.

[14] On letters of recommendation see Kim, *Form and Structure*; on 3 Jn 12 see below ch. 3, p. 119.

[15] White, *Form and Function* does include notification of a coming visit among the transitional devices in the body of a Greek letter but can point to little uniformity of expression.

[16] See F.W. Funk, 'The Apostolic Parousia', in *Christian History and Interpretation*, ed. W. Farmer et al., Cambridge 1967, 249–68.

[17] 2 Jn: πολλὰ ἔχων ... γράφειν 3 Jn: πολλὰ εἶχον γράψαι
  οὐκ ἐβουλήθην   οὐ θέλω
  διὰ χάρτου καὶ μέλανος   διὰ μέλανος καὶ καλάμου
  ἐλπίζω γενέσθαι πρὸς ὑμᾶς ἐλπίζω ... σε ἰδεῖν καὶ ...
  καὶ ... λαλῆσαι   λαλήσομεν

On the textual confusion prompted by these differences see below ch. 3, p. 122. 'Our joy may be complete': cf. Jn 3.29; 15.11; 16.24; 17.13; 1 Jn 1.4. See below p.99.

[18] *BGU* II.632, ll.14ff. ''Ασπασαι Μάξιμον πολλὰ καὶ. ... 'Ασπάζεταί σε ἡ σύμβιός μου...' Rom 16.3–16,21–23; Col 4.10–15 etc.

However, the words of 3 Jn 15 'The friends greet you; greet the friends by name' particularly echo the papyri both in the phrase, only here in the New Testament, 'by name' (κατ' ὄνομα) and in the general reference to 'the friends'.[19]

Comparison here with the papyri warns us against reading too deep a meaning into the words of 2 and 3 John. The same may be true in other details. 3 John is addressed to the beloved (ἀγαπητέ) Gaius; while 'ἀγαπητός' is characteristically Christian, the secular equivalent 'φίλτατος' is regularly found in greetings of business letters without any implication that the partners stand in a closely affectionate relationship.[20] Whether the 'lady' (κυρία) of the address of 2 John is to be explained by epistolary conventions is more debatable. In the light of the papyri where the term is very common in addressing or speaking of a wife, mother, sister, or 'dear friend', 2 John could be addressed to 'the lady Electa' or to an anonymous, elect 'lady' or 'dear friend';[21] however, we shall see that 'Electa' (ἐκλεκτή) is unlikely to be a name and 'the elect lady' more probably represents a or the church, giving 'lady' its full weight.[22]

Although both letters reflect contemporary epistolary conventions, it is 3 John of whom this is true to an extent unique

---

[19] P. Mich. (Papyri and Ostraca from Karanis (Michigan Papyri vol. 8), ed. H.C. Youtie and J.G. Winter, Michigan 1951) 491, ll.19–20, 'ἀσπάζομαι τοὺς φιλοῦντάς σε πάντας κατ' ὄνομα'; also P. Mich. 476, l.31; 477, ll.43–4; 479, ll.20–21 (all second century). On the looseness of the use of 'φίλος' in these contexts see H. Koskenniemi, Studien zur Idee und Phraseologie des griechischen Briefes bis 400 n. Chr., Helsinki 1956, 116f.

[20] Koskenniemi, Studien, 95–104; F.X.J. Exler, The Form of the Ancient Greek Letter, Washington 1923, 54, 63 both note that 'φιλτάτος' like 'τιμιωτάτος' is used in official as well as 'family' letters.

[21] P. Mich. 491, ll.1–2, 'Ἀπολινᾶρις Ταῆσι τῇ μητρεὶ καὶ κυρίᾳ πολλὰ χαίρειν'. On this interpretation of 2 John see J. Rendel Harris, 'The Problem of the Address in the Second Epistle of John' Exp VI.3 (1901) 194–203: H. Meecham, Light from Ancient Letters, London 1923, 118; J.H. Moulton and G. Milligan, The Vocabulary of the Greek Testament, London 1914–29, art. 'κυρία'.

[22] See below ch. 3, p. 65.

in the New Testament while 2 John adopts a more conscious 'apostolic' pattern within a Johannine framework. Examples of 3 John's uses of common formulae have already been seen, but most striking is the health wish in v. 2, 'In all respects I pray that you are prospering and are well' (περὶ πάντων εὔχομαί σε εὐοδοῦσθαι καὶ ὑγιαίνειν).

The letter from Antonios Maximos quoted above illustrates the health wish that is particularly common in letters of the second and third centuries AD, and which was probably introduced in the first century, 'Before all I pray that you are well'.[23] In the Egyptian papyri this seems to have replaced the earlier form which appears more widely in both Greek and Latin letters from the third century BC to the first century AD, 'If you are well, it is good. I myself am well'.[24] 'Being well' (ὑγιαίνειν) is the usual wish in the new form, sometimes combined with other benefits, but 'prospering' (εὐοδοῦσθαι) is rare.[25] It is remarkable that this conventional health wish is to be found nowhere else in the New Testament or Apostolic Fathers, neither are any of the epistolary formulae using 'to be well' which are so common in the papyri.

---

[23] *BGU* II.632, ll.3–4, 'πρὸ μὲν πάντων εὔχομαι σε ὑγιαίνειν'. Koskenniemi, *Studien*, 134–9 dates the new form to the beginning of the second century but a transitional form is represented by *BGU* IV.1205, (28 BC) ll.1–3, 'ὑγειαίνειν καθάπερ εὔχομαι' and there are also first century letters where the formula comes at the close, e.g. *P. Oxy.* (*The Oxyrhynchus Papyri*, Part 2, ed. B.P. Grenfell and A.S. Hunt, London 1899) 292, ll.11–13. *BGU* II.530, ll.3–4 would seem to be a first century example of a similar formula at the beginning. The formula is found in second century Latin letters: *P. Mich.* (ed. cit.) 467, l.2, 'ante omnen opto te fortem esse'; also *P. Mich.* (ed. cit.) 468; ctr. Seneca, *Epist. Mor.* XV.1 (ed. cit., 94).

[24] The basic Greek form was 'εἰ ἔρρωσαι, εὖ ἂν ἔχοι· ὑγίαινον δὲ κ'αὐτός' and the Latin, 'si vales, bene est; ego valeo'. There are many variations in the Greek but the Latin seems to have been more rigid.

[25] 'εὐοδοῦσθαι' and 'ὑγιαίνειν' are found together in *P. Oxy.* 1680 (ed. cit., vol. 14, London 1920) (fourth century AD) but I have not been able to find them anywhere else.

In the papyri the wish is made '*before* all' (πρὸ παντός or πρὸ πάντων), understood in a temporal or local sense, or as '*above* all',[26] while '(you) are well' (ὑγιαίνειν) is sometimes also qualified by the phrase 'continually', '*through* all' (διὰ παντός or πάντων).[27] The form we find in 3 John, 'in all respects' ('*concerning* all', περὶ πάντων) does not seem to be otherwise attested.[28] There are no grounds for textual emendation or translation in conformity with the common formula,[29] and despite its position at the beginning of the clause, the phrase most naturally goes with 'prosper and are well', rather than with 'I pray'. We may have here a rare, personal or regional variation—remembering that the formula is not otherwise attested outside Egypt—but it can hardly be shown to be more 'Christian' or 'spiritual', as has been claimed.[30]

The majority of Greek private letters from the fourth century BC to the fourth century AD open 'A to B greetings' (χαίρειν). While other words of greeting may be used, it always takes the form of a verb in the infinitive; this and the use of the third

[26] 'πρὸ τῶν ὅλων' is also found; see Exler, *Ancient Greek Letter*, 112 and Koskenniemi, *Studien*, 139 on the translation of the phrase.

[27] When 'διὰ παντὸς' qualifies the infinitive it does not come at the start of the clause.

[28] *BGU* III.885, ll.1–2 have been reconstructed by the editors to read 'Θεόκτιστ[ος Ἀπολλωνίῳ τῷ φιλτάτῳ χαίρειν.] Περὶ πάντω[ν εὔχομαί σε ὑγιαίνειν]' (AD 70–80). This was noted by F. Ziemann, *De Epistularum Graecarum formulis sollemnibus Quaestiones Selectae*, Diss. Haliis, 1910; however the fragmentary state of the papyrus means little weight can be placed on this sole 'parallel' to 3 John.

[29] AV: 'Above all things'; N. Turner, in J.H. Moulton, *A Grammar of New Testament Greek*, vol. 4 *Style*, Edinburgh 1976, 270 'before all'. J. Rendel Harris, 'A Study in Letter Writing', *Exp* V.8 (1898) 161–80, emends to 'πρὸ πάντων' (167); so also F.W. Funk, 'Form and Structure', 425, n. 7 suggesting the mistake arose from Christian copyists who only knew the Christian formula (presumably 'εὐχαριστῶ ... περὶ πάντων ὑμῶν', 1 Thess 1.2).

[30] J.A. Robinson, *St. Paul's Epistle to the Ephesians*, London 1903, 278. Koskenniemi, *Studien*, 135 and Ziemann, *De Epistularum Graecarum*, 319 use 3 John as evidence of the spread of the formula beyond Egypt, but see ch. 1, p. 11 and n. 20 for arguments locating 3 John in Egypt.

person rather than the first and second ('I to you') has its ultimate origins in the spoken words of a messenger, 'A says to B, Rejoice'.[31] Similarly Semitic letters also use the third person of sender and recipient in the greeting, but there the central word of greeting is a noun, usually 'peace' (šlm), but sometimes coupled with 'mercy/favour' or 'prosperity' (rḥm, šrrh).[32] Occasionally 'peace' comes on its own after the names of the sender and recipient, like the Greek infinitive, but more frequently there is a separate clause expressing a prayer that God or the gods may grant peace or that peace may be multiplied for the recipient.[33] Significantly, Jews writing in Greek use the Greek conventions of greeting and farewell, even when the same people when writing in Aramaic or Hebrew follow the Semitic conventions, as is illustrated by the Bar Kochba letters.[34]

Against this background it is remarkable that in the New Testament only James and the letter of the Jerusalem church in Acts 15.23–29, other than the letter of the Roman Claudius Lysias in Acts 23.26–30, use the Greek 'χαίρειν' formula. Paul's letters open distinctively 'Paul ... to ... , grace to you and peace from God our Father and the Lord Jesus Christ'. The contrast with the Greek formula is clear; although written in Greek the structure with its separate clause and element of hope or prayer is closer to the Semitic greeting, but the use of 'grace' (χάρις) has no indisputable pre-Christian precedent. The background of Paul's greeting cannot be analysed here, but it is undoubtedly distinctively Pauline, reflecting the importance of grace in his

---

[31] See Exler, *Ancient Greek Letter*, 32–3, 52 and Koskenniemi, *Studien* 161–3 for other verbs; see also J.M. Lieu, ' "Grace to you and peace": The Apostolic Greeting', *JRLB* 68 (1985) 161–78.

[32] See J.A. Fitzmyer, 'Some Notes on Aramaic Epistolography' in *Studies in Ancient Letter Writing*, Semeia 22, ed. J.L. White, Chico 1981, 25–58 (revised from *JBL* 93 (1974) 201–225; also Lieu, ' "Grace to you and peace" ', 165.

[33] See Lieu, ' "Grace to you and peace" ', 165–6.

[34] ibid., 166–7. The same is true of the closing formulae.

thinking.[35] The influence of the Pauline greeting can be seen in the use of the 'grace' formula in the other New Testament letters with greetings, excepting 3 John and James. Possibly inspired by Jewish or Scriptural precedent 'mercy' is added in 1 and 2 Timothy (and in Jude and 2 John) and a verb 'be multiplied', a common Semitic form, is supplied in 1 and 2 Peter and Jude.[36] The formula continued to exert some influence beyond the New Testament period, but it soon died out as Greek convention proved dominant.[37]

In this context the contrast between 2 and 3 John is evident. 3 John, alone of the New Testament letters with prescripts, fails to use either the Pauline greeting or, despite its other links with the Greek epistolary tradition, the conventional 'χαίρειν' greeting. Among the papyri, the absence of a greeting word is particularly characteristic of more 'official' letters, and this may also be true of Semitic letters.[38] There are 'literary' letters which use the letter form purely as a cloak and these lack both a greeting word and other epistolary conventions, but in their artificiality they do not present a parallel with 3 John.[39] 3 John,

---

[35] ibid., 167–70; on this section see also the different approach of K. Berger, 'Apostelbrief und apostolische Rede: Zum Formula frühchristlicher Briefe', *ZNW* 65 (1974) 190–231 who puts more stress on the influence of the 'Testament' form on the Pauline letters.

[36] The use of 'be multiplied' is found in Dan 3:31 LXX; on its influence in Jewish and Christian letters see Lieu, ' "Grace to you and peace" ', 173.

[37] ibid., 174–7.

[38] Exler, *Ancient Greek Letter*, 56, 64; Fitzmyer, 'Aramaic Epistolography', 33.

[39] Such letters include the 'philosophical' letters of Anarchasis, the Cynics or Apollonius of Tyana and the 'imaginary' letters of Alciphron, Aelian or Philostratus; see the collection in R. Hercher, *Epistolographi Graeci*, Paris 1873; A.R. Benner and F.H. Fobes, *The Letters of Alciphron, Aelian and Philostratus*, London and Cambridge, Mass. 1949. The suggestion that 'χαίρειν' has been lost in copying (Schnackenburg, *Johannesbriefe*, 320, n. 2) is a counsel of despair. It is unlikely that 2 and 3 John are novelistic inventions (as suggested by E. Hirsch, *Studien zum vierten Evangelium*, Tübingen 1936, 177–8).

in both its lack of a greeting word and its idiosyncratic health wish remains something of an enigma.

In contrast, 2 John, which like other New Testament letters has no health wish, opens with a considerably expanded greeting. The form found in 3 John, 'The Elder to . . . , whom I love in truth'—which could be understood in the light of secular parallels[40]—is here extended as the author includes with himself 'all who know the truth' in loving the elect lady, and qualifies this as being 'through' the truth which permanently abides in this circle of love; the language and emphasis on 'truth' is now distinctively Johannine.[41] Then follows the greeting, 'There will be with us grace, mercy, peace from God the Father and from Jesus Christ, the Son of the Father, in truth and love' (ἔσται μεθ' ἡμῶν χάρις ἔλεος εἰρήνη παρὰ θεοῦ πατρὸς καὶ παρὰ Ἰησοῦ Χριστοῦ τοῦ υἱοῦ τοῦ πατρὸς ἐν ἀληθείᾳ καὶ ἀγάπῃ). Dependence on the Pauline-type greeting is obvious, especially as neither 'grace' nor the phrase 'God (the) Father' are Johannine;[42] more particularly, the addition of 'mercy' (also not Johannine) and the description of God as 'the Father' rather than 'our Father' parallel the development of the formula in the Pastoral Epistles.[43] However, Johannine assimilation is present in the addition of 'in truth and love' and in the description of Jesus as 'the Son of the Father', while the emphatic statement 'will be with us' in contrast to the implied wish of the Pauline

---

[40] P. Fay. (Fayum Towns and their Papyri, ed. B.P. Grenfell, A.S. Hunt, D. Hogarth, London 1900) 118, ll.25–6 'ἀσπάζου τοὺς φιλοῦντές σε πάντες πρὸς ἀλήθιαν.' See ch. 3, p. 70.

[41] See ch. 3, pp. 68–70.

[42] 'χάρις' only comes in the v.l. of 3 Jn 4 in the Epistles and in 1.14–17 in the Gospel; while God as Father or the Father is important in the Johannine literature this phrase (θεὸς πατήρ) does not otherwise occur.

[43] 1 and 2 Timothy add 'mercy, to the Pauline 'Grace and peace' and they, along with Titus, also omit 'to you' after 'Grace' and describe God as 'Father' instead of the Pauline 'our Father'; 2 John shares these features. See Lieu, ' "Grace to you and peace" ', 170–72.

formula gives the greeting a theological twist we shall see to be characteristic of 2 John.[44]

To turn to the end of the letters, Greek letters, if they had a closing salutation, usually concluded with one of a number of words all of which might be translated as 'farewell'.[45] In the New Testament only Acts 15.29 follows this convention; the Pauline pattern, also followed elsewhere, is 'Grace (be) with you', often with some expansion.[46] Although this has been added in a few manuscripts of 2 John, neither letter originally had any farewell after the closing exchange of greetings.[47] However, 3 John prefixes these with the words 'Peace to you' (εἰρήνη σοι, v. 15), a translation of a common Semitic greeting, but one not regularly used in letters.[48] The closest epistolary parallel to this is the closing benediction of 1 Peter, 'Peace to you all who are in Christ',[49] but more significant may be the same words addressed by the risen Jesus to his disciples in the Fourth Gospel (Jn 20.19,21,26), perhaps conveying a clear note of authority.[50] Other New Testament letters use a benediction or a doxology in a similar position not as part of the final

---

[44] See below ch. 3, pp. 69–70.

[45] ἔρρωσο, ἔρρωσθε, εὐτύχει, διευτύχει, or ἐρρῶσθαί σε εὔχομαι; see Koskenniemi, *Studien*, 151f.

[46] See the discussion of the 'Grace' benediction by H. Gamble, *The Textual History of the Letter to the Romans*, Studies and Documents 42, Michigan 1977, 65–7. Hebrews and Revelation also close with a grace formula; in line with his general use of secular conventions Ignatius closes his letters with 'ἔρρωσθε'.

[47] 'ἡ χάρις μετὰ σου' is added at the end of 2 Jn 13 by a few Greek witnesses and some MSS of the Vulgate, presumably reflecting liturgical usage, although a similar addition has not been made to 3 John.

[48] 'שלם לך'. On opening formulae in Aramaic letters see above p. 45 and nn. 32–3; while 'שלם' is used in concluding farewells it does not come in this formula, see Fitzmyer, 'Aramaic Epistolography', 36. It is not attested in any Hebrew letters (D. Pardee, *Handbook of Ancient Hebrew Letters*, Chico 1982). The bar Kochba letters close with a form not otherwise attested, 'Be at peace' 'הוו שלם/הוא שלם' (ibid.).

[49] 1 Pet 5.14 'Εἰρήνη ὑμῖν πᾶσιν τοῖς ἐν Χριστῷ'; see also Gal 6.16; Eph 6.23.

[50] See Barrett, *Gospel*, 568.

farewells but as a climax to the section, often of exhortation, which precedes, before then concluding with exchange of greetings and the grace formula.[51] While it is characteristic of 3 John that the benediction takes the simplest possible form with no explicit mention of God or Christ, the comparison with other New Testament letters acts as a reminder that even 3 John cannot only be understood in relation to the contemporary secular letter tradition.

This is a point needing emphasis. In the light of the papyri discoveries A. Deissmann made much of the distinction between the 'letter', natural, artless and ephemeral, and the 'epistle', bearing the form of a letter but in reality designed for publication; for him we should start from Paul's 'letters', recognising the more derivative nature of the Catholic 'epistles'.[52] While the possibility of pressing Deissmann's distinction and of applying it to the New Testament has rightly been questioned, and the more literary and self-conscious character of Paul's letters has been recognised,[53] it is they which have still provided the starting point for the analysis of the New Testament letters as *letters*. As we have seen, the results have been misleading and it might be better to recognise that it is 2 and 3 John which can most fruitfully be compared with the papyri letters, and primarily 3 John. For most of the affinities which 2 John has with the secular epistolary model are the forms it shares with the Third Epistle, while it also has links with the rather different tradition of the 'Pauline' letter pattern, and with Johannine thought.[54] 3 John's relationship with contemporary non-Christian letters, unique in the New Testament and

[51] See Gamble, *Textual History*, 67–73; J.L. White, 'St Paul and the Apostolic Letter tradition', *CBQ* 45 (1983) 433–44, 442.

[52] A. Deissmann, *Bible Studies*, Edinburgh 1901, 3–59.

[53] White, 'Apostolic Letter', 434–5.

[54] See above pp. 39–41, 47; the only parallel to the secular form to be found in 2 and not 3 John is the use of 'κυρία' and the phrase 'ἐρωτῶ σε, κυρία' (2 Jn 5), see n. 12 above.

Apostolic Fathers, is, as we shall see, consonant with the general character of its vocabulary and thought;[55] perhaps it is that uniqueness which should occasion greater surprise, highlighting the distinctiveness of the New Testament letter tradition.

This contrast between 2 and 3 John shows that as letters as well as in relation to their canonical history they defy treatment as a 'pair of inseparable twins'. The contrast is not simply that between a letter directed to a community and one sent to a private individual. In the first place such a difference does not demand a different epistolary form; Philemon, the Pastorals and Ignatius's letter to Polycarp follow the same pattern as letters to communities, while official Roman letters of the time sent to communities use the same epistolary conventions as do private letters, even praying for their health![56] However, it is also questionable whether the difference between 2 and 3 John is so simple, for the amount of common material, the 'personal' addresses in 2 John and the references to brethren, friends and the church in 3 John forbid a contrast between a community and a private letter.[57] Moreover, personal names and references, often highly ambiguous to us, to conflicts and attacks on authority, such as characterise 3 John, are common in Paul's letters and do not align 2 John with other New Testament letters and set 3 John apart on its own.

[55] See below ch. 3, p. 123.

[56] See the letter from Mark Anthony to the cities of Plarasa and Aphrodisias (39–35 BC) where Mark Anthony greets (χαίρειν) the rulers, council and people and goes on to say 'If you (pl.) are well it is good; I myself am well together with the army' (Text in R.K. Sherk, *Roman Documents from the Greek East*, Maryland 1969, 163f.).

[57] Both letters envisage visits by the Elder and it would be arbitrary to call one official and the other personal; the abrupt greeting and final peace wish give 3 John a note of pastoral authority. For the argument that 2 John's divergence from secular models in contrast to 3 John is because of its religious message which means it 'is more than a merely personal letter' see J.L. Houlden, *A Commentary on the Johannine Epistles*, London 1973, 141; Schnackenburg, *Johannesbriefe*, 295.

Rather, the distinction between 2 and 3 John must be pressed in a different direction. 3 John reads as a genuine letter according to the conventions of its age. That it is written from one who sees himself in a position of authority may be implied by the absence of a greeting word and, in a different way, by the allusive 'Peace to you'. 2 John, however, is of a different type. For the same author here to use the 'Christian' benedictory greeting must be deliberate. In its initial conception that greeting had a distinct theological significance; grace and peace are God's gifts of salvation and they are offered not as from the sender of the letter but 'from God', firmly placing the sender as the mediator of those gifts.[58] Whether the author of 2 John was conscious of this precise significance may be questionable, but he is writing with a formality and authority and, as it were, 'apostolic manner'.[59] The same conscious intent is echoed in other aspects of the letter, in the emphatic 'will be with us', in the probable personification of the church as 'the elect lady', and in the lack of any clear personal references. 2 John is more consciously constructed than 3 John and, in a sense, more artificial; even if a letter, it is more than *just* a letter.

[58] Berger, 'Apostelbrief', 202–4; Lieu, ' "Grace to you and peace" ', 170.

[59] The phrase comes from Ignatius, *Trall* Praes.; although Ignatius himself uses the Greek 'χαίρειν' formula his prescripts do have something of the elaborate quality of the Pauline openings.

Chapter Three

THE LETTERS OF THE 'PRESBYTER'

The 'Presbyter'

If the preceding chapters suggest that both the common ground and the contrast between 2 and 3 John point to an intriguing history, this emerges yet more clearly in the detailed exegesis of the letters, and perhaps nowhere more clearly than in the vexed problem of the address.

As we have seen, both letters open with the standard form, 'A to B', but the way in which the author names himself has yet to find a satisfactory explanation—'The Elder' (ὁ πρεσβύτερος). In contemporary letters the name of the sender was frequently accompanied by his title or office, but here we apparently have the title or office without a personal name.[1] Clearly the designation must have functioned as a name—it must have been as well known as the author's own name and have been particularly appropriate in the context of these letters. The difference between 2 and 3 John makes it difficult to decide how selfconscious the use might be; 2 John with its address to 'the elect lady' might encourage reading 'the Elder' in a similarly symbolic or metaphorical sense,[2] but this is questionable in 3 John where the recipient is simply 'Gaius', surely the real name of a real person.

Our problem lies in the variety of ways the term 'Elder' could be used, and yet far from having a surfeit of possibilities, none quite fits 2 and 3 John. Fundamentally and most naturally

[1] It is unlikely that the name has dropped out or been intentionally removed as suggested by E. Schwartz, *Über den Tod der Söhne Zebedaei*, Berlin 1904, 52. On the reading 'Iohannes senior' in 2 Jn 1 see ch.1, p. 28 and n. 84.

[2] On the metaphorical meaning of 'the elect lady' see below pp. 65–6 and nn. 42–6.

'Elders' (οἱ πρεσβύτεροι) are those who, being more advanced in age, wisdom or social standing, hold special authority whether or not within a formally constituted office; invariably it is a corporate term: 'Elders' work in groups.

Thus in the Graeco-Roman world 'πρεσβύτεροι' formed the governing bodies of villages or of a variety of associations,[3] while in the New Testament they are Jewish officials, and particularly members of the group who, along with the chief priests and scribes, formed the Sanhedrin.[4] Whether or not related to this technical use, in the Christian church 'Elders'/'Presbyters' also came to hold an authoritative position in the local community (Acts 20.17 etc.), apparently as a group, and only later as part of a threefold 'bishops, elders and deacons'.[5] The absence of a distinguishing personal name or of the name of a local church makes a reference to an essentially collegiate office unlikely. The main proponent of such a view is E. Käsemann who saw the author of the Epistles and Gospel as one such 'presbyter' who had been excommunicated for the 'heretical' views expressed in the Gospel but who, continuing as a 'lone wolf', held on to the title of the office he had once held.[6] Quite apart from the credibility of Käsemann's whole thesis, to

[3] Deissmann, *Bible Studies*, 154–7; H. Hauschlidt, 'Πρεσβύτεροι in Agypten im I–III Jahrhundert n Chr.', *ZNW* 4 (1903) 235–42; F. Poland, *Geschichte des griechischen Vereinswesens*, Leipzig 1909, 373.

[4] e.g. Mt 16.21; 21.23; 26.3 etc. On the question of the Jewish use of 'πρεσβύτερος' outside Palestine see G. Bornkamm, art. 'πρέσβυς', *TDNT* VI, 651–80, 660–1; A.E. Harvey, 'Elders', *JThS* NS 25 (1974) 318–32. It is unlikely that the author was an ex-member of the Sanhedrin as suggested by E.C. Selwyn, *The Christian Prophets and the Prophetic Apocalypse*, London 1900, 133f. (identifying the author of these Epistles and of the Apocalypse).

[5] Bornkamm, 'πρέσβυς', 662–8; Harvey, 'Elders', questions whether there is sufficient evidence that they formed an organised council or were dependent on a similar Jewish institution.

[6] E. Käsemann, 'Ketzer und Zeuge', *ZThK* 48 (1951) 292–311; in 'Zur Johannes-Interpretation in England', *Exegetische Versuche und Besinnungen* II, Göttingen 1964, 131–33, n. 1 he admitted himself convinced by arguments for the different authorship of the Gospel and Epistles.

which we shall return, for a man who was rejected by and who to some extent rejected the ecclesiastical 'establishment', so to cling to and exalt his former ecclesiastical office seems hardly probable.

However, there is some evidence of 'monarchical' or single ruling elders, mainly in Egypt but possibly elsewhere in the early period when considerable variety of practice and terminology might be expected; alternatively we might envisage the emergence of a leader among the elders (*praeses presbyterii*) especially in the light of Polycarp's words in his letter to the Philippians, 'Polycarp and the Elders with him'.[7] A number of interpreters have seen the Elder of 2 and 3 John in such a role, having sole or primary responsibility for a local church (the 'elect sister' of 2 Jn 13), although writing to members of other communities.[8] Yet it is doubtful whether this can explain our enigmatic 'The Elder', for while possibly self-explanatory in 3 John if Gaius was a member of the author's church, the absolute use of the title in 2 John when writing to another church implies a recognition which is not tied to a single community.

Hence the designation 'πρεσβύτερος' is unlikely to signal status within the ecclesiastical structure of the church as known to us; it is clearly the term which identifies the author to those who belong to the same Christian tradition as he. Yet it must be

[7] For a single ruling elder see Athanasius, *C. Arianos* 63 (PG 25:363); Eutychius, *Annales* (PG 91:982D) says there was no bishop in Egypt until the time of Demetrius (beginning of 3rd C.). E. Schweizer, *Church Order in the New Testament*, London 1961, §9b, n. 422 sees a reference in 1 Pet 5.3 to a part of a church or a local church under a single presbyter. Polycarp, *Philipp* 1.1 'Πολύκαρπος καὶ οἱ σὺν αὐτῷ πρεσβύτεροι'.

[8] Houlden, *Epistles*, 5; K. Donfried, 'Ecclesiastical Authority in 2–3 John', in *L'Évangile de Jean*, ed. M. de Jonge, Gembloux 1977, 325–33. E. Haenchen, 'Neue Literatur zu den Johannesbriefen', *ThR* 26 (1960/61) 1–43, 267–91, 290–1 sees the author as 'praeses presbyterii' like Polycarp, but also as a bearer of tradition in the sense discussed below. See below ch. 4, p. 152 and nn. 74–75.

more than the affectionate epithet by which he was known to his friends, 'The Old Man',[9] for the question of authority runs through both letters and that authority would need to be established in their openings.

These difficulties have led many interpreters to appeal to 'the Elder' or 'Presbyter' as a semi-technical designation of a 'bearer of tradition' and a 'disciple of the Apostles'. According to this understanding, 'the Elders' as a group primarily associated with Asia Minor formed a bridge between the Apostles and the post-Apostolic church. As a member of this group the author would have held a sufficiently significant position among the Christians of the area to be able to refer to himself simply as 'The Elder'.[10]

The existence of such a group has been deduced from an oft-quoted passage of Papias reported by Eusebius and from Irenaeus's frequent references to Elders as his authorities. Papias, so he himself claimed, sought only to use such material as could be authenticated as coming from the Lord and from those who were his disciples:

> If then at any time someone came who had followed the Elders, I asked the words of the Elders; what Andrew or what Peter said or what Philip or what Thomas or James or John or Matthew or any other of the disciples of the Lord (said), and the things Aristion and the Elder John (ὁ πρεσβύτερος Ἰωάννης), the disciples of the Lord, were saying. For I did not think that things from books would be of as much value for me as things from the living and abiding voice.[11]

Irenaeus specifically refers to 'the Elders who lived with John

---

[9] An appropriate nickname for the long-lived John of Ephesus whom tradition identified with the Apostle: Eusebius, *HE* III.18.1–3; 20.9 (all references from Eusebius, *HE* are taken from GCS 9); see above ch. 1, p. 31 and n. 92.

[10] This view is succinctly put by C.H. Dodd, *The Johannine Epistles*, London 1946, 155–6.

[11] Eusebius, *HE* III.39.4.

55

the disciple of the Lord in Asia' some of whom had also seen and heard other Apostles. These Elders can themselves be called 'the disciples of the Apostles'.[12]

The term is also used by other writers as a designation for earlier authorities; Eusebius himself uses it to refer to Irenaeus among others while outside Asia Minor its most important use is by Clement of Alexandria in whose writings it refers in the plural to those who pass on traditions and in the singular to a particular authority quoted anonymously.[13] Only by Irenaeus are the Elders explicitly called disciples of the Apostles.

Much has been built on this basis. Papias's Elders have somehow justified seeing the author of the Epistles not only as a disciple of the Apostles and witness to Apostolic tradition, but also as a charismatic figure, a prophet-teacher of the early type or one with a 'patriarchal', non-institutional authority over a whole province.[14] Keeping closer to Papias's words, others have grasped the reference to 'the Elder John' and, following a tradition we found in Jerome, have ascribed at least the minor Epistles to him, thus combining the author's self-designation as 'The Elder' and the traditional ascription to 'John' by the theory of an early confusion between the Elder John and the Apostle.[15]

The attraction of the hypothesis is obvious, but the sources can scarcely bear the weight of the elaborate and fanciful constructions built upon them. In the first place, the passage of Papias is not without ambiguity. From the wording and grammatical construction 'the Elders' could refer either to the

---

[12] Irenaeus, *AH* II.22.5; V.5.1; also IV.27.1; V.36.1 (following the text of the SC edition).

[13] Eusebius *HE* V.8.1; Clement of Alexandria, *Ecl. Proph.* XI.1; XXVII.1, 4 (GCS 17, 139, 144–5) see Eusebius, *HE* VI.13.8–9; 14.4–5.

[14] See below ch. 4, pp. 151–2 and nn. 71–3.

[15] See above ch. 1, pp. 12–3 and nn. 24–30; so for example, A.v. Harnack, *Über den dritten Johannesbrief*, TU 15.3b., Leipzig 1897.

Apostles or to those who could report their words.[16] J.B. Lightfoot's magisterial pronouncement that the view which distinguishes between the Elders and the Apostles, seeing the former as disciples of the latter, 'demands such a violent wresting of the grammatical construction in the passage of Papias that it is not likely to find much favour'[17] has proved a false prophecy. It is now that view which is the more popular one in modern scholarship, although the alternative possibility that the Elders at least included the Apostles has sometimes provided a justification for the Apostle John, as the author of the Epistles, so designating himself;[18] this latter approach can also hold that Papias's 'Elder John' is not a separate person but the Apostle John, aged but still alive at that time.

More fundamental is the weakness of the assumption that the Elders formed a defined group in Asia Minor. Papias gives no hint as to where his Elders might be found; even if he had once learned directly from them, his dependence on the reports of others about their words when he wrote his *Expositions* in Hierapolis near Colossae and Laodicaea suggests they were not immediately available.[19]

The issue is more complex in Irenaeus and cannot be

---

[16] Thus 'what Andrew . . . said' (τί Ἀνδρέας . . . εἶπεν) may be parallel with or give the content of 'the words of the elders' (τοὺς τῶν πρεσβυτέρων λόγους); in the former case Andrew etc. would be among the Elders; the change of tense and of construction from 'what Andrew . . . *said*' and 'the things Aristion . . . *were saying*' (λέγουσιν) adds to the uncertainty.

[17] J.B. Lightfoot, *Essays on the Work entitled 'Supernatural Religion'*, London 1880, 145.

[18] So originally Schnackenburg, *Johannesbriefe*, 1st edition, Freiburg 1953, 263–4 although in the 6th edition he leaves the question open (296); others who argue that the term could include the Apostles are J. Munck, 'Presbyters and Disciples of the Lord', *HThR* 52 (1952) 223–43; T. Zahn, 'Apostel und Apostelschüler in der Provinz Asien', *Forschungen* VI, Leipzig 1900, 109–51.

[19] Although the phrase in the previous section 'ὅσα ποτε παρὰ τῶν πρεσβυτέρων καλῶς ἔμαθον' may imply direct learning from the Elders at one stage.

separated from his own understanding of the crux of the conflict with Gnosticism. Essential weapons in his attack, and yet also the very bulwarks he sees as set at nought by his opponents, are Scripture and its valid interpretation, the teaching of the Lord and the preaching of his words by his disciples, and the tradition which conveys and guarantees this within the church, along with the structures of the church itself, its unity, unanimity and its authorities.[20] By appealing to 'the Elders' Irenaeus unites all these, although the variety both in the terms used and in those to whom they might refer—including non-Christian authorities—reflects the more complex reality.[21] He can move from speaking of Elders as authorities for tradition to Elders as officials within the church, in whose number are bishops, thus combining the succession of bishops with the continuity of Apostolic tradition—which helps his cause but obscures for us the historical identity of the Elders to whose traditions and interpretations he appeals.[22]

Irenaeus does refer, as already noted, to the Elders who knew John in Asia, some of whom had also seen other Apostles, and he implicitly includes Papias among these Elders, describing him as a 'hearer of John' (*Adv Haer* V.33). Eusebius denies that Papias

[20] See G. Vallée, 'Theological and non-Theological Motives in Irenaeus's Refutation of the Gnostics', in *Jewish and Christian Self-definition*, ed. E.P. Sanders, I, 174–85.

[21] The terms he uses include 'ὁ κρείσσων ἡμῶν' (Lat.: superior nobis?), 'πρεσβύτης', 'τις τῶν προβεβηκότων' and, only in the Latin translation, 'quidam ex veteribus', 'hi qui ante nos fuerunt', 'quidam ante nos'; 'senior' probably represents 'πρεσβύτερος' or 'πρεσβύτης'. In *AH* III.23.3 and IV.41.2 non-Christian authorities may be cited.

[22] Irenaeus speaks of the apostolic tradition as continued through the succession of Elders and Bishops (*AH* I.27.1; IV.26.2f) in view of the lack of any clear break between IV.26 (succession of Elders) and IV.27 (Scriptural interpretation handed down by a 'certain Elder') it is difficult to draw a sharp line between Elders in the church and as authorities, as does J.B. Lightfoot, *St Paul's Epistle to the Philippians*, London 1908, 228f.; see also Bornkamm, 'πρέσβυς', 676f. and A. Ehrhardt, *The Apostolic Succession*, London 1953, 109ff.

made this claim, although he acknowledges his link with the, for him separate, 'Elder John'—but Eusebius, with his prejudice against Papias and his millenarian teaching, would not want to associate him with the Apostles.[23] What then was Irenaeus's knowledge of 'the Elders'? Most of his references to what the Elders said or taught could refer to oral or written sources and some have argued that most of these are in effect drawn from Papias,[24] and from the same source may have come the link with the Apostles which was so crucial to his argument. It is of course a notorious problem that not only the association of the Elders with John of Ephesus, but also the whole related tradition of the long sojourn of John the Apostle in Ephesus cannot be confidently traced before the time of Irenaeus.[25] We must add to this the nature of the teaching he ascribes to the Elders— including millenarian interpretations and questionable traditions about Jesus—which renders improbable their close link with Jesus or with the first Apostles.[26]

The depiction of the Elders as a defined group of reliable bearers of the tradition of the Apostles may well be a simplistic and anachronistic reconstruction intiated by Irenaeus and developed by more recent scholars in an attempt to bridge the confused and complex period between the Apostles and later generations. The fluidity with which other authors use the title lends little support to the attempt to see the Elders as such a

[23] Eusebius, *HE* III.39.2; see also his description of Papias as of 'very little intelligence' (III.39.13). A. Gustafsson, 'Eusebius' Principles in handling his sources as found in his Church History Books I–VII', in *Studia Patristica* IV, TU 79, Berlin 1961, 428–41 argues that Eusebius did not have direct access to Papias's works.

[24] See the discussion in Bornkamm, 'πρέσβυς', 677–8.

[25] See Gunther, 'Early Identifications'; H.B. Swete, 'John of Ephesus', *JThS* 17 (1916) 375–8; J. Regul, *Die antimarcionitischen Evanglienprologe*, Freiburg 1969, 134–5 argues that Irenaeus's association of the Elders with John might be solely based on their knowledge of Revelation (*AH* V.30.1).

[26] See *AH* II.22.5; V.33.3; 36.1–2; however, this raises questions about the origin and antiquity of early Christian millenarian teaching.

recognisable body, neither can the possible currency of the term in Asia Minor to designate earlier authorities prove that such authorities were primarily to be found in Asia Minor.[27]

Yet even were we to rely on what Papias and Irenaeus do say about the Elders, they are there, as in later authors, associated mainly with traditions about New Testament books and the interpretation of Scripture, serving to authenticate traditions and to provide continuity. There is nothing to suggest that they exercised any disciplinary authority or control unless in virtue of their personality or some additional status—Polycarp, even if designated an 'Elder' in this sense by Irenaeus, drew his authority both from his ecclesiastical position and from his personality, as is demonstrated in the story of his encounter with Marcion.[28] Status as 'one of Papias's Elders' cannot be taken to imply a recognised authority in the life of the early church. Neither do terms such as 'charismatic' or 'itinerant' find support in the sources, and certainly not in Papias's bland reference to the 'coming' of the followers of the Elders.[29] It is true that Eusebius does refer to those who followed the Apostles, spreading the Gospel and building up the churches, but he knows little about them and probably assumes their existence as part of his idealised view of the purity and the unity of the early church.[30] We shall meet again the picture of charismatic figures holding wide pastoral authority but certainly they cannot be seen behind Papias's and Irenaeus's shadowy references to the

---

[27] R.P.C. Hanson, *Tradition*, 35ff. suggests that the 'Elders' are the result of a 2nd century attempt to bridge the gap with the Apostles; some scholars have located the Elders in Jerusalem because of the Jewish-Christian links of their millenarian teaching; see B.W. Bacon, 'Date and Habitat of the Elders of Papias', *ZNW* 12 (1911) 176–8.

[28] Eusebius, *HE* V.20.4–8; Irenaeus, *AH* III.3.4.

[29] Bornkamm, 'πρέσβυς', 677 argues that they were itinerant on the basis of the use of 'ἔρχεσθαι' instead of 'παρακολουθεῖν' which is used of their relationship with the Elders; see further below.

[30] Eusebius, *HE* III.37.

Elders, and neither can the latter then be used to identify the Elder of 2 and 3 John.[31]

The fruits of the imagination have been even more abundant in the reconstruction of 'the Elder John'. It is often forgotten that we know nothing about him beyond the brief reference already quoted from Papias. We have already traced his assocation with Ephesus to Eusebius who was combining Papias's allusion with Dionysius of Alexandria's mention of two memorials 'of John' in Ephesus; his authorship of Revelation, supported by Eusebius, was later contested in favour of his responsibility for 2 and 3 John, a suggestion we first meet in Jerome.[32] That he was a disciple of the Apostle John, and other modern, more detailed reconstructions of his career are founded not on any other sources but on the desire to solve problems of the authorship of the Johannine corpus about which we have no certain reliable traditions.[33] Yet even the initial reference in Papias must remain shrouded in ambiguity; that he should be

---

[31] Thus Bornkamm, 'πρέσβυς', 672, n. 125 overstates the case by saying 'with confidence that there was an honorary group of elders' and that they were 'peculiarly if not exclusively the normative guarantors of the Johannine tradition' and when he suggests (678, n. 174) 'may we with tongue in cheek call them one of the first theological faculties in the form presupposed in Iren.?'!

[32] See ch. 1, pp. 13–14 and nn. 27–28.

[33] Some have tried to introduce a more precise identification of the Elder John into the text of Papias; thus for 'οι του κυριου μαθηται' (the disciples of the Lord), Bacon, 'Date and Habitat', 185 reads 'οι τουτω μαθηται' (disciples of these, ie the apostles), while W. Larfeld, 'Das Zeugnis des Papias über die beiden Johannes von Ephesus', *NKZ* 33 (1922) 490–512 reads 'οι του ιω μαθηται' (the disciples of John). A. Mingana, 'The Authorship of the Fourth Gospel. A New Document', *JRLB* 14 (1930) 333–39 describes a Syriac MS referring to a 'John the Younger' as a disciple of the Apostle whom Mingana identifies with Papias's second John; cf. *Apost. Const.* VII.46 where John was consecrated 'a me Ioanne' as bishop of Ephesus. For a criticism of the misuse of Papias and the proliferation of Johns see G. Dix, 'The Use and Abuse of Papias on the Fourth Gospel', *Theol* 24 (1932) 8–20 and J. Donovan, 'The Elder John and Other Johns', *IER* 31 (1928) 337–50.

distinguished from the Apostle John is not totally beyond doubt while the epithet 'elder' has variously been taken as identifying him with the 'Elders' already mentioned in the passage, or as an elder of a local church so designated in distinction from the Apostle, or as establishing a link with the tradition of the aged John of Ephesus.[34] Eusebius gives us no clue as to how he took the epithet and we have no additional information on which to make an independent decision. All that the text, if not corrupt, tells us is that he was a disciple of the Lord, which most naturally means of Jesus during his lifetime, and that he was the authority of some of Papias's material, possibly including his report about the origin of Mark's Gospel and perhaps some of his millenarian doctrines.[35] We know nothing about where he lived or what his position in the life of the church may have been.

When discussing the origin of Mark's Gospel Papias cites his source simply as 'the Elder', just as Irenaeus and Clement of Alexandria each refer to a particular authority anonymously as 'the Elder' as well as appealing more generally to 'the Elders' in the plural.[36] That one could refer to oneself as 'the Elder' in this fashion is far less probable; it is an appeal to an earlier generation or respected individual as the source and authority for teaching. Papias uses it of those before him while Irenaeus seems to include Papias among the Elders; in due course Eusebius lists

[34] The combination of a title of respect with a personal name is strange; J. Munck, 'Presbyters and Disciples' compares 'The Grand Old Man' as used of Gladstone which would never be prefixed to his name as 'The Grand Old Man Gladstone'; yet the particular mention of his ecclesiastical office seems equally strange in the context.

[35] For 'the elder's' traditions about Mark see Eusebius, *HE* III.39.15; however, it is not obvious from Eusebius's account that the Elder (John) was the source of Papias's millenarian views.

[36] For Papias see n. 35; 'Elder' used in the singular; Irenaeus, *AH* IV.27.1f.; 30.1–31.1; Clement of Alexandria, *Ecl. Proph.* L.1; *In Epist. Iohannis Prima* 1.1 (GCS 17, 150, 210); plural: Irenaeus, *AH* V.33.3; 36.1; Clement of Alexandria, *Ecl. Proph.* XXVII.1 (GCS 17, 144); *Protepticus* XI.113.1 (GCS Clemens Alexandrinus I, 79).

Irenaeus among them. The title reflects a later generation's estimate of their predecessors, not one's own estimate of oneself! It would hardly belong in the opening of a letter.

That Papias's Elders are relevant to an understanding of the author of 2 and 3 John is therefore highly doubtful. Yet this is to admit that none of the many uses of the term are directly relevant. It would be attractive to see in the absolute use a self-conscious claim to the title in a unique sense—the Elder *par excellence*—and we might then think of Clement of Alexandria's later assertion that the true elder is not necessarily one appointed by men but he who 'does and teaches the things of the Lord', namely the true 'gnostic' for Clement, a member of a spiritual elite.[37] This, with its implicit criticism of the church office, might seem to accord with Johannine thought,[38] but it would perhaps be too sophisticated for the author of 2 and 3 John.

Certainly the title can hardly avoid implying some claim to seniority in the Christian faith and this is reinforced by his reference to his readers as 'children', but to conlude that the author was thus representing himself as *the* bearer of Johannine tradition or that there is a Wisdom or 'school' background is giving the language more content than it can carry.[39] We can only conclude that although some clue may well lie in the

[37] Clement of Alexandria, *Strom.* VI.106 (GCS 52, 485); M. Hornschuh, 'Das Leben des Origenes und die Entstehung der alexandrinischen Schule', *ZKG* 71 (1960) 1–25, 193–214, 201 asks whether the use of 'presbyters' of teachers in Clement might express a critical relationship with the church office and even be a self-designation.

[38] A Kragerud, *Der Lieblingsjünger im Johannesevangelium*, Oslo 1959, 110f. sees the article (ὁ πρεσβύτερος) as implying 'par excellence'. See further below ch. 4, pp. 156–8.

[39] R.E. Brown, *The Epistles of John*, New York 1982, 213–4 links the use of 'children' (τέκνα) with Wisdom language and with the father-children relationship of the passing on of tradition; for Johannine Christianity as a 'school' see also R. Culpepper, *The Johannine School*, SBLDS 26, Missoula 1975, esp. 261–90.

complex of material we have studied,[40] the title remains oblique and we cannot use it to interpret the Epistles—rather it may only be illuminated from the Epistles themselves.

2 John

Our study so far would lead us to expect to discover an uneasy relationship between 2 John and its 'twin', the Third Epistle. In its history it could be found rather in the company of 1 John and as a letter it stands caught between bearing the marks of a genuine correspondence and suggesting hints of a more artificial construction. To turn to the text in detail is to find this expectation confirmed and expanded. Yet we shall see that what can be read as a pale version of 1 John does in fact have its own deliberate structure and purpose.

The Greeting

1–3

1 Ὁ πρεσβύτερος ἐκλεκτῇ κυρίᾳ καὶ τοῖς τέκνοις αὐτῆς, οὓς ἐγὼ ἀγαπῶ ἐν ἀληθείᾳ, καὶ οὐκ ἐγὼ μόνος ἀλλὰ καὶ πάντες οἱ ἐγνωκότες τὴν ἀλήθειαν, 2 διὰ τὴν ἀλήθειαν τὴν μένουσαν ἐν ἡμῖν καὶ μεθ' ἡμῶν ἔσται εἰς τὸν αἰῶνα. 3 ἔσται μεθ' ἡμῶν χάρις ἔλεος εἰρήνη παρὰ θεοῦ πατρὸς καὶ παρὰ Ἰησοῦ Χριστοῦ τοῦ υἱοῦ τοῦ πατρὸς ἐν ἀληθείᾳ καὶ ἀγάπῃ.

The Elder to the elect lady and her children, whom I love in truth, and not I alone but also all who know the truth, through the truth which remains in us and will be with us for ever. There

---

[40] Although we have stressed the paucity of evidence for many modern reconstructions the material remains tantalising, not least the possibility of some link between 'the Elder' of 2 and 3 John, the disciple 'who would not die' of Jn 21, Papias's 'Elder John' and the tradition of the long-lived John of Ephesus; each of these figures, together with Papias's 'Elders' remains enigmatic.

will be with us grace, mercy, peace from God the Father and from Jesus Christ the Son of the Father in truth and love.

The anonymity of the author of the letter is apparently matched by the anonymity of its recipient.[41] Moreover, while it is true that 'lady' (κυρία) is used in the papyri letters in affectionate respect addressing a mother, sister or close friend, the use of 'elect' and the tone of the letter imply something more formal here, and indeed are best explained by the suggestion that the letter is addressed to a church rather than to a particular Christian matron and her family.[42] On the same grounds we need not suppose that the church met in the house of, or was headed by, a 'lady'; it is more likely that this is a personification of the church and as such is part of a rich conceptual tradition with firm biblical roots but also with pagan parallels.[43]

[41] 'Your elect sister' in v. 13 prohibits reading 'Electa' as a proper name while an article would be expected before 'ἐκλεκτῇ' (elect) if 'κυρία' were a proper name. Some older commentaries do read Kyria—F. Lücke, *A Commentary on the Epistles of St John*, Edinburgh 1837, 322; J.H.A. Ebrard, *Biblical Commentary on the Epistles of St John*, Edinburgh 1860, 377f.

[42] For the patristic view of the letter as to an individual see ch. 1 p. 31, n. 94 and for this in the light of the papyri, ch. 2, p. 42, n. 21; such scholars then speculate as to why she is the head of the household; Rendel Harris, 'Problem of the Address' concludes she is a widow of the tribe of Ruth. D. Pape, *God and Women*, London 1976, 206 sees the prevalent interpretation of the 'lady' as a church as another example of the failure of scholarship to acknowledge the importance of women in the New Testament, but her positive arguments are weak. E. Gaugler, *Die Johannesbriefe*, Zurich 1964, 283 offers a compromise—she is a Christian woman whose home hosts a church meeting.

[43] For pagan parallels and the use of 'κυρία' of a political community in dedication stones see F.J. Dolger, 'DOMINA MATER ECCLESIA und die "Herrin" im zweiten Johannesbriefe', in *Antike und Christentum* V, Munster 1936, 211–17; for the discussion of its possible use in a synagogue inscription see N. Hyldahl, 'A supposed Synagogue Inscription', *NTS* 25 (1978/9) 396–8. The origins of the concept of the church as 'mother', have been much discussed with some suggesting influence from gnosticism, Oriental cults or the imperial cult; see J.C. Plumpe, *Mater Ecclesia*, Washington 1943 and the review by C.Mohrmann in *VigChr* 2 (1948) 57–8. There is some evidence linking the concept with Asia Minor (ibid.).

Jerusalem is portrayed vividly as a woman in Isaiah, and later in Baruch and 2 Esdras, while Paul contrasts the earthly with the heavenly Jerusalem through an allegory of Hagar and Sarah.[44] The new Jerusalem is represented as a bride in Rev 21.1, as is the church in 2 Cor 11.2 and Eph 5.25f. Referring to a specific church, presumably at Rome, 1 Pet 5.13 speaks of 'the elect one (fem.) in Babylon', and probably it was with this passage in mind that Clement of Alexandria wrote of 2 John, 'It was written to a certain Babylonian "Electa" by name, but it signifies the election of the holy church'.[45] Outside the New Testament, in the *Odes of Solomon* 33.5 'the perfect virgin' may represent the church, while in the *Visions* of Hermas a woman, addressed as 'lady' (κυρία) clearly does so (*Vis* I.2.2f.; II.4.1f. etc.). There Hermas has to be told who she is (*Vis* II.4.1), whereas in the letter from the Churches of Lyons and Vienne 'the virgin mother' (ἡ παρθένος μήτηρ) is used of the church without any explanation, showing that the metaphor was now well established (Eusebius, *HE* V.1.45). More directly part of the background to 2 John, it is possible that in the Gospel of John there is a prefigurement of the church in the mother of Jesus.[46]

However, the use of this imagery in the address of a letter is without parallel,[47] and points to the selfconscious use of the letter form in 2 John. The reference to 'your elect sister' with

[44] Is 54; Baruch 4–5; 2 Esdras 9–10; Gal 4.21f. See H.J. Gibbins, 'The Second Epistle of St John', *Exp* VI.6 (1902) 228–36; VI.12 (1905) 412–24.

[45] For Clement's comment see ch. 1, p. 29, n. 89.

[46] See A. Feuillet, 'La récherche du Christ dans la Nouvelle Alliance d'après la Christophanie de Jo.20.11–18', in *L'homme devant Dieu* I, Aubier 1963, 93–112 and the caution of J. McHugh, *The Mother of Jesus in the New Testament*, London 1975, 351–403.

[47] R.M. Grant, 'Notes on Gnosis', *VigChr* 11 (1957) 145–51 suggests that Ptolemaeus's letter to 'Flora' is addressed to the Christian church in Rome with reference to Ioannes Lydus, *De Mensibus* IV.73 who gives the city a mystical name (Ἔρως), a political name (Ῥῶμα) and a priestly name (Φλῶρα). However, the letter uses 2nd person sing. throughout with no hint of a wider readership.

her children in v. 13 suggests that an individual church is intended as the recipient of the letter, although the absence of any more specific characterisation of the church speaks against such a restriction.

The language itself reflects the author's understanding of the church. 'Elect' (ἐκλεκτός) does not occur elsewhere in the Johannine corpus,[48] although in the Gospel the verb 'to choose' (ἐκλέγομαι) is used, for it is fundamental to the disciples' relationship with Jesus that *he* has chosen them (Jn 6.70; 13.18; 15.16,19). The adjective 'elect'/'chosen' is used increasingly in the New Testament and Apostolic Fathers in the plural of Christians, no doubt because of its biblical use for Israel as 'an elect people' (1 Pet 2.9 with reference to Is 43.20 etc.). This, together with its use in eschatological contexts of those whose ultimate salvation is assured (Mk 13.20,22,27), puts the emphasis on the inherent or achieved nature of Christian status in relation to the world and to God rather than on the act or the initiator of that choosing.

Thus the phrase, **'the elect lady'**, used as an address, does imply a concentration on the divine calling and status of the church rather than on her historical form. This suggests that, despite the apparently specific situation behind 2 John, the letter probably had a wider catholic purpose, at least within the Johannine circle.

If, then, the 'lady' is the church, **'her children'**, who are also greeted, must be its members.[49] In a rather different use of the image, but one with many parallels, the Elder addresses Gaius in 3 John as 'my child', just as a 'spiritual' father or teacher does his protégé.[50] The Greek word used in both Epistles is 'τέκνον', in

[48] Except of Jesus at Jn 1.34 by P[5vid] ℵ* b e ff[2*] sy; electus filius a ff[2c] sa.
[49] As in Is 54; Baruch 4–5; Gal 4.21–31; Hermas, *Vis* III.9.
[50] 3 Jn 4; cf. A. Oepke, art. 'παῖς', *TDNT* V, 636–54, 638–9. The author speaks of '*my* children' in 3 John but not in 2 John, not because the community of 2 John was not brought to faith by him (so Haenchen, 'Neue Literatur', 285), but because of the image of the lady and *her* children.

common with the New Testament and other parallels; in contrast, the Gospel and First Epistle use the rare diminutive forms 'τεκνία', 'παιδία' in address to the disciples or members of the community, reserving 'τέκνον' for describing spiritual origin, 'children of God', 'Abraham' or 'the devil'.[51]

Just as the address of the letter may well be intended to point beyond its apparently private guise, so what follows confirms that the author is not sending a purely personal missive but writes within a circle of those whose standing in the faith is mutually acknowledged—**'not I alone but also all who know the truth'** are those who **'love in truth'** the elect lady and her children. Whereas in the Gospel it is promised to those who are faithful to Jesus's teaching that they 'will know the truth and the truth will make (them) free' (Jn 8.32), here the phrase is a definition of the true believer, as evident in the use of the perfect tense, 'know' (lit. 'have known').[52]

There is a (Johannine) circle of mutual love; it is also a circle which is best characterised by the word 'truth'. Love is 'in truth', it is given by all who 'know the truth', all this is **'through the truth which remains in us and will be with us'**,[53] while loosely appended to the whole greeting is the phrase **'in truth and love'.** The term 'truth' (ἀλήθεια) comes with

[51] 'τέκνα τοῦ θεοῦ' Jn 1.12; 11.52; 1 Jn 3.1,2,10; 5.2; 'τέκνα τοῦ Ἀβρααμ' Jn 8.39; 'τέκνα τοῦ διαβόλου' 1 Jn 3.10; 'τεκνία' Jn 13.33; 1 Jn 2.1,12,28; 3.7,18; 4.4; 5.21; 'παιδία' Jn 21.5; 1 Jn 2.14,18. For 'τέκνον' used by a 'missionary' see 1 Tim 1.2; 2 Tim 1.2; 1 Cor 4.14,17. 'τεκνία' is found as a v.l. at Gal 4.19.

[52] See 1 Jn 2.21 where it is said the readers do know the truth using 'οἶδα'; in both cases the possession of 'the truth' distinguishes the true believer. Brown, *Epistles*, 681 suggests 'those who have come to know the truth' was a 'self-description used by members of the Johannine community'.

[53] On the participle followed by a finite verb see F. Blass & A. Debrunner, *A Greek Grammar of the New Testament and other early Christian Literature*, translated and revised by R.W. Funk, Chicago & Cambridge 1961 (B.D.), §468(3). Turner, *Style*, 137 calls this a Semitism. For 'μένουσαν' A reads 'ἐνοικοῦσαν' and 33 *pc* co read' 'οὖσαν'; the omission of 'διὰ τὴν ἀλήθειαν' by some witnesses is presumably by haplography.

surprising frequency in 2 and 3 John—eleven times (in 1 Jn 9 times; in Jn 25 times)—but often (six times) in the phrase 'in truth'; of the five occurrences in 2 John, four are here packed into the greeting, the fifth coming in the phrase 'walking in truth' (v. 4). While truth is undoubtedly an important term in the Johannine corpus, there is little feel here of the significance the term has in 1 John and the Gospel. In 1 John 'truth' is characteristically used in a dualist framework in contrast to falsehood (explicitly in 1.6,8; 2.4,21; 4.6 and by implication in 2.21; 3.18, 19; 5.6). Despite the polemical note of both Epistles, and particularly 2 John, that dualist use is not explicit and the vocabulary of falsehood is missing, even from the description of the 'deceivers' who are no longer 'false prophets' (v. 7, cf. 1 Jn 4.1).[54] The Gospel also does not use 'truth' in explicit contrast to falsehood—'doing the truth' is contrasted with lying in 1 Jn 1.6 but with doing wrong in Jn 3.21—but it does use it in a bewildering variety of ways clearly reflecting a rich background, but with a meaning which often includes ideas of norm, revelation and divine reality.[55]

That richness and weight of meaning can hardly be read into 'truth' here in 2 Jn 1–3 (or, probably, into its other occurrences in the minor Epistles); rather it would seem to be preeminently that which can characterise the community and its members. Truth belongs to the community—it 'remains in us and will be with us for ever'—rather than the community to the truth (as in Jn 8.32; 18.37). The increased use of the prepositional phrase 'in truth', whose meaning is not always obvious, and particularly the final 'in truth and love' here, suggests that the term is becoming a catchword or slogan for what is, in the author's

---

[54] See Appendix 1, Table E. 1 John's dualist use of light vs. darkness is also missing from 2 and 3 John.

[55] On 'truth' in the Johannine writings see F. Büchsel, *Der Begriff der Wahrheit in dem Evangelium und den Briefen Johannes*, Gütersloh 1911; R. Bultmann, art. 'ἀλήθεια' D, *TDNT* I, 241–7.

eyes, genuinely Johannine.[56] Yet to see it here as meaning 'the true teaching' or 'Christian faith', similar to the use of 'faith' in the Pastoral Epistles,[57] is to give it too great precision. Indeed, while increasingly looking like a Johannine slogan, this weakening of truth has also brought it closer to its conventional use, 'sincerely', in the letters of the day.[58]

The assurance of the abiding possession of truth is continued as 'grace, mercy, peace' are offered, not as a blessing as in the original Pauline form of the greeting from which this is derived, but as a statement of the confidence of a self-conscious elect: **'There will be with us grace, mercy, peace'.**[59] As we have seen, the Pauline form already signified not merely a conventional greeting but a blessing given by one (an apostle) with the authority to mediate God's salvation. In 2 John various motifs have given the greeting a more Johannine tone—the replacement of the Pauline 'ἀπό' by the more Johannine 'παρά' (from), unusually also repeated before 'the Son', the description of Jesus as **'the Son of the Father'**—a unique phrase sounding like an emphatic 'Johanneism'—instead of as 'Lord', and the addition of 'in truth and love';[60] strengthened by these the greeting gives the letter more than a merely personal authority, and it is this note we must expect to find continued as we pursue the argument of the letter.

[56] The closest parallel to this combination of truth and love comes in 3 Jn 3, 6 'witness to your truth/love'.

[57] So R. Bergmeier, 'Zum Verfasserproblem des II and III Johannesbriefes', ZNW 57 (1966) 93–100; he is opposed by R. Schnackenburg, 'Zum Begriff der "Wahrheit" in den beiden kleinen Johannesbriefen', BZ 11 (1967) 253–7.

[58] See P. Fay 118 cited in ch. 2, n. 40. Hence it is difficult to say dogmatically that it could not mean or could not be taken to mean 'sincerely' simply because of its Johannine context; see below p. 119f for a similar position in 3 Jn 12.

[59] On the greeting see ch. 2, pp. 47–8 and nn. 42–3. 'ὑμῶν' is read by some witnesses (as also in v. 2) and omitted by others.

[60] 'παρά' is used frequently in John (33 times), but not all in 1 John. The omission of the Pauline 'Lord' (κύριος) before Jesus Christ and the stress on him as Son of the Father is characteristic of Johannine thought, see Brown, Epistles, 169. ℵ has a number of variants in this verse.

The Love Command and the Tradition of the Community
4-6

4 Ἐχάρην λίαν ὅτι εὕρηκα ἐκ τῶν τέκνων σου περιπατοῦντας ἐν ἀληθείᾳ καθὼς ἐντολὴν ἐλάβομεν παρὰ τοῦ πατρός. 5 καὶ νῦν ἐρωτῶ σε, κυρία, οὐχ ὡς ἐντολὴν καινὴν γράφων σοι ἀλλὰ ἣν εἴχομεν ἀπ' ἀρχῆς, ἵνα ἀγαπῶμεν ἀλλήλους. 6 καὶ αὕτη ἐστὶν ἡ ἀγάπη, ἵνα περιπατῶμεν κατὰ τὰς ἐντολὰς αὐτοῦ· αὕτη ἡ ἐντολή ἐστιν, καθὼς ἠκούσατε ἀπ' ἀρχῆς, ἵνα ἐν αὐτῇ περιπατῆτε.

I rejoiced greatly when I found some of your children walking in truth, even as we received a command from the Father. And now I beseech you, lady, not as if I were writing a new command to you, but one we have had from the beginning, that we love one another. And this is love, that we walk according to his commands. This is the command, as you have heard from the beginning, that you should walk in it.

The author opens the body of his letter conventionally with an expression of joy at having found, either by news or personal encounter—the Greek permits of both—**'some of the children'** of the 'elect lady' **'walking in truth'**. This may well tell us little about the church situation envisaged[61] but merely provides a courteous way of leading into what follows. **'Walking in truth'** is a phrase peculiar to 2 and 3 John in the New Testament, although the figurative use of 'walking' for a manner of life is found in Paul (as in 'walking in' or practising 'cunning');[62] here it means more than that they were 'acting sincerely', for in 3 Jn 4 'walking in *the* truth' is used in a parallel context.[63] The Gospel and First Epistle of John use a different set

---

[61] There is no suggestion that some were therefore not faithful (C.H. Dodd, *Epistles*, 147).

[62] Eph 5.2; Rom 6.4; 2 Cor 4.2.

[63] Contrast Westcott, *Epistles*, 216, 226. Bultmann, 'ἀλήθεια', 242 translates 'acting honestly'; Schnackenburg, *Johannesbriefe*, 310 adopts the rendering accepted here although originally (1st edition) he translated 'in Wirklichkeit'. However, for the meaning 'sincerely' see n. 58.

of idioms; they speak of 'doing the truth' or 'being of the truth', and when they use the image of walking it is part of a metaphor—walking in the light or darkness, in the day or night.[64] Here in 2 and 3 John it is again tempting to see 'truth' ('the truth', 3 Jn 4) as that which is faithfully Johannine—in this case these members of the community must be living according to the principles of Johannine Christianity. From this Epistle, and more particularly from 1 John, we may suppose that these principles consisted of matters of belief and behaviour which found their coherence in loyalty to the tradition of the community and to each other. Therefore, without need of further specification, the 'elect lady' is congratulated that her 'children' are 'sound'.

In this they are following **'the command we received from the Father',** not that the command was 'to walk in truth' but that it epitomised the Johannine tradition to which they were faithful. There is a verbal echo of Jn 10.18, 'This command I received from my Father'; the echo may be a conscious appeal to the authoritative language of the Gospel for, although the reference there is to Jesus's readiness to die, neither 'receiving a command' (λαμβάνειν ἐντολὴν) nor this word for 'from' (παρά) are found in 1 John.[65] Certainly the author has, with studied courtesy, now introduced the central theme of this section, the commandment which forms the backbone of Johannine Christianity. Having excluded any inference that they have failed and denying that he is imposing a new obligation on them, he proceeds to stress the fundamental importance of the commandment **'to love one another'.**

[64] 'Doing the truth' Jn 3.21; 1 Jn 1.6; 'Being of the truth' Jn 18.37; 1 Jn 3.19. For 'walking' in the Gospel and First Epistle see Jn 8.12; 11.9,10; 12.35; 1 Jn 1.6,7; 2.11.

[65] On 'παρά' see n. 60. In assimilation to Jn 10.18 ℵ 33 *pc* read 'ἔλαβον'. The parallel leads J. Chapman, 'The Historical Setting of the Second and Third Epistles of St John', *JThS* 5 (1904) 357–68, 517–34 to see a reference to martyrdom, but there is nothing in the letter to support this.

The commandment of mutual love first appears in the Johannine tradition when it is given by Jesus to his disciples in the 'Farewell Discourses' (Jn 13.34; 15.12,17). Like the broader Synoptic 'Love your neighbour' (Mt 22.39; Mk 12.31; Lk 10.27), it probably goes back to the injunction of Lev 19.18, 'you shall love your neighbour as yourself', where 'neighbour' (רֵעַ) originally had a restricted sense—virtually 'your compatriot'.[66] This restricted sense was further developed in sectarian Judaism, even leading to the corollary, hatred of enemies, and no doubt reflecting the sense of being an elect but beleagured group within a hostile and alien environment.[67] The restriction of the command of love to fellow members of the group, unlikely to be Jesus's own intention, is reflected elsewhere in early Christian literature, largely from a theologically dualist and sectarian context like the Gospel of Thomas.[68]

In the Johannine community the restriction of love to 'one another' is given a theological rationale which sees love as a divine principle of unity,[69] but in practice it would have helped preserve the community's self-identity in the face of opposition or isolation and may also have acted as a guard against the individualism which is an implicit danger in Johannine thought.

These characteristics of the command to love one another and

[66] See Hoskyns, *Fourth Gospel*, 431; R.A. Harrisville, 'The Concept of Newness in the New Testament', *JBL* 74 (1955) 69–79, 78.

[67] So in the *Damascus Document* 6.20–1 (ed. C. Rabin, *The Zadokite Documents*, Oxford 1954, 24–5), 'They shall love each man his brother as himself'. For hatred to enemies as a corollary see 1 *QS* 1.9–11 (ed. M. Burrows, ASOR, New Haven 1951) 'That they may love all the sons of light . . . and hate all the sons of darkness'.

[68] *Gospel of Thomas* 25 (ed. A. Guillaumont et al., Leiden 1959, 19), 'Love thy brother as thy soul'. See G. Quispel, 'Qumran, John and Jewish Christianity', in *John and Qumran*, ed. J. Charlesworth, London 1972, 137–55; idem, 'Love thy Brother', *Ancient Society* 1 (1970) 83–93. Quispel argues that this reflects the intention of Jesus.

[69] See further ch. 5, p. 204 and note love as a principle of unity in Jn 17.

their development are evident in its use in the Johannine literature. The context of the first appearance of the command in the Gospel directs it specifically to the Johannine community, which is represented by the disciples, and thus restricts the exercise of that love to within the community. The pattern of their love for each other, Jesus's love for them, does not indicate a wider interpretation of 'one another' despite a passage like Jn 3.16, 'God so loved the world'. For in the Farewell Discourses (Jn 13–17) it is clear that Jesus's love for his disciples, which is to be the pattern and motive for their mutual love (15.12f.), separates them from the world and brings them into the circle of love and obedience which unites Father, Son and believers (17.23–26; 15.10. In 15.13f. love is seen in readiness to die for one's friends, the name Jesus now bestows on his disciples). Love is therefore that which must characterise the community and set them apart from the world, for the world will hate them even as it has first hated Jesus (15.18). Elsewhere in the Gospel there may be a more positive evaluation of the world but in these chapters it stands in opposition to Jesus and to the community which believes in him and practises mutual love.

1 John sees the love-command as fundamental for the community, as is witnessed by the high number of times words for 'love' and 'command' appear.[70] An additional reason for its importance is now that it is part of the tradition of the community. Whereas in the Gospel Jesus gives it as his 'new command' (ἐντολὴν καινήν: Jn 13.34), in 1 Jn 2.7–8 it is 'new' only in that it, like the community, belongs to the new age, 'a new command which is true in him and in you'; for the author it is perhaps of greater importance that the commandment is in fact 'not a new commandment but an old (παλαιά)

---

[70] See Appendix 1, Table E and note especially 'command': 1 Jn 14x, Jn 11x; 'love' (noun): 1 Jn 18x, Jn 7x; 'love' (verb): 1 Jn 28x, Jn 36x.

commandment which (they) have had from the beginning'.[71] The phrase 'from the beginning' (ἀπ' ἀρχῆς) represents a recurring theme in 1 John (1.1; 2.7,13f.24; 3.8,11); usually, as here, it must refer not to an absolute beginning (as in Jn 1.1, 'in the beginning', 'ἐν ἀρχῇ'), but to the beginning of the church's life, whether the Christian church as a whole or this particular community and the experience of its members.[72] For 1 John obedience to the commandment to love one another is constitutive for the community in two senses: a) because loyalty to that which has belonged to the community 'from the beginning' is essential for continuing in genuine 'Christian' life against the dangers of innovation (2.24), and b) because love is still a principle of unity—no-one can fail to love his brother and still be a member of the community (2.9f.)[73] In 2.3–11

---

[71] 'παλαιός' (old) does not occur in John. Thus the command is part of the tradition to which 1 John looks back; this militates against the argument that Jn 13.34 and 15.1–17, which introduce the command, are later additions to the Gospel contemporary with the Epistles (so J. Becker, 'Die Abschiedsreden Jesu im Johannesevangelium', ZNW 61 (1970) 215–46). Harrisville, 'Newness' sees the reference in 1 John as to eschatological newness, while H. Conzelmann, 'Was von Anfang war', in Neutestamentlichen Studien für R. Bultmann, ed. W. Eltester, Berlin 1954, 194–201 refers it to the newness of Christianity in the world.

[72] 'ἀρχή' is only used in this phrase in 1 John; in John the phrase comes at 8.44; 15.27. See further Conzelmann, 'Anfang'. An absolute beginning may be intended in 2.13f.; 3.8 but even here the beginning of Christian experience is possible; see I. de la Potterie, 'La Notion de la "Commencement" dans les Écrits Johanniques', in Die Kirche des Anfangs, ed. R. Schnackenburg et al., Leipzig 1977, 379–403, 396f.; H.H. Wendt, 'Der "Anfang" am Beginne des 1 Johannesbriefes', ZNW 21 (1922) 38–42. There is little evidence for a reference to baptism as argued by W. Nauck, Die Tradition und der Charakter des ersten Johannesbriefes, Tübingen 1953, 85.

[73] 'Brother' must mean a fellow member of the community; so H. Schlier, 'Die Bruderliebe nach dem Evangelium und den Briefen Johannes', in Mélanges Bibliques au Beda Rigaux, ed. A. Descamps and A. de Halleux, Gembloux 1970, 234–45; ctr. V. Furnish, The Love Command in the New Testament, London 1973, 151, R. Bultmann, The Johannine Epistles, Philadelphia 1973, 28–9.

knowledge of God, keeping the commandments, loving the brethren, being in the light etc. are all facets of the one reality— the assurance of 'being of God' which mere external membership of the community might not guarantee.

We can hardly avoid the conclusion that 2 John builds on the language and assumptions of the First Epistle. The eschatological newness of the commandment is now forgotten—**'not as if I were writing a new command to you'**—in favour of it being **'one we have had from the beginning'**.[74] This crucial 'from the beginning' (ἀπ' ἀρχῆς) is repeated twice in the two verses, and given even more emphasis as the real significance of the commandment by the absence of any practical content to the latter. The only content of love— **'and this is love'**—appears to be **'that we walk according to his commands'**, a statement apparently dependent on 1 Jn 5.3, 'For this is love *of God*, that we keep his commands'. 2 John, however, lacks the definition there of love as 'of God' and thus falls into the tautology that the command is to love, and to love is to follow the command.

This impression of redundancy is reinforced by the final statement that **'this is the command, as you have heard from the beginning, that you should walk in it'**. There is considerable textual confusion here, partly occasioned by cross-influence from John and 1 John, but also reflecting the ambiguity of the sense, although none of the readings remove the ambiguity entirely.[75] Common sense would suggest that the

---

[74] The reading of B P 𝕸 'ἐντολην γραφων σοι καινην' may be original as the order of words in ℵ A 33 *al* vg may be an assimilation to 1 Jn 2.7. ℵ also adds 'ἐντολην' after 'ἀλλα' (cf. sy^h 'old commandment').

[75] καθως ἠκουσατε . . . ἱνα ἐν αὐτῃ   B L P *pm* sy
ἱνα καθως ἠκουσατε . . . ἱνα ἐν αὐτῃ   ℵ A 69 *al*
ἱνα καθως ἠκουσατε . . . ἐν αὐτῃ   K 33 1739 *al* vg co

The reading of ℵ etc. is probably a conflation of the other two readings; at the beginning of the clause ℵ reads 'αὑτη ἐστιν ἡ ἐντολη', probably in assimilation to Jn 15.21; 1 Jn 3.23 (cf. also n. 74), while at the end it reads

final 'in it' refers back to 'love' at the beginning of the verse—the command is 'to walk in love', a good 'Johannine' sentiment; grammatical sense suggests 'in it' refers to the nearest antecedent, the command. The tautology which ensues, that the command, as heard from the beginning, is to walk in it (the command), may be partly avoided if we paraphrase, 'This, then, is the command which, as you have heard from the beginning, you should live by.'[76]

The overall effect of the passage is to stress the fundamental and essential character of the command as the command known from the beginning rather than its content of love or its application. Although the Elder starts by beseeching 'the lady', his request has no content—'that we love one another' is the definition of the command rather than the content of his request.[77] There are no grounds for supposing that there was some lack of love in the community. The appeal to the command is an appeal to tradition. It is made by bringing together language and phrases from the Gospel and 1 John—hence the appeal to Jn 10.18 whose effect has been to make the love command originate not from Jesus as in the Farewell Discourses, but from God, a step already implied in 1 John.[78] It would seem there is a development from John, where mutual love is fundamental, to 1 John where this is balanced by the

'περιπατησητε'. The reading of B is probably to be preferred here, although if the longer reading were original (ℵ A etc.), the two alternatives could be attempts at simplification.

[76] Ctr. Westcott, *Epistles*, 218 who refers 'ἐν αὐτῇ' to 'ἀγάπη'; the confusion may be partly caused by 2 John's use of 'περιπατεῖν' (see below).

[77] Against Westcott, *Epistles*, 217 and Dodd, *Epistles*, 147 who take 'ἵνα ἀγαπῶμεν' as dependent on 'ἐρωτῶ', but then we might expect the 2nd pl. 'ἀγαπῆτε'; Brown, *Epistles*, 664 combines both options. For 2 John's epexegetic use of 'ἵνα' see the earlier uses in this verse.

[78] On the command as God's in 1 John see 1 Jn 5.3 and below ch. 5, p. 199 on the ambiguity of 'his'; there is nothing in the context in 2 Jn 6 to suggest 'his' (αὐτοῦ) refers to Jesus.

foundational nature of the command itself, to the position we
have found in 2 John. Alongside this it is strange that while John
and 1 John (and Revelation) talk about 'keeping' (τηρεῖν) the
commands, 2 John talks of 'walking (περιπατεῖν) according to'
(and possibly 'in') them—a reflection of the way that in 2 and 3
John we find both continuity and changes of language and ideas
from John and 1 John.[79] However, within the framework and
argument of 2 John these verses clearly provide an appeal to
loyalty to the community's origins and as such act as a battle cry
and inspiration to what follows.

False Teaching—a denial of the tradition

7

7 Ὅτι πολλοὶ πλάνοι ἐξῆλθον εἰς τὸν κόσμον, οἱ μὴ
ὁμολογοῦντες Ἰησοῦν Χριστὸν ἐρχόμενον ἐν σαρκί· οὗτός ἐστιν
ὁ πλάνος καὶ ὁ ἀντίχριστος.

For many deceivers have gone out into the world, who do not
confess Jesus Christ coming in flesh. Such is the deceiver and the
antichrist.

It would be difficult to understand this verse without a
knowledge of 1 John, and particularly 1 Jn 2.18ff. and 4.1f.:

Children, it is the last hour, and just as you heard that the
antichrist is coming, so now many antichrists have come. From
this we know that it is the last hour. They went out from us but
they were not of us; for if they had been of us they would have
remained with us . . . Who is the liar but he who denies that Jesus

[79] 'Keeping (τηρεῖν) the commands or (his) word is found regularly in John
and 1 John (see below p. 179) and also in Rev 3.8,10; 12.17; 14.12; 22.7,9 but
otherwise only in Mt 19.17 and 1 Tim 6.14 in the New Testament; for 2 John's
'walk according to' (περιπατεῖν κατά) compare Mk 7.5.

is the Christ; this is the antichrist, he who denies the Father and the Son. (1 Jn 2.18ff.)
Beloved, do not believe every spirit, but test the spirits to see whether they are of God, for (ὅτι) many false prophets have gone out into the world. By this you know the spirit of God; every spirit which confesses Jesus Christ having come in flesh is of God and every spirit which does not confess Jesus is not of God. This is that (spirit) of the antichrist which you have heard is coming and now is in the world already. (1 Jn 4.1ff.)

Without the 'eschatological' understanding of the term 'antichrist' in these passages its sudden introduction in 2 John would make little sense, especially when it is remembered that these are the first occurrences of the term and that it comes nowhere else in the New Testament or Apostolic Fathers besides the possibly dependent passage in Polycarp, *Philipp* 7.1. The introduction 'for' (ὅτι) only loosely follows what precedes and may come from 1 Jn 4.1 where the spirits are to be tested '*for* many false prophets have gone out into the world', where the Greek is close to that of 2 John (ὅτι πολλοὶ ψευδοπροφῆται ἐξεληλύθασιν εἰς τὸν κόσμον). For the interpretation of 2 John we may note three important points in these passages from 1 John.

a) Although the term 'antichrist' was apparently coined by 1 John, the idea behind it, the so-called 'Antichrist' Legend, of a final opponent of God embodying the forces of wickedness, is much older and has a complex religious and historical background.[80] Other New Testament passages also refer to a final manifestation of wickedness in opposition to God and in these we find a common nucleus of ideas including the appearance of one or many falseprophets (ψευδοπροφήτης) and the use of signs and wonders (σημεῖα, τέρατα, δυνάμεις) by

[80] W. Bousset, *The Antichrist Legend*, London 1896, and W. Meeks, *The Prophet King*, NT.S 14, Leiden 1967, 47–55 represent two contrasting positions; see also Schnackenburg, *Johannesbriefe*, 145–9.

which many are led astray (ἀποπλανᾶν, πλανᾶν).[81]

That 1 John reflects this tradition can be seen in the use of the term 'falseprophets' (4.1), in the phrase 'the spirit of error' (τὸ πνεῦμα τῆς πλάνης 4.6, cf. πλανᾶν) and in the explicit eschatological reference to 'the last hour' (2.18). Recognition of this as traditional terminology means we cannot assume that the opponents were, or claimed to be, prophets possessed of the spirit. However, the author has not utilised the theme of 'signs and wonders' because he identified the historical appearance of people who were essentially teachers with the manifestation of the antichrist—thus historicizing eschatology. In this way the question of true faith or teaching has been introduced into the traditional picture of the 'Antichrist', a most important step in the development of the heresiological tradition and in the attitude to apostates and heretics.[82]

b) These false teachers had been members of the community. From the author's viewpoint they had left the community, thus proving that they had never been true members (2.19), but the letter implies that they were a continuing threat and that the division was not yet absolute—perhaps the faithful were a minority. In saying 'they have gone out into the world' the author uses terminology which could imply mission and 1 Jn 4.5 does suggest that their propaganda met with some success—'They are of the world; therefore they speak of the world and the world hears them'.[83]

[81] E.g. Mt 24.11; Mk 13.22; Rev 19.20; 2 Thess 2.8–12; *Didache*, 16.4f.; *Apoc Peter* 2 (ET in E. Hennecke, *New Testament Apocrypha*, ed. W. Schneemelcher, London 1963–5, II, 668–83).

[82] On this step in Jude see F. Wisse, 'The Epistle of Jude in the History of Heresiology', in *Essays on Nag Hammadi Texts in Honour of Alexander Böhlig*, ed. M. Krause, Leiden 1972, 133–43.

[83] N.H. Cassem, 'A Grammatical and Contextual Inventory of the Use of "κόσμος" in the Johannine Corpus', *NTS* 19 (1972) 81–91 sees 'to go (out) in the world', used of Jesus in the Gospel and of the false teachers in 1 John, as a technical term for a prophetic or messianic mission; see also F. Hahn, *Mission in the New Testament*, London 1965, 152–63.

c) Faced with this danger the spirits must be tested and the decisive test is belief *about*, and not simply *in*, Jesus. It is probably both impossible and misguided to attempt to identify the false teachers by the confession of 'Jesus Christ having come in (the) flesh' ('Ιησοῦν Χριστὸν ἐν σαρκὶ ἐληλυθότα 4.2). Impossible because it is difficult to see what view is being countered here and because the language is too imprecise to be matched against any later, more finely articulated heresy. For example, one very common candidate, a docetism which rejected the physical reality of Jesus's body, would however best be refuted by a statement *that* Jesus Christ came in the flesh and this grammatically would require an accusative and infinitive construction, (such as is found in some witnesses to this verse and in Polycarp, *Philipp* 7.1).[84] The original text here with the participle is probably either a confession of Jesus *as* the Christ who came in the flesh or of Jesus Christ *as* (the one) who came in the flesh.[85] Likewise a gnostic divorce between the human Jesus and the divine Christ which descended at the baptism and left before the crucifixion, a view which denied the real involvement of the divine with humanity, would be more fittingly combatted by the assertion that 'the Christ', the divine

---

[84] For Polycarp see ch. 1 p. 7, n. 5; B here reads the infinitive 'ἐληλυθεναι'. The commentators show some disagreement in determining whether Cerinthus's doctrine was docetic; thus the commentaries of Bultmann, Holtzmann and Westcott identify Cerinthianism as docetism and as the heresy here, C. Gore, *The Epistles of St John*, London 1920, 116 argues in favour of Cerinthianism here, denying that docetism is involved, while H. Braun, 'Literar-Analyse und theologische Schichtung im ersten Johannesbriefe', *ZThK* 48 (1951) 262–92, 290 denies that Cerinthus is in mind and identifies the heresy with docetism. See also J.M. Lieu, 'Authority to Become Children of God: A Study of 1 John', *NT* 23 (1981) 210–28.

[85] 'ὁμολογεῖν' can be followed by a 'ὅτι' clause, by an infinitive, by a double accusative or by a direct object but, unlike other verbs of thinking and saying, not by a participle unless this supplies the predicative accusative; see B.D. §416(3); the translations suggested in the text assume a double accusative construction, although conceivably the whole clause could represent the direct object.

being or aeon, rather than 'Jesus Christ', had come in the flesh. Indeed, if, as often supposed, it is a gnostic heresy such as that of Cerinthus which is in view, we would expect a more explicit denial of the other components of his doctrine.[86]

In fact, the attempt at identification is in any case certainly misguided, because the author himself does not seek to define the erroneous confession of the false teachers. The full confession, which, as we have stressed, is not in the form of a statement about Jesus, is ascribed to the spirit which is of God. The spirit of error, whose views if representing a specific heresy we might expect to be fully articulated, is only said to fail to confess Jesus (πᾶν πνεῦμα ὃ μὴ ὁμολογεῖ τὸν Ἰησοῦν).[87] Elsewhere in the Epistle confession or belief is centred on the question of Jesus as the Son of God or Christ (2.22; 4.15; 5.1,5) and there are no grounds for supposing that these simpler forms are subordinate to the longer and ambiguous confession and so must be interpreted in its light. The author's own Christology, beyond the repetition of traditional formulae, is not well articulated and hence Christological error as he sees it is expressed purely in terms of the denial of such formulae. Moreover the confession of 4.2 under discussion is set in the context of the community's obligation to 'test the spirits' from which it is clear that the author's prime concern is not with the schismatics but with the community.

The author of 2 John has based the warning of v. 7 on the passages from the First Epistle which have been quoted, but this was not because an identical situation had arisen. The force of the dictum has changed in these three aspects.

[86] See Lieu, 'Authority to Become Children of God', 212; on the problem of ascertaining Cerinthus's theology see A.F.J. Klijn and G.J. Reinink, *Patristic Evidence for Jewish-Christian Sects*, Leiden 1973, 3–19.

[87] Unless 'ὁ λύει τὸν Ἰησοῦν' should be read with many Latin witnesses; even then, only in the light of later Gnostic thought could this be taken as a reference to a division between the human Jesus and the divine Christ, see Braun, 'Literar-Analyse', 289.

a) No longer is it said to be 'false prophets' but instead **'deceivers'** (πλάνοι) who have gone out into the world. 'Deceiver' is not used in 1 John, although the cognate noun 'error' and the verb 'to lead astray' are; conversely, 'falsehood' (ψεῦδος) and its cognates, regularly used in contrast to 'truth' in 1 John, are nowhere used in 2 or 3 John.[88] Along with the disappearance of any reference to false prophets, there is also neither here nor anywhere in the letter, any mention of the spirit either of God or of error. In 1 John the true confession is set within the context of the testing of the spirits—something that has been necessitated by the appearance of some who were false—but this context has been lost in 2 John. This may reflect the change in understanding of true and false belief which is more clearly expressed in the use of 'teaching' (διδαχή) in v. 9; a growing dogmatism might no longer see error or confession of faith in 'spirit' terms.

b) As in 1 John it is said that these deceivers **'have gone out into the world'** (ἐξῆλθον εἰς τὸν κόσμον)[89] but, unlike the First Epistle, it is not said that their point of departure was the community; instead the implication of v. 10, 'If anyone comes to you', is that the community has yet to encounter such heretics, a different situation from that of 1 John. The threat is an external and 'seductive' one rather than one of internal conflict. The author has taken the language of going out 'into the world' from 1 John but for him it indicates no more than the rise of false teachers.[90] So also the thought of the world standing in opposition to the community and responding to the message

---

[88] 'πλάνος' (deceiver): 2 Jn 2x, 1 Jn 0; 'πλάνη' (error): 2 Jn 0, 1 Jn 1x; 'πλανᾶν' (to lead astray) 2 Jn 0, 1 Jn 3x; for the vocabulary associated with falsehood see Appendix 1, Table E.

[89] 2 John's use of the aorist instead of the perfect of 1 John may be only a matter of stylistic preference. Possibly because of the following 'εἰς' some MSS read 'εἰσηλθον'.

[90] Thus it need not refer to 'going out' from the devil (so Brooke, *Epistles*, 175) or secession from the community (Brown, *Epistles*, 668).

of those who have gone out into it is not automatically to be carried over from 1 John to 2 John.

c) Within this change of context from internal 'testing the spirits', the confession of Jesus gains a different significance. In 1 Jn 4.2f. the interest is focused on the dualist contrast between the spirit of God and that which is not of God, between the spirit of truth and the spirit of error, and between those who are of God and those who are of the world. The confession fits into this dualist framework, and hence is expressed both positively and negatively. In 2 John the reference is only to those who fail to make the right confession—**'who do not confess'**. The loss of the dualist context means attention is now concentrated on the confession and on its role as a defining characteristic of the deceivers. This in turn highlights the change in wording of the confession itself.

The present participle **'Jesus Christ *coming* in (the) flesh'** ('Ιησοῦν Χριστὸν ἐρχόμενον ἐν σαρκί), instead of the perfect of 1 Jn 4.2, 'having come' (ἐληλυθότα), *grammatically* makes a reference to the past fact of the incarnation improbable.[91] Since in the Greek of the New Testament period the future of 'to come' (ἰέναι) was not frequently used and the present could be used with future meaning,[92] the most natural translation *grammatically* would be a reference to a future coming 'in the flesh'.

In fact, few modern scholars have followed the grammar to discover a debate about the fleshly parousia of Jesus.[93] Against

[91] Although a present participle can refer to action prior to the main verb, it is usually marked as such by a temporal adverb or represents durative or frequentative action (see H.G. Meecham, 'The Present Participle of Antecedent Action—Some New Testament Instances', *ET* 64 (1953) 285–6). The Vulgate 'venientem' marks a correction of the Old Latin 'venisse' just as in the Syriac the Harklean reads a participle in place of the perfect tense of the Philoxenian.

[92] B.D. §101. In the New Testament only Luke and Hebrews use 'ἰέναι'; cf. Jn 16.13; 18.4; 14.3 for the use of 'ἔρχεσθαι' with future meaning.

[93] Westcott, *Epistles*, 218; Gore, *Epistles*, 226f.; E. Schwartz, *Über den Tod*,

the objection that this is to be 'in glory' and not 'in flesh' it must be pointed out that antidocetic polemic in the early church could emphasise not only the 'fleshly' incarnation, death, resurrection and ascension of Jesus but also his coming again 'in the same flesh'.[94] A more cogent objection, however, is the absence of anything in the context to suggest a reference to the parousia, especially in isolation from any stress on the incarnation.

The majority of scholars have assumed that the confession of 2 Jn 7 is to be explained by that of 1 Jn 4.2. While some give no explanation of the change of tense of participle or suggest grammatical weakness by the author, others see the present as signifying the timeless significance of the incarnation, or that it is an abiding fact, the continuing mode of the Redeemer's existence, or even that it implies a denial of the possibility and not just the fact of the incarnation.[95] That the present tense of the

---

147; this interpretation has been revived by G. Strecker, 'Die Anfänge der johanneischen Schule', NTS 32 (1986) 31–47, 35; on Oecumenius see ch. 1, p. 32, n. 96. Ep. Barn. VI.9 to which Brooke, Epistles, 175, n. 1 appeals is not relevant.

[94] The objection is made by Bultmann, Epistles, 112 and Schnackenburg, Johannesbriefe, 313. For Jesus's coming again as 'in the same flesh' see Irenaeus, AH III.16.8; Tertullian, De Carne Christi XVI.1; XXIV.4. Opposition to this can already be found in the 3rd(?) century anonymous commentary edited by C.H. Turner, 'Documents', JThS 5 (1904) 218–41, IV.8f.

[95] With no explanation, R.R. Williams, The Letters of John and James, Cambridge 1965, 65; grammatical weakness, Dodd, Epistles, 149; timeless significance, Schnackenburg, Johannesbriefe, 313, S. Smalley, 1,2,3 John, Waco, Texas 1984, 329–30; continuing mode of the Redeemer's existence, Brooke, Epistles, 175, Brown, Epistles, 670, I.H. Marshall, The Epistles of John, Michigan 1978, 70–1 ('is and remains flesh'), and from a different perspective W. Thüsing, Die Johannesbriefe, Düsseldorf 1970, 107 ('His incarnation continues to be actively present in the lives of the disciples.'); denial of the possibility, A. Plummer, The Epistles of St John, Cambridge 1884, 180. H. Windisch, Die Katholischen Briefe, 3rd ed. by H. Preisker, Tübingen 1951, 139 describes it as a 'doctrinal formulation' (lehrsatzmässige Formulierung); similarly H. Holtzmann, Briefe und Offenbarung Johannes, Leipzig and Freiburg 1893, 270.

verb 'to come' would be the most natural way of expressing timeless significance, abiding fact or even possibility seems highly unlikely—even if such ideas were not too sophisticated and abstract for our author or for first century Christianity generally. Such arguments have a note of desperation about them and ascribe to the author either too abstruse or too weak a sense of what he was doing.

The analysis of the letter so far has suggested that the key to the interpretation of 2 John lies in its relation to the material it imitates or modifies, in particular from the Gospel and First Epistle. Clearly 2 Jn 7 does reflect 1 Jn 4.2, but equally clearly it also changes its emphasis, and the present participle 'coming' must be part of this change. A further change is in the move of 'in flesh' to a weaker, less emphatic position after the participle.[96] The participle 'coming' (ἐρχόμενον) recalls the epithet 'he who comes' (ὁ ἐρχόμενος) in the Gospel, which features as part of popular Messianic expectation ('he who is to come into the world', Jn 6.14; 11.27), but which is also used of Jesus as 'he who comes from heaven' or 'from above' (Jn 3.31). In the latter case the present tense is used because of the contrast with 'he who is (ὁ ὤν) of the earth' to make the point that Jesus, although 'on earth' during his minstry, was not 'of the earth' but 'of heaven' or 'from above' and yet he had come into the world. These parallels do not justify seeing in 2 Jn 7 a reference to the incarnation, and they are distinguished from it by the article 'he who' (ὁ),[97] but they may have provided the author with a description of Jesus more in accord with Johannine tradition than 'having come', if this had no particular force or meaning for him. The author would hardly have introduced the ambiguous present participle if he had wished to oppose gnosticism or

[96] See E.A. Abbott, *Johannine Grammar*, London 1906, §2553.

[97] Bultmann, *Epistles*, 112 appeals to the Johannine parallels; Selwyn, *The Christian Prophets*, 133f. sees the absence of the article as a solecism typical of the author of Revelation to whom he attributes 2 and 3 John.

docetism or any specific heresy or had so understood the force of the original.

The loss of the wider dualist context and the reference only to the negative 'not confessing' means that the confession functions primarily as a characterisation of the opponents. Yet they are not characterised as specific, recognisable heretics but in terms of Johannine tradition, they are those who fail to confess Jesus as Johannine thought acknowledges him—**'such is the deceiver and the antichrist'**.[98]

In this way vv. 5–6 and 7 together encapsulate two fundamental elements of Johannine teaching: the heritage of Johannine Christianity summarised in the commandment and the threat of opposition to what distinctively belongs to that Christianity. In so doing they form the backcloth to the main thrust of the letter in the following verses.

Loyalty to the tradition

8–9

8 βλέπετε ἑαυτούς, ἵνα μὴ ἀπολέσητε ἃ εἰργασάμεθα ἀλλὰ μισθὸν πλήρη ἀπολάβητε.

9 Πᾶς ὁ προάγων καὶ μὴ μένων ἐν τῇ διδαχῇ τοῦ Χριστοῦ θεὸν οὐκ ἔχει · ὁ μένων ἐν τῇ διδαχῇ, οὗτος καὶ τὸν πατέρα καὶ τὸν υἱὸν ἔχει.

Take heed for yourselves, that you do not lose that for which we have worked, but receive a full reward. Everyone who leads forward and does not remain in the teaching of Christ does not have God. He who remains in the teaching, he has both the Father and the Son.

Although 2 John has not taken from 1 John the interpretation

---

[98] Some witnesses of the Old Latin and a few Greek minuscules improve the continuity by reading the plural. 1 John does not use the noun 'deceiver' but does use the verb, see n. 88 above.

of the appearance of 'the antichrist' as a sign of the 'last hour', this injunction to **'take heed'** is given eschatological force by the use of language common in eschatological contexts outside the Johannine literature. In Mk 13.23, after the prophecy of the rise of false christs and false prophets who will endeavour to lead even the elect astray by signs and wonders, come the words, 'Take heed for yourselves (ὑμεῖς δὲ βλέπετε), I have told you everything in advance'.[99] The author therefore now leaves his close dependence on earlier Johannine tradition as he comes to the main theme of his letter in language which is markedly non-Johannine.[100]

The vocabulary of 'working' (ἐργάζεσθαι), 'reward' (μισθός) and 'losing' (ἀπολλύναι) has many New Testament parallels, for, however, it may be related to faith, the concept of a final reward is firmly fixed in much of the New Testament, although less so in the Johannine writings. Interpretation here is complicated by textual uncertainty. While the Majority text reads the first person plural throughout (we do not lose—we have worked—we receive), a number of old and reliable witnesses read the second person plural in each case (you do not lose etc.); there is also scanty but strong evidence for a change from the second person in the first and third verbs to the first person in the second, the text and translation adopted here.[101] This text, represented primarily by Codex Vaticanus(B), has the force of intrinsic probabilty on its side in that it could explain

---

[99] This may have influenced the addition to v. 11 found in some Latin witnesses, 'Ecce praedixi vobis ne (*or* ut) in diem domini (*or* dei [+ nostri] non) condemnemini (*or* confundamini)'. See Ps. Augustine, *Speculum* 50 (CSEL 12, 517).

[100] Note the number of words from this section listed in Appendix I, Table A(b). J. Rendel Harris, 'Problem of the Address' sees a reference here to Ruth 2.12 (see above n. 42).

[101] ἀπολεσητε ... ἀπολαβητε   ℵ c (ἀπολησθε ℵ*) A B 33 *al* latt sy co.
ἀπολεσωμεν ... ἀπολαβωμεν   P 𝔐
ειργασασθε   ℵ A 33 latt bo sy^ph, htxt
εἰργασαμεθα (B* ἠργ-)   B P 𝔐 sa sy^h mg

both the alternative readings as the results of the verbs being assimilated to each other. It has been rejected by many recent scholars in favour of the second person throughout on the grounds that the switch to the first person 'we have worked' involves too self-conscious a claim by the author and implies he brought the community to faith, something supposedly denied by his refusal to call them 'my children', whereas 'you have worked' could be interpreted in a thoroughly Johannine sense with work as faith and eternal life as the reward, after the pattern of Jn 6.27ff.[102] Such arguments are hardly conclusive; it is the image of the members of the community as the children of the 'elect lady' which does not permit them to be the Elder's offspring, while the alteration between second and first person is characteristic enough of the author's style (cf. vv. 5–6) not to imply an unusually self-conscious note here. The meaning is that all (Johannine) Christians have worked; it is for this particular community to see that they do not fail to attain their **'full reward'**.[103]

Neither reward nor work need further definition; the language of Christian exhortation and expectation is being used to add force to the author's point. Yet this in itself reveals a significant difference from 1 John in the attitude to false teaching. The reference to false teachers in 1 John comes in the

[102] The reading of B is rejected by Tischendorf, H. v. Soden, *Die Schriften des Neuen Testament*, Göttingen 1913, Harnack, *Zur Revision*, Haenchen, 'Neue Literatur' and the commentaries of Bultmann, K. Grayston (*The Johannine Epistles*, London 1984), Holtzmann, Schnackenburg (who lists others, 314, n. 4) and Windisch. Schnackenburg appeals to Jn 6.27ff., while A. v. Harnack, 'Das "Wir" in den johanneischen Schriften', *SPAW* (1923) 95–113, 97 argues 'we' would imply too selfconscious a claim; Westcott, *Epistles*, 219 suggests the author is associating himself with all the apostolic teachers.

[103] Brown, *Epistles*, 672–3 interprets 'full' in the light of Johannine eschatology but this may be reading too much into the phrase. L here reads 'πληρης' (i.e. treating it as indeclinable, see B.D. §137(1) and ctr. the confusing comment of Brown, loc. cit.).

context of testing the spirits and of the community's assurance of victory over the world. Despite the need to 'test the spirits' and the warning against those 'who would lead them astray' (2.26), there is no real thought of any reward they are in danger of losing, for, being 'of God', they have already 'conquered them' (4.4) and, in possession of an 'anointing', they are in no need of teaching (2.27). If the assurance of victory must be balanced by a self-interrogation marked by statements such as 'If we say . . .', the arena of questioning is not future reward but the validity of present Christian standing—do we 'deceive ourselves', is 'the truth in us' (1.6ff)? The appearance of false-teachers, even if it does mark the last hour, is as much a witness to what it means to belong to God or to the world (4.1–6).[104] This note of assured victory no longer sounds in 2 John; in the battle over loyalty to the tradition the reward may yet be lost and counter-measures must be devised.

This point must be spelt out more clearly in language with a stronger Johannine ring. Failure to remain within the confines of true teaching will inevitably mean failing 'to have God', less eschatological but presumably concomitant with 'losing a reward'. Again we have a clear echo of 1 John and particularly of a verse which follows the first reference to the antichrists quoted earlier:

This is the antichrist, he who denies the Father and the Son. Everyone who denies the Son does not have the Father; he who confesses the Son also has the Father. (1 Jn 2.22–23)

2 Jn 9 shares with this verse the parallelism which is typical of Johannine style; it also shares the phrase, which only comes in these two places in the New Testament, 'to have the Father' (ἔχειν τὸν Πατέρα), while 'to have the Son' comes in 1 Jn 5.12 as a condition of having life. 'To have God' is not found in 1 John

---

[104] Lieu, 'Authority to become children of God', 215–19.

but is clearly modelled on the other two formulations which are peculiarly Johannine.[105]

The common ground with this passage from 1 John, perhaps signifying a literary relationship, makes the difference of expression in 2 Jn 9 more noticeable. In 1 John 'he who does not have the Father' is the one who denies the Son, namely the antichrist, or his representative, the subject of the preceding passage. There is no explicit link with the antichrist and his failure to confess in 2 John; instead he who does not possess God is **'he who leads forward and does not remain within the teaching of Christ'**.

What is the fault in being one 'who leads forward' (προάγων)? The textual variations witness to the uncertainty of the earlier copyists and translators,[106] but modern scholars have been more confident in building on seeing in 2 Jn 7 a gnostic heresy by recognising here these gnostics' own claims to be 'progressives', possessed of higher knowledge or more advanced doctrine. This claim is one the author can take and turn to mockery in the manner of 2 Tim 3.13, 'They will advance to the worse'.[107]

In fact there is little to support seeing here a further reference to the gnostic opponents of the letter, this time in their own words. There is no evidence from Christian, philosophical or gnostic circles for the absolute use of the verb we have here,

---

[105] See H. Hanse, art. 'ἔχειν', *TDNT* II, 816–27, 823. The similarity of style led R. Bultmann, 'Analyse des ersten Johannesbriefes', in *Festgabe für A. Jülicher*, Tübingen 1927, 138–58 to suggest that the verse is dependent on the source he found behind 1 John, although 'προάγων' and 'διδαχῇ τοῦ Χριστοῦ' have been introduced by the author.

[106] 'ὁ προαγων' ℵ A B *pc* vg co; 'ο παραβαινων' P 𝔐 sy. See ch. 1, p. 34, n. 104.

[107] 2 Jn 9 is paralleled with 2 Tim 3.13 by G. Stählin, art, 'προκόπτειν', *TDNT* VI, 703–19 and by W. Bousset, *Kyrios Christos*, Nashville 1970, 443, n. 71. For 'προάγειν' as a 'Schlagwort der Gnostiker' see Windisch, *Katholischen Briefe*, 139 and Gaugler, *Johannesbriefe*, 287.

'προάγειν', as meaning 'to be advanced' intellectually or spiritually. The basic meaning of the verb is to go before someone or something, and when used metaphorically, 'to excel', an accompanying noun is necessary to provide the sphere of excellence.[108] The usual verb 'to progress', one with a long technical history in Greek thought, is 'προκόπτειν', the verb used in the passage above in 2 Timothy and frequently in both Christian and Gnostic sources, where it is indeed a proper achievement.[109] It is unlikely that 'προάγειν' would be used by Gnostics in a synonymous sense as a claim to superiority because it is used in gnostic texts in a very different sense, 'to emanate' (trans.).[110] Interestingly the word used to translate 'προάγων' in the Sahidic version of 2 John is used of emanations coming forth in the *Gospel of the Egyptians* from Nag Hammadi.[111]

Clearly 'leading forward' is the author's own term of censure and is not used in any technical sense, nor can it be used to identify the opponents of the letter. Despite its apparently emphatic position at the beginning of the verse, it is not 'leading

---

[108] E.g. 'Advancing (προάγων) much beyond his contemporaries in (*dat.*) understanding and training' (ed. W. Dittenberger, *Orientis Graeci Inscriptiones Selectae*, Leipzig 1903–5, 323); similarly Demosthenes, *De Corona* 181. Although sometimes cited with reference to this verse, Sirach 20.27 uses the reflexive pronoun (προάξει ἑαυτὸν); Aristotle, *Phys* 184a19, cited by Liddell & Scott as meaning 'to advance', refers to the path of investigation.

[109] E.g. 'Let us try to make progress (προκόπτειν) in the commands of the Lord', *2 Clement* 17.3; similarly Clement of Alexandria, *Ecl. Proph.* XIX.1. For Gnostic use see *Interpretation of Knowledge* (N.H. XI.1) 16.32 'But is someone making progress (προκοπτ-) in the Word?'; similarly *Discourse on the Eighth and Ninth* (N.H. VI.6) 54.6–9, 14 where the noun 'προκοπη' is used.

[110] E.g. 'He [Simon Magus] produced (προάγαγων) himself from himself and manifested to himself his own thought', Hippolytus, *Elenchus* VI.18.6 (GCS 26, 144); similarly Clement of Alexandria, *Extr. Theod.* 33.3; 41.2, 4. (GCS 17, 117, 119).

[111] *Gospel of the Egyptians* (N.H. IV.2) 50.4, 13, 29 using the verb ' ϣⲱⲣⲡ' which is also used in the Sahidic of 2 Jn 9; however the Greek 'προάγειν' does not seem to have been taken over into Coptic as a loan word in this sense as was 'προέρχεσθαι' (to emanate [intrans.]) (N.H. IV.41.7f. etc.).

forward' but 'remaining' or 'not remaining in the teaching' which expresses the decisive criterion for 'having God', for it is this which is repeated in both parts of the antithesis. 'Leading forward' is an extension of 'not remaining'; both participles are governed by the one article ('he whō') while their order is determined by the dependence of 'in the teaching' on 'not remaining'. If the verb has been chosen because of its root meaning the implication may be that he who does not remain within the true doctrine may also seek to persuade others to follow his example, as might do the potential visitors in v. 10.[112] More certainly, the rejection of forward movement reflects the essentially conservative nature of Johannine thought which is already sounded in the emphasis on abiding in the teaching of Christ.

'Abiding' (μένειν) is distinctively used in John and 1 John of the believer's relationship with Jesus (Jn 6.56; 15.4–7; 1 Jn 2.6,24,27) or with God (1 Jn 2.24).[113] Abiding in teaching is a very different concept. Jn 8.31, 'If you abide in my word' is less of a parallel than it sounds, for in the context the idea is of commitment to Jesus himself, rather than to his teaching as self-contained doctrine; the exhortations in 1 Jn 2.24,27 to let 'that which they heard from the beginning' or 'the anointing' remain

---

[112] C.F. Evans, 'I will go before you into Galilee', *JThS* NS 5 (1954) 3–18 suggests the translation 'he who takes the lead'; H.H. Wendt, 'Zum zweiten und dritten Johannesbrief', *ZNW* 23 (1924) 18–27, 23 combines two ideas in the translation 'Führer Vorangehenden' (identified with Diotrephes). In *Die Johannesbriefe und das johanneische Christentum*, Halle 1925, 21, 27 he translates 'jeder, der Anführer ist', again seeing him as a gnostic. N. Turner, in J.H. Moulton, *A Grammar of New Testament Greek*, vol. 3, *Syntax*, Edinburgh 1963, 51 gives *P. Lond.* 21, l.15 as a parallel to the contrast between 'μένειν' and 'προάγειν' but the emphasis seems different—'May you not only abide (μενειν) by these [instructions?] but also proceed further (ἐπι μειζονα προαγειν)'.

[113] Becker, 'Abschiedsreden' notes the restriction of this use to passages in the Gospel which he classifies as redactional (6.56; 15.1–17) and cites this as further evidence for assigning them to a stage parallel to the Epistles.

in them, although they reverse the image, are a little closer in that they counsel the steadfast maintenance of unity with the teaching or tradition received. Even closer parallels can be found outside the Johannine corpus in the growing emphasis on loyalty to the faith received in the later New Testament writings (Acts 14.22; Col 1.25; 1 Tim 2.15; 2 Tim 3.14, 'As for you remain in those things you have learned and are assured of.').[114]

The relevance of these parallels is confirmed by the contrast with 1 John where it was confession of the Son which was decisive for 'having the Father'; here in 2 Jn 9 it is remaining in **'the teaching (of Christ)'.** Whether this is teaching about Christ as in v. 7 (objective genitive) or the teaching from Christ as in vv. 5–6 (subjective genitive) makes little difference.[115] 1 John talks of adherence to a person, 2 John of loyalty to 'teaching', a body of doctrine. The noun 'teaching' does not appear in 1 John,[116] which, although it urges loyalty to the tradition received, tends to use more dynamic language, 'that which you have heard' (2.24; cf. 2.7). Where teaching does come as a verb, it is an inward experience from 'the anointing' rather than something imposed from outside (2.27). However, that reliance on inward experience may have proved inadequate, as is implied by the exhortation to test the spirits, even within the community. Perhaps to avoid such a danger, 2 John reflects both here and in the treatment of the commandment a growing concentration on the community's tradition or teaching as the given focus for faithfulness. We do not know what constituted 'the teaching', whether it is a

[114] H. Conzelmann, 'Anfang' labels 1 John a 'Johannine Pastoral' because of its interest in tradition, but 2 John has a better claim to the title.

[115] 'About Christ': Bultmann; 'Of Christ': Brown, Schnackenburg, Westcott. Many commentators allow for either. 'του χριστου' is repeated after the second 'διδαχη' by many manuscripts.

[116] Appendix 1, Table A(b); in Rev 1–3 it is only used of heretical teaching.

reference to the tradition just summarised in the Epistle or points to a written document such as the Gospel or one of its sources or even I John. However, in introducing this reference to 'the teaching' as a criterion for having **'the Father and the Son'**,[117] the explicit connection with the deceivers and their confession has, as we have seen, been lost confirming the impression that we are not to see here specific heretics to be opposed but a pastiche of Johannine themes which together provide the background for the injunction to follow.

In Defence of the Tradition

10-11

10 εἴ τις ἔρχεται πρὸς ὑμᾶς καὶ ταύτην τὴν διδαχὴν οὐ φέρει, μὴ λαμβάνετε αὐτὸν εἰς οἰκίαν καὶ χαίρειν αὐτῷ μὴ λέγετε· 11 ὁ λέγων γὰρ αὐτῷ χαίρειν κοινωνεῖ τοῖς ἔργοις αὐτοῦ τοῖς πονηροῖς.

If anyone comes to you and does not bear this teaching, do not receive him into your home and do not give him a greeting. For he who greets him shares in his evil deeds.

Repeated summons to loyalty to the tradition of the community, and warnings of the final reward yet in jeopardy now reach their goal in this stern refusal of hospitality to anyone who does not bear 'this teaching'. It is not a question of the outbreak of heresy and schism within the community as in I John, but of dealing with those who visit the community from outside but are suspected of failing to conform to the community's tradition. These were almost certainly not casual visitors but travelling Christians carrying out missionary work

---

[117] 'and the Son' may be an echo of the confession of the Son in I Jn 2.23. A 33 *pc* vg reverse the order (και τον υιον και τον πατερα), a reading accepted by Harnack, *Zur Revision*, 72 as more appropriate to the context.

like the 'brethren' of 3 Jn 5–8 and/or teaching the Christian communities like the apostles and prophets of the *Didache* (see below). There is ample evidence that such itinerant teachers were a feature of the early church, and particularly of Asia Minor and of Syria, either of which have been suggested as the home of the Johannine literature.[118] Inevitably they created problems, especially when their teaching was not in line with the community's own tradition, and ways of testing them had to evolve, as perhaps already in Rev 2.2, 'You tested those who call themselves apostles and are not, and you found them false'. This is an area of considerable importance in the history of the early church, and is one to which we shall return in the next chapter. It suggests that the author of 2 John was seeking to meet a problem which was not necessarily that of Christianity against a clearly recognisable heretical gnosticism but more probably one where boundaries were fluid and not readily identifiable. In this context, two closely related factors stand out in his reaction:

(a) The condition of acceptance is that the visitor should **'bear this teaching'.** A similar injunction to this is found in the *Didache,* 'Whoever comes and teaches you all these things already mentioned (τὰ προειρημένα), receive him. But if the teacher himself has turned back and teaches a different doctrine (ἄλλην διδαχὴν) to destroy, do not listen to him' (11. 1–2). Both refer back to what has been said earlier rather than to any set doctrinal formulation or issue. It is this which gives 2 John its coherence; the love command is part of the tradition of the community; it is abiding in the teaching rather than the confession of faith which determines whether one 'has God'; measures against those who do not bear this teaching are

---

[118] See ch. 4, pp. 129,131 n. 20. We know little about travellng teachers or about any other aspect of the organisation of the church in Egypt, the other, least probable, suggested home of the Johannine literature.

justified because of 'the antichrist', the opponent of Johannine tradition; without due heed all may be lost.

(b) What is denied is being **'received into the home'** or 'house' (οἰκίαν), which could equally refer to private hospitality or to reception into the house in which the church met—the two are not mutually exclusive.[119] For even a greeting to be forbidden, whatever the given reason, seems hardly a Christian action or one marked by love. Certainly the **'greeting'** (χαίρειν) probably has a weightier note than a conventional 'Hello' (Mt. 10.11f.), but more central is the feeling that any compliance, apparent or genuine, has dire consequences. Even to give a greeting is **'to share in his evil deeds'**—to 'have fellowship' (κοινωνεῖ) with them[120]—and therefore presumably also to lose one's reward. Heretical teaching is so insidious and lethal a danger that total avoidance is the only solution, as it was also for Ignatius, who urged the Christians of Smyrna not to receive or even meet, never mind speak to, those 'beasts in the form of men' who held docetic views—but he did at least allow prayer for the repentance of such creatures (*Smyrn* 4.1; 7.2)! The development of the interpretation of heretical teaching as a manifestation of the final eschatological opposition to God fostered this attitude—it would be impossible either to have any dealings with or even to attempt to convert such enemies of God.[121] However, 1 John had already shown little concern over those who had left the community, saying with a note of bland

---

[119] See ch. 4, p. 132. For a discussion of the range of meaning of 'οἰκία' see P. Stuhlmacher, *Der Brief an Philemon*, Zurich 1975, 70–75; O. Michel, art. 'οἶκος' etc., *TDNT* V, 119–34.

[120] 1 John does not use 'κοινωνεῖν' but it does use the phrase 'κοινωνίαν ἔχειν' (to have fellowship). J. Moffatt, *Introduction to the New Testament*, 3rd edition, London 1918, 480f. sees this as a sign of different authorship. On the addition to this verse in some Latin witnesses see n. 99; A. v. Harnack, 'Zur Textkritik und Christologie der Schriften des Johannes', *SPAW* (1915) 534–73, 570, n. 1 argues it may have had a Greek origin.

[121] See Wisse, 'Epistle of Jude'.

assurance, 'You are of God, children, and you have conquered them'. 'We know that we are of God and the whole world lies under the evil one' (1 Jn 4.4; 5.19). A community with such an exclusive outlook, who felt in possession of the truth and in no need of further teaching (1 Jn 2.20f., 27), could easily go on to exclude categorically any who did not belong to their tradition.

However, that 2 John reflects a common problem, especially of the post-apostolic age, and a common need to give (apostolic) authority to a reaffirmation of tradition and to uncompromising rejection of those who do not adhere to it, is shown by a passage from the pseudonymous *Third Epistle to the Corinthians*, which is certainly independent but which shows remarkable parallels in language and ideas:

> And if anyone remains (μένει) in the rule which he received through the blessed prophets and the holy Gospel, he will receive a reward (μισθὸν λήμψεται). If anyone transgresses (παραβένει) these things, the fire is with him and with those who travel ahead (προοδοιπορούντων) in this manner; impious men who are the offspring of vipers. Turn away from these (ἀποτρέπεσθε) in the power of the Lord, and may peace be with you.(*3 Cor* 36–39)[122]

Final Greetings

12–13

12 Πολλὰ ἔχων ὑμῖν γράφειν οὐκ ἐβουλήθην διὰ χάρτου καὶ μέλανος, ἀλλὰ ἐλπίζω γενέσθαι πρὸς ὑμᾶς καὶ στόμα πρὸς στόμα λαλῆσαι, ἵνα ἡ χαρὰ ἡμῶν πεπληρωμένη ᾖ.

13 Ἀσπάζεταί σε τὰ τέκνα τῆς ἀδελφῆς σου τῆς ἐκλεκτῆς.

---

[122] *P. Bodmer* X, ed. M. Testuz, *Papyrus Bodmer X–XII*, Cologny-Genève 1959, 9–45. H. v. Campenhausen, *Ecclesiastical Authority and Spiritual Power in the Church of the First Three Centuries*, London 1969, 145–6 sees the beginning of formal excommunication in *3 Cor*, but bases this on Harnack's reconstruction of the text before the discovery of *P. Bodmer* X.

Although I have much to write to you I did not wish to do so by pen and ink; but I hope to come to you and to speak face to face, that our joy may be fulfilled. The children of your elect sister greet you.

Since in closing his letter the Elder follows the conventions of his day it is hazardous to seek to cull much historical information from the passage;[123] certainly it does not necessitate the picture of the Elder exercising authority over a number of churches through pastoral visits. That the purpose of any visit is **'that our joy may be fulfilled'**[124] reflects the tendency for Johannine language to become slogans in 2 John. In the Farewell Discourses of the Gospel the fulfilment of joy is a promise given to the disciples (Jn 15.11; 16.24; 17.13); this is an 'eschatological' joy not limited to human emotions but marking the fulfilment of God's purposes as when the pain of childbirth reaches its goal in the joy of the child that is born (16.21–22; cf.3.29). When the words are used as the purpose of the First Epistle (1 Jn 1.4), some of this depth is lost although the joy remains the consequence of fellowship not only with the author but also with the Father and the Son. Here in 2 John the words have become trivialised, a polite common-place culled from the jargon of the Johannine communities or perhaps from imitation of 1 John.

The closing greeting from **'the children of your elect sister'** suggests that the author is writing from one specific community[125] to another (or others) (cf. 1 Pet 5.13), but might

---

[123] See ch. 2, p. 41, n. 17; G. Schunack, *Die Briefe des Johannes*, Zurich 1982, 108–9 succinctly shows how appeal to this part of 2 John complicates the picture of 'the elder' gained from 3 John. The parallel with 3 John has led to a number of textual variants.

[124] '*Your* (ὑμων) joy' is read by A B *al* lat bo. A similar variation occurs at 1 Jn 1.4 where B supports ℵ in reading 'our' (ἡμων); this may give some support to B here.

[125] This is made more explicit by the addition of 'ἐκκλησιας' (church) in some witnesses; a few go further and add 'της ἐν Ἐφεσῳ' following the tradition of the Ephesian residence of John. See also ch. 2, p. 48, n. 47 for the addition of a grace formula.

this be little more than a literary device chosen in faithfulness to the epistolary form but in fact, like the address to 'the elect lady', equally applicable to any Johannine community?

This possibility is part of a question which runs through the whole of 2 John. There has been much to suggest that the letter relates as much to Johannine tradition and Johannine communities as a whole, as to the specific problems of any one church. The primary purpose of the letter would appear to be the injunction to avoid any visiting preachers bearing deviant doctrine—deviancy being defined in terms of departure from Johannine tradition. 2 John thus meets a gap left by 1 John, which, although it introduced the eschatological interpretation of false teaching, had not really dealt with the problem of how to counter it. The impression of a specific community, members and heretics has given way in our study to a sense of generalisation and characterisation. The letter form may have been chosen because, possibly after the Pauline pattern, it had become a standard way of conveying teaching to the church, the opening greeting, whether or not involving pseudonymity, expressing the authority behind that greeting. The parallels but greater clumsiness of the final paragraph compared with that of 3 John may reflect the same artificiality we saw in that opening greeting.[126] If 2 John did have this wider goal, this may explain its early association and survival with 1 John; both were, and would have been preserved as, pastoral letters for Johannine Christianity. The particular value then of 2 John will be not what it may tell us 'historically' about the pastoral role of the Elder or the development of heresy in Johannine ranks, but what it reveals of the development of problems and solutions, language and theology in Johannine Christianity.

[126] See ch. 2, p. 41, n. 17. The adversative use of the participle (πολλὰ ἔχων) and the failure to repeat the verb 'to write' after 'I did not wish' (οὐκ ἐβουλήθην) is more clumsy than 3 John's 'I had . . . but I did not wish . . . to write'.

3 John

Of all the letters in the New Testament 3 John comes closest to the secular letters of the time, sharing with them brevity and frequently only allusive or ambiguous references to the background events. This means it has little of the artificiality and conscious construction of 2 John, here as in its historical, literary and theological relationship with the rest of the Johannine corpus, standing awkwardly with its 'twin'. If the survival of the letter—and most recent interpretations of its contents—indicates the importance of the events to which it refers, any attempt at reconstruction must deal not only with the ambiguity of its references to events but also with this ambivalence of its relation with its New Testament partners.

The Greeting

1–2

1 Ὁ πρεσβύτερος Γαΐῳ τῷ ἀγαπητῷ, ὃν ἐγὼ ἀγαπῶ ἐν ἀληθείᾳ.
2 Ἀγαπητέ, περὶ πάντων εὔχομαί σε εὐοδοῦσθαι καὶ ὑγιαίνειν, καθὼς εὐοδοῦταί σου ἡ ψυχή.

The Elder to the beloved Gaius, whom I love in truth. Beloved, in all respects I pray that you are prospering and are well, just as your soul does prosper.

'Gaius', the recipient of the letter, is otherwise unknown[127]

---

[127] There is no reason to identify him with the Gaius of Rom 16.23; 1 Cor 1.14 (as already done by Ambrosiaster, *Comm. in Ep. ad Rom.* 16.23 (see ch. 1, n. 33)); according to *Apost. Const.* VII.46 Gaius was consecrated bishop of Pergamum but there is no indication whether the Gaius of Corinthians or of 3 John is in mind. For other attempts to identify him see J. Chapman, 'Historical Setting'; V. Bartlett, 'The Historical Setting of the Second and Third Epistles of St John', *JThS* 6 (1905) 204–16.

and little can be drawn from 3 John itself about him. The epithet **'beloved'** is an epistolary courtesy common in the addresses of contemporary letters, particularly Christian ones; although it is also a Johannine term, the addition of the words 'whom I love in truth' suggests it might otherwise be read as mere convention.[128] Although the theme of 'truth' is not developed here as it is in the greeting of 2 John, **'whom I love in truth'** probably here also expresses not sincere affection so much as a relationship determined by membership of the Johannine circle for which 'truth' was a characterising term. Later the Elder will include Gaius among 'my children' (v. 4), which may be the address of a missionary to his convert or simply that of a teacher who views his protégés as his offspring.[129]

In contrast to 2 John's theologically deliberate use of the 'apostolic' 'Grace and peace' formula, 3 John lacks any greeting word in the address, perhaps, as we saw earlier,[130] but not necessarily, giving the letter an extra note of authority. In a way strikingly unique in the New Testament, the address is followed by a form approximating to the secular conventional health wish, **'in all respects I pray that you are prospering and are well'**. There are, as we have noted, anomalies and apparently a recognition that such a wish might appear misleading—**'just as your soul does prosper'**. It is neither in the author's interests nor part of his style (cf. v. 3, 'just as you do walk in truth') to imply any deficiency on Gaius's part, and, in any case, as the letter well illustrates, material advancement is not the only consideration.

---

[128] So U. v. Wilamowitz-Möllendorf, 'Lesefruchte', *Hermes* 33 (1898) 529–31; 'ἀγαπητός' is the only term which 3 John shares with 1 John but not with 2 John; Berger, 'Apostelbrief', 211–12 sees it as a 'Testament' term but it is probably wider than this, see ch. 2, p. 42 and n. 20.

[129] 2 Tim 1.2; see also above n. 50.

[130] Ch. 2, p. 46.

Gaius's faithful support of 'the brethren'

3–8

3 ἐχάρην γὰρ λίαν ἐρχομένων ἀδελφῶν καὶ μαρτυρούντων σου τῇ ἀληθείᾳ, καθὼς σὺ ἐν ἀληθείᾳ περιπατεῖς. 4 μειζοτέραν τούτων οὐκ ἔχω χαράν, ἵνα ἀκούω τὰ ἐμὰ τέκνα ἐν τῇ ἀληθείᾳ περιπατοῦντα.

5 Ἀγαπητέ, πιστὸν ποιεῖς ὃ ἐὰν ἐργάσῃ εἰς τοὺς ἀδελφοὺς καὶ τοῦτο ξένους, 6 οἳ ἐμαρτύρησάν σου τῇ ἀγάπῃ ἐνώπιον ἐκκλησίας, οὓς καλῶς ποιήσεις προπέμψας ἀξίως τοῦ θεοῦ · 7 ὑπὲρ γὰρ τοῦ ὀνόματος ἐξῆλθον μηδὲν λαμβάνοντες ἀπὸ τῶν ἐθνικῶν. 8 ἡμεῖς οὖν ὀφείλομεν ὑπολαμβάνειν τοὺς τοιούτους, ἵνα συνεργοὶ γινώμεθα τῇ ἀληθείᾳ.

For I rejoiced greatly when brothers came and bore witness to your truth, just as you do walk in truth. I have no greater joy than this, to hear of my children walking in the truth. Beloved you act faithfully in whatever you work towards the brothers – and strangers at that, – who have born witness to your love before the church; please send these forward worthily of God. For they have gone out for the sake of the name, taking nothing from the Gentiles. Therefore we ought to help such that we may be fellow-workers with the truth.

The main subject of the letter is certain travelling brethren who, in the eyes of the Elder, merit support. Indeed, to support them is to have fellowship with the truth, to be faithful and reliable in Johannine terms. This is the view and behaviour which the Elder wishes to commend to Gaius but he approaches his subject carefully. Preumably both the advocacy and the care are necessitated by the adverse reaction of Diotrephes referred to in v. 9f.

The subject is approached by the conventional expression of joy which enables the author to commend Gaius first for his fidelity to truth just as later he commends him for his love. In both cases the commendation is based on the reports of 'the brethren'; firstly they **'bear witness to your truth'**, the present participle (μαρτυρούντων) suggesting a more general or repeated testimony, while in the second instance they **'bore witness to your love'**, suggesting a specific occasion (aorist ἐμαρτύρησάν).[131]

The parallel linking of 'truth' and 'love' recalls the way they are brought together at the close of the greeting of 2 John; they are the cardinal and characteristic virtues of Johannine Christianity, and like the more patent 'love', Gaius's 'truth' must refer to his behaviour as in conformity with these virtues. It is important that, despite the high proportion of non-Johannine vocabulary we shall find in 3 John, Gaius's integrity is being measured by Johannine standards.

The brethren have testified to Gaius's 'truth' (σου τῇ ἀληθείᾳ); such is the author's main wish for his protegés – he has **'no greater joy than to hear of my children walking in the truth'** (ἐν τῇ ἀληθείᾳ περιπατοῦντα).[132] Despite the absence of the article the meaning must be the same when the Elder affirms that dependence on a report implies no doubt, **'just as you do walk in truth';**[133] as we argued for 2 Jn 4, 'walking in truth' means more than 'sincere behaviour', it is behaviour in conformity with Johannine standards of belief and behaviour.

The author has now moved away from epistolary niceties to

[131] The parallelism shows that there is no link with the use of 'μαρτυρεῖν τῇ ἀληθείᾳ' in Jn 5.33; 18.37 or with its use in the papyri of vouching for the correctness of a document.

[132] Reading 'χαραν' (joy) with the majority of witnesses against 'χαριν' (which could also be translated as 'delight') read by B *pc* vg bo; although accepted by W.H. and Harnack, *Zur Revision*, 72 the reading of B etc. may have been introduced for its theological overtones. On 'μειζοτέραν' see B.D. §61(2). In 2 Jn 4 'in truth' follows the verb whereas in both occurrences in 3 John it preceeds it; this is another of those slight variations between 2 and 3 John which only might point to the 'secondary' nature of 2 John.

[133] Thus we should not translate 'as you do actually walk' or see the 'καθώς' as introducing reported speech (so G. Bonnaccorsi as reported by B.D. §453(2)).

the main burden of his letter, but his words remain ambiguous and perhaps guarded. The brethren had given a testimony to Gaius's love **'before the Church'**—a specific occasion and place is clearly in mind. It is characteristic that 'church' (ἐκκλησία) comes three times in 3 John—here presumably of the Elder's community and in vv. 9–10 of that dominated by his enemy Diotrephes—but is a word which is notoriously absent from the rest of the Johannine corpus.[134] As such it is one of a number of significant 'ecclesiastical' terms which 3 John shares with other New Testament writings but not with the Gospel or other Epistles with their lack of 'institutional' language.

Despite this apparent specificity, the Elder's words of praise are surprisingly imprecise, 'You act faithfully in whatever you work towards the brothers'. **'In whatever you work towards the brothers'** is indefinite both in content and construction,[135] albeit the further qualification of these men as **'strangers at that'**[136] indicates that the 'work' must have been hospitality—though unknown to Gaius they received a welcome because they were fellow Christians. Moreover, the commendation itself, **'you act faithfully'**, in using the present tense (πιστὸν ποιεῖς) also points away from any particular, past action. The phrase itself is unusual with no obvious parallels, but most probably it reflects the common use of 'πιστός' as an attribute or epithet of Christians, believing and faithful.[137] Here the neuter

---

[134] However, its use here shows that the author does not reserve the term for the structure he rejects as suggested by E. Schweizer, *Church Order*, §12c; the absence of the article is probably due to the preposition (see B.D. §255) and does not mean the word is used non-technically as 'the assembled body of Christians' (so Brooke, *Epistles*, 184 comparing 1 Cor 14.19).

[135] See S. Langdon, 'History of the use of ἐάν for ἄν in Relative Clauses', *American Journal of Philology* 24 (1903) 447–51 who argues that this usage stresses the abstract, conditional aspect of the relative clause.

[136] Some witnesses read 'καὶ εἰς τους' in an attempt to ease the construction.

[137] See J.H. Moulton and W.F. Howard, *A Grammar of New Testament Greek* Vol. II, *Accidence and Word Formation*, Edinburgh 1929, 163.

adjective is being used adverbially and means to act as a believer should—a non-Johannine equivalent for 'walking in truth'.

The overall impression of the rather tortured language is that the Elder is advancing his case with great caution—Gaius has yet to be totally won for the cause and the writer is keen to emphasise that he is casting no doubts on Gaius's integrity and reliability, but rather is building on a commitment already demonstrated. Possibly Gaius had already shown hospitality but the author uses this imprecise language to extend the commendation to every such occasion; alternatively he may have been noted as a loyal member by earlier visitors to the community and the Elder wishes to channel this reliability into a concrete form. He has assured Gaius that there is no doubt as to his faithfulness, but in saying 'you act faithfully' he uses the present tense to look forward to further acts of such faithfulness, which he now intends to specify.[138]

More precisely Gaius is now requested to **'send forward the brethren worthily of God'**. In early Christian usage 'sending forward' (προπέμπειν) acquired a technical meaning in missionary contexts of patronage or financial sponsorship for the journey, a meaning it does not have in its non-biblical background.[139] Clearly this is intended here as the author proceeds **'we ought to help such that we may be fellow-workers with the truth',** with 'helping' (ὑπολαμβάνειν) implying active support.[140] Again we are in a world apart from

---

[138] Cf. the interpretation of B. Weiss, *Die Katholischen Briefe*, TU 8.3, Leipzig 1892 also adopted by Harnack, *dritten Johannesbrief* that v. 5 refers to the future and that 'πιστὸν ποιεῖς' means that Gaius will behave in a way confirming the Elder's expectations based on his earlier behaviour.

[139] Acts 15.3; (20.38; 21.5); Rom 15.24; 1 Cor 16.6, 11; 2 Cor 1.16; Tit 3.13; Polycarp, *Philipp.* 1.1. The basic meaning of the verb is 'to send before' and hence 'to conduct, escort'. C changes the construction reading 'ποιησας προπεμψεις'. On 'καλῶς ποιεῖς' see ch. 2, p. 40, n. 12.

[140] Only here in the New Testament but cf. Josephus, *C. Apion* I.247 for supporting with food etc. The more common term, 'ἀπολαμβανειν', is read by a number of witnesses.

the rest of the Johannine corpus where there is little technical missionary language or interest; 'to send forward' (προπέμπειν) and 'fellow-worker' (συνεργός) are words which otherwise in the New Testament occur only in Pauline and related texts, primarily in missionary contexts.[141] Similarly, 'worthily' (ἀξίως) comes only here (v. 6) and in Pauline writings in the New Testament, although the frequency of the phrase 'worthily of God' (ἀξίως τοῦ θεοῦ) in non-biblical Greek makes this of less significance.[142] Indeed it is notable that this is the first occurrence of 'God' in the letter and that each time the word appears it is in a phrase which could be taken from tradition (v. 11, 'to be of God' and 'to see God'). This underlines the strange absence of any distinctively Christian teaching about God or any reference to 'Jesus', 'Christ', 'Son' or 'Father' in 3 John.

That the people Gaius is asked to help are missionaries is confirmed when it is said **'they have gone out for the sake of the name'**.[143] In 1 and 2 John 'to go out' (ἐξέρχεσθαι) is used only of the antichrists, and the use of this 'mission' terminology of them may reflect the ambivalence of those letters towards missionary work. Here 'for the sake of the name' uses 'the name' in an absolute sense unusual in the New Testament. The nearest parallel is Acts 5.41 where the apostles rejoice to be thought

[141] For 'προπέμπειν' see n. 139; 'συνεργός', Rom 16.3, 9, 21; 1 Cor 3.9; 2 Cor 1.24; 8.23; Phil 2.25; 4.3; Col 4.11; 1 Thess 3.2; Philem 1, 24; it does not occur in the Apostolic Fathers. In Paul the noun is never followed by the dative of person or thing as here in 3 John and in some classical examples (see below n. 150).

[142] Rom 16.2; Eph 4.1; Phil 1.27; Col 1.10; 1 Thess 2.12. A. Deissmann, *Bible Studies*, 248 gives examples from inscriptions.

[143] Harnack, *dritten Johannesbrief* denies that these are the same brothers as those of v. 3 whom he identifies as members of Gaius's community; this seems less probable than that they are the same 'ἀδελφοί', and the term may be restricted to missionaries. The context does not support Chapman's argument ('Historical Setting') that 'for the sake of the name' means because of persecution (cf. Acts 5.41; 9.16; 21.13).

worthy to suffer 'for the sake of the name'; there the context makes it clear that the name is that of Jesus, as it is so often in the New Testament where the Old Testament use of 'the name' as the presence and power of God was transferred to Jesus, so that belief, baptism, prayer or suffering are 'in the name' or 'for the sake of the name' of Jesus or the Lord.[144] Later, 'the Name' did come to be used absolutely and played an important role in Christian—especially Jewish Christian—theology.[145] This later development can hardly be read back into 3 John nor is there evidence to support the argument that in Johannine thought 'the Name' was a term for Jesus.[146] Rather the continuity between 'worthily of God' and 'for the sake of the name' suggests that the name is that of God—it is for his sake they have gone out and they should be treated appropriately.[147]

In **'taking nothing from the Gentiles'**—ἐθνικοί (otherwise only used by Matthew) perhaps because the more common 'ἔθνος' is used in John's Gospel of the Jewish nation[148]—they conformed to standard Christian practice, not living by begging from their hearers in contrast to many of the mendicant preachers of the age.[149]

Who these 'brethren' were or from where they have come is

[144] Acts 5.40–41; 9.16; Rom 1.5 etc.; cf. also Phil 2.9; Jas 2.7.

[145] J. Danielou, *The Theology of Jewish Christianity*, London 1964, 147–63; J.E. Menard, 'Les Élucubrations de l'Evangelium Veritatis sur le "Nom" ', *Studia Montis Regii* V, Montreal 1962, 185–214. For the later absolute use of 'the Name' see Hermas, *Vis* III.2.1; *Sim* VIII.10.3; Ignatius, *Eph* 3.1; 7.1.

[146] Contrast the other apparent 'absolute' use in the NT where the context provides the reference to Jesus, Acts 5.41; seeing the problem some witnesses have added 'αὐτοῦ'. G. Quispel, 'Het Johannesevangelie en de Gnosis', *NedThT* 11 (1956–7) 173–203, 197f. suggested 'the Name' was a Johannine term for Jesus; similarly Brown, *Epistles*, 712.

[147] So the commentaries of B. Weiss, J.H.A. Ebrard, F. Lücke, but most modern commentaries refer it to Jesus.

[148] 'ἐθνικός': Mt 5.47; 6.7; 18.17 with derogatory overtones; 'ἔθνος' of the Jewish nation in Jn 11.48, 50–2; 18.35. 'ἐθνῶν' is read by the Majorty text here.

[149] E.g. Lucian, *Fugitivi* 14 (ed. A. Harmon, London and Cambridge, Mass. 1936, 70).

not stated. It may well be implied that they have visited the Elder on more than one occasion (v. 3 ἐρχομένων represents the imperfect), but it is not said they have been sent by him. Neither are any numbers given—there may have been only two following the dominical injunction (Mk 6.7). Certainly they cannot be cited as evidence of a centrally organised missionary organisation behind 3 John or in the New Testament era.

We have in this section a catena of words and phrases otherwise foreign to the Johannine corpus, often having more in common with the Pauline writings, and this presents one of the enigmas of 3 John which often appears to be using ideas and forms distant from the other Johannine writings. And yet the purpose of this support for missionary activity, unexpected in the Johannine world, is **'that we may be fellow-workers with truth'**, (not 'fellow-workers [with them] in the cause of truth');[150] 'truth' appears to be virtually personified but must surely represent the Johannine norm and ideal—to help such brethren is to align oneself fully with the spirit of Johannine Christianity![151] The parallel-in-reverse with 2 Jn 10–11 is provocative; there 'not helping' (μὴ λαμβάνετε cf. ὑπολαμβάνειν) those failing to bear right teaching is advocated lest one be found 'to have fellowship' (κοινωνεῖ cf. 'fellow-workers', συνεργοί) with their 'evil deeds' (τοῖς ἔργοις ... πονηροῖς cf. 'truth', τῇ ἀληθείᾳ). Nothing here is said about the doctrine of the brethren but a question must be raised by this

---

[150] Paul uses the genitive after 'συνεργός' (n. 141) but the dative is found in classical authors (e.g. Thucydides, III.63); I. de la Potterie, 'L'arrière-fond du thème johannique de verité', *Studia Evangelica* I, TU 73, Berlin 1959, 277–94 sees the construction as Jewish, cf. *Clem. Hom.* XVII.9. See also D. Hall, 'Fellow-workers with the Gospel', *ET* 85 (1973–4) 119–20.

[151] However, Büchsel, *Begriff der Wahrheit*, 51–3 goes too far in saying that truth has ontological reality and independence here; Brown, *Epistles*, 715 gives truth a christological reference here (as does Haenchen, 'Neue Literatur', 283 for v. 12) but this too is reading more into the verse than 3 John on its own justifies. ℵ* A read 'ἐκκλησίᾳ', an early attempt at a similar interpretation!

parallel as also by the reaction of Diotrephes which the Elder now reports.

The Conflict with Diotrephes

9–10

9 Ἔγραψά τι τῇ ἐκκλησίᾳ· ἀλλ' ὁ φιλοπρωτεύων αὐτῶν Διοτρέφης οὐκ ἐπιδέχεται ἡμᾶς. 10 διὰ τοῦτο, ἐὰν ἔλθω, ὑπομνήσω αὐτοῦ τὰ ἔργα ἃ ποιεῖ λόγοις πονηροῖς φλυαρῶν ἡμᾶς, καὶ μὴ ἀρκούμενος ἐπὶ τούτοις οὔτε αὐτὸς ἐπιδέχεται τοὺς ἀδελφοὺς καὶ τοὺς βουλομένους κωλύει καὶ ἐκ τῆς ἐκκλησίας ἐκβάλλει.

I have written something to the church; but Diotrephes, who loves to be first among them, does not receive us. Therefore, if I come I shall bring up the actions he does, slandering us with evil words and, not content with this, he even does not receive the brethren and those who wish to he forbids and casts out of the church.

The Elder must appeal to Gaius because he cannot gain the support of **'the church'** and presumably assumes his earlier letter, no doubt on the same subject, to have been suppressed or rejected.[152] 'The church' is not further identified neither is it clear whether Gaius was one of its members. If he was then he

---

[152] Grayston, Epistles, 160–1, Strecker, 'Die Anfänge', 37 and H. Thyen, 'Entwicklungen innerhalb der johanneischen Theologie und Kirche im Spiegel von Joh 21 und der Lieblingsjüngertexte des Evangeliums', in L'Évangile de Jean, ed. M. de Jonge, 259–99 have revived the suggestion that the letter was 2 John; however, this is hard to sustain in the light of our study of 2 John and because the following words do not suggest that Diotrephes had over-reacted to 2 John as is suggested by Grayston. The reading 'ἔγραψα ἄν' of ℵᶜ 33 al latt sy probably represents an attempt to avoid the problem of a lost letter although it is accepted by Harnack, Zur Revision, 73; B sa read 'ἔγραψας τι' which may be a misspelling or represent a genuine alternative, 'you have written' (so Brown, Epistles, 716); the Majority reading 'ἔγραψα' is probably an attempt at simplification.

would have known of Diotrephes's action and the Elder's
account would be giving his side of the story while reminding
Gaius of the treatment he could receive if he responded to the
appeal. If he was not—and this may be supported by the
description of Diotrephes as wanting authority over 'them'
(φιλοπρωτεύων αὐτῶν) and not over 'you'—then its identity
must have been obvious to Gaius, perhaps even without the
reference to Diotrephes. That the term 'church' is unique to
3 John among the Gospel and Epistles has already been noted,
but its use in v. 6 prohibits the suggestion that its use here
denotes a derogatory use of the enemy camp's own self-
appellation.[153]

'Diotrephes', of whom we again know nothing outside this
letter, is condemned for his **'desire for pre-eminence'**; the
verb used here (φιλοπρωτεύειν) is not attested earlier although
the adjective is used by hellenistic writers in conjunction with
the ambition for tyranny.[154] Whether or not a tyrant, the
passage indicates that he was not merely ambitious but was
actually in a position where he could determine the conduct of
the community, presumably with the support of the majority of
its members. Inasmuch as we only have the Elder's account the
text itself does not determine whether such dominance was
based on personal strength of character and self-assertion or on
some more official position; neither does it decide the grounds
of the Elder's reaction—justified anger against an upstart,
rejection of the hierarchical office itself or resentment at being
opposed regardless of his opponent's actual status and character.
What he does condemn is both Diotrephes's attitude towards
himself and his treatment of the 'brethren'.

---

[153] See above p. 105 n. 134.

[154] Plutarch, *Solon* 95B. However, similar forms are used in a positive sense
in inscriptions to benefactors, e.g. φιλότιμος, cf. Poland, *Geschichte*, 411f.;
hence, it is possible that this is a parody or rejection of a 'secular' designation of
honour.

(a) In the first place, despite the Elder's letter, Diotrephes **'does not receive us'**—so presumably the letter will be of no avail. Exactly the same language is used of Diotrephes's attitude to the brethren—he does not 'receive' them (οὐκ ἐπιδέχεται ἡμᾶς ... οὔτε ἐπιδέχεται τοὺς ἀδελφούς); in both cases the use of the present tense suggests a consistent attitude rather than a single act of hostility. Clearly in not 'receiving' the brethren Diotrephes must be denying them entry into the community and hospitality, but the same can hardly be meant of his attitude to the Elder since the latter speaks only of an abortive letter and seems to envisage a visit (v. 10, 'If I come'). The problem of what the Elder means when he complains that Diotrephes 'does not receive us' is complicated by the plural 'us' (ἡμᾶς) after the singular 'I' at the beginning of this and the following verse ('I wrote', 'I come'). The same alternation occurs in the next verse—'If I come, I shall bring up . . . he slanders us',—while the first person plural of v. 12 ('we bear witness . . . our witness') may be part of the same issue. This alternation between first person singular and plural may be nothing more than a matter of style which can readily be paralleled in papyri letters.[155] For some interpreters, however, it contains a vital clue to the meaning of the letter; in 1 Jn 1.1 and Jn 21.24 the first person plural is used in a context of witness and tradition which has led many to talk of the Johannine 'we' of authority or of a claim to association with eyewitness tradition. If this is the case here Diotrephes is not simply rejecting the Elder on personal grounds but is repudiating the generation and tradition he represents and the authority that is therefore his.[156] It is doubtful whether the letter can support such an interpretation, neither is it demanded by the language. The verb 'ἐπιδέχεσθαι' primarily means to 'receive' and does not of itself imply recognition of authority

[155] See E. Mayser, *Grammatik der griechischen Papyri aus der Ptolemäerzeit* II.1, Berlin 1926, 40f.
[156] See Harnack, 'Das "Wir" '; Brown, *Epistles*, 717.

unless that is entailed in the status of the person being received;[157] it is not obvious that the plural 'us' can imply such a significance. More probably the 'us' emphasises the parallel and the link between Diotrephes's attitude to the Elder and to the brethren. In ignoring the Elder's letter and its request as well as those he supports Diotrephes is rejecting the Elder and all he stands for— or that at least is how the Elder sees it. The language of 'not receiving' is too imprecise to speak of rejection of authority or of excommunication[158]—Diotrephes is simply failing to do what he 'ought' to be doing.

(b) Not only this, Diotrephes adds to this rejection by **'slandering us with evil words'**—something the Elder sees as more than a personal slight (us—ἡμᾶς).[159] This does little to clarify the situation; the slander may have been the abusive language of personal vindictiveness or may have contained charges of a more serious nature which the Elder could only see as defamatory.

(c) Diotrephes's hostility even extends to the brethren whom **'he does not receive'**, clearly refusing them entry or hospitality. Since the Elder complains that Diotrephes does this because he **'is not content'** with his defamation of the Elder, the implication may be that it was their link with the Elder which told so heavily against 'the brethren'. Just as those 'slanders' may have contained for Diotrephes charges justifying his behaviour, so too may have been the reasons for which he turned away the brethren. Certainly the refusal of hospitality must have meant the refusal of support for the mission on which the brethren were engaged.

[157] E.g. 1 Macc 10.1. A. Ehrhardt, 'Christianity before the Apostles' Creed', *HThR* 55 (1962) 74–119, 91 compares the Lukan use of 'ἀποδέχεσθαι' signifying both acceptance of doctrine and provision of hospitality.

[158] Against Käsemann, 'Ketzer und Zeuge' who argues for the excommunication of the Elder; 'ἐκβάλλειν' is only used of Diotrephes's response to members of his community wishing to help the brethren.

[159] C vg read 'εἰς ἡμας'.

(d) That Diotrephes's response was more serious than personal animosity is even more strongly suggested by the charge that he **'forbids those who wish'** to help the brethren **'and expels them from the church'**.[160] Again the present tense suggests this was his consistent attitude and not something he only tried to do[161]—and thus he must have had the support of the majority of his community. We must assume that either Gaius had not yet shown such hospitality or that he was not a member of Diotrephes's church. The parallel with 2 Jn 10–11 is unmistakable. There hospitality or even a greeting is to be denied one failing to bear right doctrine, for even to give a greeting is to share in the faithless man's evil deeds; here the travelling brethren are refused hospitality or the fellowship of the church, while those who seek to help them, presumably sharing their culpability, share also in the exclusion from the community. Here nothing is said of the doctrine of the brethren, but the parallel may suggest that Diotrephes suspected them of false belief or rejected their status and rights as Christian missionaries for reasons not stated—and this may have constituted the much resented 'slander'.

The precise status of Diotrephes's reaction remains ambiguous; to say he 'excommunicated' some members of his church may imply too formal a structure and authority, although this is precisely the question we do not have the evidence to solve. The Elder's reaction is even more equivocal; he defends neither himself nor the brethren and speaks only of a possible visit ('if I come') when he **'will bring up Diotrephes's behaviour'**. There is nothing here to imply public censure or rebuke;[162] the verb essentially means to remind

---

[160] 'ἐπιδεχομενους' is read for 'βουλομενους' by C *pc* it sy[ph. hmg] sa; ℵ *pc* omit ἐκ before της ἐκκλησιας.

[161] Against Haenchen, 'Neue Literatur', 283.

[162] As is suggested by Schnackenburg, *Johannesbriefe*, 327 and M. Goguel, *L'Église Primitive*, Paris 1947, 254 comparing 1 Cor 5. 2 Tim 2.14 which is

or mention and probably the Elder can only hope to give his interpretation of events and to show the injustice of Diotrephes's actions to all concerned. C.H. Dodd's words remain true: 'The language which he uses ... suggests that the Presbyter is not too sure of his ground. He can do no more than stake his personal influence and prestige against those of Diotrephes'.[163] But what was this 'personal influence and prestige' and how persuasive would its effect be?

Taking sides with the 'good'

11–12

> 11 'Αγαπητέ, μὴ μιμοῦ τὸ κακὸν ἀλλὰ τὸ ἀγαθόν. ὁ ἀγαθοποιῶν ἐκ τοῦ θεοῦ ἐστιν· ὁ κακοποιῶν οὐχ ἑώρακεν τὸν θεόν. 12 Δημητρίῳ μεμαρτύρηται ὑπὸ πάντων καὶ ὑπὸ αὐτῆς τῆς ἀληθείας· καὶ ἡμεῖς δὲ μαρτυροῦμεν, καὶ οἶδας ὅτι ἡ μαρτυρία ἡμῶν ἀληθής ἐστιν.

Beloved, do not imitate evil but good. He who does good is of God; he who does evil has not seen God. Witness is borne to Demetrius by all and by the truth itself; and we also bear witness, and you know that our witness is true.

It has become clear that Gaius must take sides and there can be no doubt that the choice is not simply between two viable alternatives. It is a matter of choosing good or evil; Diotrephes must be the one who does evil, who, by implication, **'has not seen God'**, while in contrast to him is set chiastically one Demetrius who (v. 12) is worthy of imitation, who clearly 'does good' and is 'of God'.[164]

sometimes cited for the sense of admonition does not justify a sense of rebuke here.

[163] Dodd, *Epistles*, 165.

[164] Contrast T. Horvath, '3 Jn 11b. An Early Ecumenical Creed?', *ET* 85 (1973) 339–40 who gives the verse universal reference—acts of charity are more important than acceptance or rejection of Jesus.

The exhortation is given in an antithetical structure which is Johannine in style and particularly reminiscent of 1 Jn 3.6ff.:

> Everyone who remains in him does not sin; everyone who sins has not seen him nor known him. . . . He who does righteousness is righteous . . . he who does sin is of the devil . . . everyone who does not do righteousness is not of God.

In both the antithesis explores the relationship between behaviour ('doing') and being 'of God' or seeing 'him'; since being 'of God' is a typically Johannine idiom with no precise parallel in other New Testament writings the link between the two passages appears particularly strong.[165] However, the points of difference are such that we must wonder whether the Johannine guise is more than skin deep. In the passage from 1 John 'he who sins' is said not to have 'seen him', with the context clearly showing that 'him' refers to Jesus, however that claim to have seen Jesus might be understood; here the assertion is that he who does evil has not 'seen *God*', unusual in that the general Johannine and biblical emphasis is that no-one can see God anyway.[166] The verse from 1 John, which taken out of context would be ambiguous, or something like it, could have provided a model for the statement of 3 Jn 11; the overall effect of course is to underline this Epistle's remarkable silence about Jesus and its reference only to 'God'.[167]

It is the language of 'doing good' and 'evil', however, which is most removed from Johannine thought. 'Good' (ἀγαθός) and 'evil' (κακός) occur only a very few times in the Gospel and not at all in the other Epistles of John, while the compound verbs 'to

---

[165] Jn 8.47; 1 Jn 3.10; 4.2,6. Houlden, *Epistles*, 154 suggests that if a series of aphorisms does lie behind 1 John, this may be one of them; Bultmann, 'Analyse', 148 sees the verse as only modelled on the style of the source document he posits for 1 John, because of its unJohannine 'ἀγαθοποιεῖν'.

[166] Jn 1.18; 6.46; 1 Jn 4.12,20 etc.

[167] See above p. 107.

do good' or 'evil' (ἀγαθοποιεῖν; κακοποιεῖν) are not found at all in the rest of the Johannine corpus.[168] The Johannine writings prefer to speak of 'doing the truth', 'walking in the light', 'loving one another' and, in I John, 'doing righteousness' as in the verse quoted. The verb 'to do good', unlike its opposite, 'to do evil', does not occur in classical Greek, although it is found in some astrological papyri meaning 'to exert a favourable influence'. Reflecting its use in the Septuagint meaning 'to show favour to' or 'to benefit', it is used in Mark and Luke, but it is only in I Peter and the Apostolic Fathers that it comes to gain the more explicit sense of 'doing what is morally right' and to be seen as a necessary quality for Christians.[169] This is probably the force we should give it here, with 'to do evil', as elsewhere in the New Testament, only being used to express the opposite, and it may be of some significance that for Hermas (*Mand* VIII.10) 'doing good' (ἀγαθοποίησις) is manifested in hospitality. It would seem that although 3 John can use Johannine terminology and values, these are being combined with language from the developing ethical terminology of non-Johannine Christianity, something confirmed by the earlier use of 'acting faithfully' and of ecclesiastical and mission language.

Despite the apparently well-supported attitude of Diotrephes, Gaius's true Christian standing, (that he is 'of God'), can only be assured if he imitates—another non-Johannine word more common to Pauline writings[170]—and does what is good. His pattern must be not Diotrephes but **'Demetrius'**,

---

[168] 'ἀγαθός' Jn 1.46; 5.29; 7.12; (also missing from Revelation); 'κακός' Jn 18.23,30. In Jn 5.29 'those who have done good' may refer to unbelievers.

[169] Mk 3.4; Lk 6.9,33,35 (meaning 'to benefit'); thus it is used to translate the hiphil of ' יטב ' in Num 10.32; Judg 17.13; Zeph 1.12. 'To do right' is the meaning in I Pet 2.14f.; 3.6,17; 4.19; 2 Clem 10.2; Hermas *Vis* III.4.5; 9.5; *Sim* IX.18.1; *Ep. Diognetus* 5.16. See W. Grundmann, art. 'ἀγαθοποιέω' TDNT I, 17–8.

[170] 'μιμέομαι' 2 Thess 3.7; Heb 13.7; cf. 'μιμήτης' I Cor 4.16; 11.1; Eph 5.1; I Thess 1.6; 2.14; Heb 6.12.

whose exemplary quality is made clear in the words that he has **'witness borne to him by all'**. Despite the importance of the Johannine theme of witness, especially in the Gospel,[171] the clue to these words—as to the witness borne by the brethren to Gaius's truth and love (vv. 3, 6)—would seem to lie in other non-Christian and Christian usage. Similar formulae occur frequently in inscriptions from Asia Minor and in other sources as a standard designation of honour in civic life, with the impersonal perfect passive (μεμαρτύρηται αὐτῷ) being used in the same way as here.[172] Similarly, in Acts Cornelius has a good report from the whole Jewish nation (10.22, using the present passive participle 'μαρτυρούμενος', so also of Ananias in Acts 22.12). Frequently, however, the term is employed to express a more formal sense of approbation especially of those worthy of office or of imitation, such as the 'seven' of Acts 6.3 or widows in 1 Tim 5.10. *1 Clement* makes good use of the theme in condemning the deposition from office of those who were not only appointed by the apostles but who have also blamelessly fulfilled their ministry and have for a long time 'been approved by all' (μεμαρτυρημένους ὑπὸ πάντων, using the perfect passive, 44.3); earlier the readers have been urged 'to become imitators' (μιμηταὶ γενώμεθα) of the prophets of old and of those who 'are approved' or 'testified to' (τοὺς μεμαρτυρημένους), including Abraham, Job, Moses and 'the well commended David' (ὁ μεμαρτυρημένος Δαυείδ) (*1 Clem* 17.1ff; 18.1; cf. Heb 11.2). That Demetrius is described in the same terms (using the perfect passive) as 'having testimony borne to him by all'

---

[171] See A. Trites, *The New Testament Concept of Witness*, SNTS MS 31, Cambridge 1977, 78–127; J. Beutler, *Martyria: Traditionsgeschichtliche Untersuchungen zum Zeugnisthema bei Johannes*, Frankfurt 1972.

[172] See L. Robert, *Hellenica* 13 (1965) 207; Deissmann, *Bible Studies*, 265. H. Strathmann, art. 'μαρτύς' *TDNT* IV, 474–514, 496 recognises the sense of 'a good report' in 3 John but only cites Christian parallels; however, here as elsewhere, 3 John should be set in its wider non-Christian context.

(μεμαρτύρηται ὑπὸ πάντων), may suggest not only that he is worthy of honour but also of imitation.

We need not, therefore, assume, as do so many commentators, that Demetrius was one of the missionaries or (and) the letter-bearer, and that the letter, or this part of it, acts as a 'letter of recommendation' for him.[173] Letters of recommendation (ἐπιστολαὶ συστατικαί) represent an important epistolary genre with a characteristic vocabulary and structure not found here; in such letters the standard verb used to commend the person concerned is 'to recommend' (συνιστάναι) and there then usually follows a specific request on their behalf or a statement of appreciation (cf. Rom 16.1–2).[174] Where the verb 'to witness' (μαρτυρεῖν) is used, it is to say that the person recommended will later be able to bear witness of his host's kindness to the writer of the letter—as perhaps in vv. 3 and 6 of Gaius's hospitality to the brethren, but not relevant to the credentials given to Demetrius.[175]

The validity of these credentials are confirmed in that they are supported **'by the truth itself'**.[176] Again, this could be read in a thoroughly Johannine sense—Demetrius's approval is upheld by the very spirit and norm of Johannine Christianity;[177] it

[173] So Brooke, *Epistles*, 192; Schnackenburg, *Johannesbriefe*, 330 and many others. A.J. Malherbe, 'The Inhospitality of Diotrephes', in *God's Christ and his People*, ed. J. Jervell and W. Meeks, Oslo 1977, 222–32 develops a comprehensive interpretation of 3 John against the background of hospitality and letters of recommendation.

[174] See C-H Kim, *Form and Structure*; K. Treu, 'Christliche Empfehlungs-Schemabriefe auf Papyrus', in *Zetesis*, Antwerp 1973, 629–36 who cites letters from the 3rd to 5th centuries which follow a common pattern of asking the recipient to receive (παρα-/προσδεξαι) a 'brother' 'through whom I address you'.

[175] So *P. Oslo* 55, l.13 and *P. Oxy* 1064 (Vol.7 London 1910), l.12 both of which are cited by Malherbe although without recognising that this militates against seeing 3 Jn 12 as a letter of recommendation.

[176] For 'της ἀληθειας' A* P[74]* read 'της ἐκκλησιας' and C sy[ph, hmg] have a composite reading.

[177] Haenchen, 'Neue Literatur', 283.

would make equal sense in a more secular context where a man on trial could be said to be 'condemned by his own life and by truth' or where oligarchs are 'classified by truth itself'[178]—so too the witness given Demetrius can brook no denial.

To this weight of evidence in Demetrius's favour is added finally the Elder's own testimony, about which Gaius can have no doubt, **'We also bear witness and you know that our witness is true'**. The bringing together of the themes of witness, its truth, 'knowing' and the ambiguous 'we' is unmistakeably Johannine. The most obvious parallel comes in the closing testimony to the Gospel:

> This is the disciple who is bearing witness concerning these things and has written them, and we know that his testimony is true. (Jn 21.24)

A similar attestation of witness comes in the Passion Narrative following the issue of blood and water from the side of Jesus:

> And he who has seen has borne witness, and his witness is true, and that one (ἐκεῖνος) knows that he speaks the truth that you also may believe. (Jn 19.35)

These verses look like Johannine maxims (cf. also 3.11) which have been brought in to support the important Johannine theme of witness which runs through the Gospel.[179] It would seem that in 3 John one such maxim, or an imitation of the Gospel

---

[178] Aeschines, *C. Timarch* 90 (ed. C.A. Adams, London and Cambridge, Mass. 1919, 74) 'καταμεμαρτυρημένος ὑπὸ τοῦ ἑαυτοῦ βίου καὶ τῆς ἀληθείας'; *C. Ctesip* 207 (ibid., 470) 'ὑπ᾽ αὐτῆς τῆς ἀληθείας διηριθμημένους'.

[179] See n. 171; B. Lindars, 'The Persecution of Christians in Jo 15:18–16:4a', in *Suffering and Martyrdom in the New Testament*, ed. W. Horbury and B. McNeil, Cambridge 1981, 48–69, 59 draws attention to such Johannine maxims.

passages,[180] has been used to support the approval given to Demetrius—with a consequent loss of theological depth so it functions little more than as a slogan. For this reason it is hazardous to base too much on the use of the first person plural, 'we bear witness', for while that 'we' could express the authority of the witness or the support of his party it may equally owe its origin to that Johannine nexus of themes which associates testimony with an allusive 'we'. This continuity of the theme of witness from a non-Johannine to a Johannine context is a peculiarity of 3 John which characterises the problem of the letter.[181]

The letter gives no indication of who Demetrius was or why he merited such approval.[182] No doubt he was a partisan of the Elder who had not failed to support his cause and who perhaps had shown hospitality to the brethren. Where or in what capacity the brevity of the letter leaves unsaid.

Final Greetings

13–15

13 Πολλὰ εἶχον γράψαι σοι ἀλλ᾽ οὐ θέλω διὰ μέλανος καὶ καλάμου σοι γράφειν · **14** ἐλπίζω δὲ εὐθέως σε ἰδεῖν, καὶ στόμα πρὸς στόμα λαλήσομεν.

15 Εἰρήνη σοι. ἀσπάζονταί σε οἱ φίλοι. ἀσπάζου τοὺς φίλους κατ᾽ ὄνομα.

I have much to write to you, but I do not want to write to you by ink and pen; but I hope to see you very soon, and we shall

---

[180] See Brooke, *Epistles*, 194; Westcott, *Epistles*, 231 argues that Jn 21.24 is an echo of this verse. The reading of the plural 'οἴδατε' by the Majority text may be an assimilation to the Gospel passage (we know), or influenced by the church use of 3 John.

[181] The language of 'loving in truth' and 'witness by the truth' shows a similar ambivalence between its Johannine and non-Johannine backgrounds.

[182] Although he has been variously identified with known figures in the early church; see the authors cited in n. 127.

speak face to face. Peace to you. The friends greet you. Greet the friends by name.

The apology for the brevity of his letter and the other closing epistolary courtesies follow the same pattern as those of 2 John but somewhat less clumsily and with minor changes of language which have given rise to considerable textual confusion.[183] Unless it is a matter of imitation by 2 John to give epistolary verisimilitude this must have been the author's conventional way of closing his letters. If so the hope of an imminent personal encounter may, despite the **'very soon'**, belong to farewell pleasantries as much as to useful historical background for the letter. Whereas 2 John explicitly spoke of a visit, the Elder's hope here merely 'to see' (σε ἰδεῖν) Gaius is far less precise.

In surprising contrast with the more Greek conventions of the letter comes the Semitic benediction **'Peace to you'**. Such benedictions were used in Christian letters, as for example in I Pet 5.14, 'Peace to you all who are in Christ', although Johannine authority would have been provided by Jesus's use of this greeting in the resurrection appearances in the Gospel (Jn 20.19,21,26 'Peace to you (pl.)')[184] The benediction may have become a conventional Christian greeting but it may be another of these surprising notes of Johannine authority which we have found in 3 John.

The final greetings conform again to the conventions of contemporary letters. Greetings to or from 'friends' are too common for us to conclude from the Elder's transmission of greetings to and from **'the friends'** that they constituted a circumscribed and perhaps small **('by name')** group, or that this was a distinctively Johannine term for members of the

---

[183] For 'γραψαι σοι' many witnesses read 'γραφειν' and for οὐ θελω' A reads 'οὐκ ἐβουληθην', in each case following 2 Jn 12; there are also minor variations of order.

[184] See ch. 2, p. 48 and nn. 49–50.

group (as in Jn 15.15).[185] The Elder closes his letter as he began it, like countless other people did every day.

Herein lies the enigma of 3 John. In language and style the letter shows as much familiarity with the secular conventions of the age as any New Testament Epistle—we may think of the health wish and the general use of the word 'God'. Much of the main import of the letter is expressed in terms which one suspects the author of the Gospel or of 1 John would not have used, language which was becoming technical in other parts of the church and which is shared with Paul, with Peter or with the Apostolic Fathers rather than with the rest of the Johannine corpus. There is too a precision of expression different from that of the Gospel and other Epistles. And yet Johannine style and language would appear to be very much part of the author's tradition, for they come in his mannerisms and idioms as well as in explicit parallels with other Johannine writings—although they have lost theological depth and do not express the most important points of the letter.

When we turn to the situation which provoked 3 John we find equal ambiguity. The Elder approaches Gaius with circumspection and surprisingly fails to make any defence of himself against the 'calumnies' of Diotrephes. Even if he does claim authority in his title, in his talk of his 'children', the use of 'we', the echo of Jn 21.24 and the benediction 'Peace to you', it is unlikely that this authority was institutionalised or uncontested.

It has become clear that 2 and 3 John, in their relation to the Gospel and First Epistle, imply a community or communities with a common self-understanding and language. The signs of change and development indicate passage of time and

---

[185] So Bousset, *Kyrios Christos*, 211; Harnack, *dritten Johannesbrief* isolates the 'friends' of the elder from the rest of the community. See above ch. 2, p. 42 and n. 19. In each case some, but not the same, witnesses read 'brethren' for 'friends'.

differences of authorship, although at this point we shall not be any more specific than that! It is against this complex and composite picture that we must seek not only to interpret 2 and 3 John, but also to see how they in turn can throw light on the history of the Johannine tradition and of the early church.

Chapter Four

'IF ANYONE COMES ...'

The Early Church Background

Whatever the differences between 2 and 3 John, besides their epistolary form and certain idioms they share both their indebtedness to the Johannine tradition and also the assumption of Christian preachers journeying from community to community and provoking the question of the appropriate response. We meet here an important phenomenon in the development of the early church and one which is widely documented and which has received much attention in recent years. There has been a tendency to dub this wandering ministry 'charismatic', setting it in contrast to the institutional local ministry, but even if we recognise this as misleading, owing as much to modern debates about the structure of the church as to the evidence of the sources themselves, it remains true that this is an area of considerable historical importance for the life of the early church.[1]

The New Testament and early Christian literature reflects the very high degree of mobility among Christians whether in service of the Gospel or for more secular or commercial reasons. No doubt the consequent exchange of ideas and traditions was important both in encouraging a sense of unity and in creating unity through common participation in a growing collection of traditions of diverse origin. Thus we may think of the travelling

[1] Among earlier studies that of A. v. Harnack, *Lehre der zwölf Apostel*, TU 2.1, 2, Leipzig 1886, stands out; among recent work that of G. Theissen (see below nn. 6, 10, 18) has been very influential. For the ideological motives behind Harnack's approach see A. Zimmermann, *Die urchristlichen Lehrer*, Tübingen 1984, 36ff.

both by members of the various communities and by his opponents implied by Paul's letters, of Ignatius's enforced route through the churches of Asia Minor and Greece and of the ambassadors sent to greet him or those whose mission to the church at Antioch is of such importance to him.[2] The inns of the day were unreliable and those who could would rely on a network of acquaintances and patronage for hospitality; eschewing the Cynic practice of begging, the Christians established their own network and hospitality became a fundamental Christian virtue.[3]

Amidst this more general movement we find, as in the first or second century *Didache*, travelling 'apostles', prophets or teachers who particularly merit hospitality. There such a prophet is to be received 'as the Lord' (*Didache* 11.4), language which recalls the Gospel injunctions of Jesus that in receiving others Jesus himself is received (Jn 13.20; Lk 10.16; Mk 9.37f.); indeed Matthew's promise that he who receives a prophet will receive a prophet's reward (Mt 10.40–42), peculiar to this Gospel, may reflect a similar situation in his church to the *Didache*'s travelling prophets.[4]

---

[2] 1 Cor 1.11; Phil 2.25; 4.18; Col 4.12; Rom 16.1 etc.; Ignatius, *Eph* 1.3; 21.1; *Trall* 12.1; *Philad* 10–11. Acts also takes for granted lengthy travels by Paul and others.

[3] R. Hock, *The Social Context of Paul's Ministry*, Philadelphia 1980, 27–31 who emphasises the wide social cross section involved in such travelling and hospitality against the view that it was the perogative of the rich, propounded by E. Judge, *The Conversion of Rome*, Sydney 1980, 7. On begging see Epictetus, *Discourses* III.22.10 (ed. W. Oldfather, London and Cambridge, Mass. 1966, 132–4). On hospitality see Heb 13.2; 1 Pet 4.9; Hermas, *Mand* VIII.10; *Sim* IX.27.2.

[4] See E. Schweizer, 'Law Observance and Charisma in Matthew', *NTS* 16 (1969–70) 213–30; idem, 'The Matthaean Church', *NTS* 20 (1974) 215; idem, *The Good News according to Matthew*, London 1976, 176f. However, it may be debated whether the Matthaean prophets are itinerant or local, a debate which has also entered the discussion of the *Didache*; see ed. W. Rordorf and A. Tuilier, *La Doctrine des Douze Apôtres (Didachè)*, SC 248, Paris 1948, 51–63.

The *Didache* implies that such visitors would not merely be welcomed but would be treated with honour, exercising considerable influence and probably providing a significant form of leadership within the community—'for they are your high-priests'.[5] No doubt this influence would have been the consequence both of their charismatic gifts and also of the importance of the teaching they brought for the growth of the community (*Didache* 11.2,7).

More recent study has related the early Christian tradition of asceticism to these 'wandering charismatics' as those who would have obeyed and preserved the more radical demands of the Gospel, homelessness and the loss of family, possessions and protection (Mt 5.38f.; 6.25–32; 8.20ff.; 10.23; Mk 10.29); on this basis too they would have commanded the respect of the settled communities who supported them.[6]

The identity of these figures has been much discussed. In analysing the *Didache*, A. v. Harnack related its 'apostles, prophets and teachers' to a wider body of references to these and similar configurations of gifts or offices and argued that they constituted a class who held the highest position in the early church; they exercised their ministry in the church as a whole as opposed to those officials appointed by the local church and, by wandering from place to place, were a source of the unity of the early church. Their 'appointment' was by God (Eph 4.11) through spiritual or teaching gifts and with them are to be associated the Catholic Epistles. However, as we shall see in 3 John, the future lay with the organisation of the local church.[7] Harnack's thesis has enjoyed very great popularity so that the

---

[5] *Didache* 13.3. G. Kretschmar, 'Ein Beitrag zur Frage nach dem Ursprung frühchristlicher Askese', *ZThK* 61 (1964) 27–67, 42 sees this pattern behind Revelation.

[6] G. Theissen, *The First Followers of Jesus*, London 1978, 8–16; Kretschmar, 'frühchristlicher Askese'.

[7] Harnack, *Lehre der zwölf Apostel* II, 93–107; on the triumph of the local community see idem, *dritten Johannesbrief*, 27.

model of early Christianity as including both the local church with its own theological and authority structures and itinerant prophets or teachers with their own theology and lifestyle, exercising a non-institutional authority within the whole church, is widely accepted and reproduced in a number of forms.[8] So too is the assumption of a conflict between the two forms of authority, for which limited support is given by *Didache* 15.2 where the church is enjoined to appoint bishops and deacons and 'not to despise them for they are your honoured men together with the prophets and teachers'.

In fact much of the evidence Harnack used for the importance of this class within the whole church fails to establish his point; most notably 1 Cor 12.28 shows that prophets, teachers and bearers of other charismatic gifts were to be found in the local community and that a simple identification of asceticism, charismatic gifts and itinerancy is unwarranted.[9] The *Didache* remains the most specific evidence for these figures and while undoubtedly there were wandering prophets in the life of the early church, comprehensive theories of their role are hazardous. So too it is difficult to move from the *Sitz im Leben* of the radical sayings of the Synoptics to identifying a continuation of the tradition elsewhere.[10]

Undoubtedly there was a wide variety of practice; the brethren of 3 John are missionaries, a subject not mentioned in the *Didache*, while Paul himself combined the functions of teaching within the community and of missionary work,

---

[8] Kretschmar, 'frühchristlicher Askese'; idem, 'Christliches Passa im 2 Jahrhundert', *RSR* 60 (1972) 287–323; A. Kragerud, *Der Lieblingsjünger*, 84–93; Bornkamm, 'πρέσβυς', 671, 676–7.

[9] See H. Greeven, 'Propheten, Lehrer, Vorsteher bei Paulus', *ZNW* 44 (1952–3) 1–43; J. Reiling, *Hermas and Christian Prophecy*, NT.S 37, Leiden 1973, 7–11; Zimmermann, *urchristlichen Lehrer*, 50f.

[10] As does G. Theissen, ' "Wir haben alles verlassen" (Mc.X.28). Nachfolge und Soziale Entwurzelung in der jüdisch-palästinischen Gesellschaft des 1 Jahrhunderts n. Chr.', *NT* 19 (1977) 161–96.

claiming a personal and controversial authority. Ignatius occupied the local church office of bishop and yet assumed the right to give advice and to be heard in other churches, as no doubt did the delegates sent to Antioch.[11]

Although there are further references to wandering 'prophets' commanding respect and honour—particularly in sources associated with Palestinian or Syrian Christianity[12]—it is notable that much of that evidence is negative, warning against the inevitable misuse provoked by the support and respect given to these itinerants. Lucian's story of Proteus Peregrinus in the second century is a tale of a charlatan quickly perceiving the benefits of such a lifestyle and achieving a position of leadership among the Christians, whose support of him and whose gullibility Lucian readily satirises.[13] It is hardly surprising that Christian sources do not expand on comparable examples, although Origin's *contra Celsum* hints at some such problems.[14] We cannot therefore know how accurate Lucian's account might be,[15] but when the *Didache* states that a true prophet will not request money, overstay his welcome, or refuse to work (11.3–5; 12.2–5), the implication is that there were spongers around.

A more serious problem was the inevitable result of the

[11] K. Lake, 'Der Strijd tusschen het oudste Christendom en de Bedriegers', *ThT* 42 (1908) 395–411 distinguishes between apostles as missionaries to non-believers and prophets as acting within the church, but the evidence is not as precise as this.

[12] See Kretschmar, 'frühchristlicher Askese'; Theissen, ' "Wir haben alles verlassen" '; G. Stanton, '5 Ezra and Matthaean Christianity in the Second Century', *JThS* NS 28 (1977) 67–83; Rordorf and Tuilier, *Didachè*, 62–3.

[13] Lucian, *Peregrinus* 11–13 (ed. A. Harmon, London and Cambridge, Mass. 1936, 12–14).

[14] Origen, *C. Celsum* III.9; VII.9–11 (SC 136, 30; 150, 34–40).

[15] G. Bagnani, 'Peregrinus Proteus and the Christians', *Historia* 4 (1955) 107–12 fully accepts the historicity of Peregrinus and dates his Christian period to AD 120–40; this perhaps is overconfident; see H.D. Betz, 'Lucian von Samosata und das Christentum', *NT* 3 (1959) 226–37.

interchange of traditions and interpretations of the Christian message which this mobility fostered, namely the problems of conflicting interpretations and of teaching found to be unacceptable. Paul himself had to deal with visitors to the churches he founded propounding different views, and he pronounces an anathema against anyone who preaches an alien Gospel (Gal 1.9). The commendation of the church of Ephesus for its detection and rejection of false apostles (Rev 2.2) reflects a similar problem, while Ignatius warns explicitly against those bringing evil doctrine (*Eph* 7.1; *Smyrn* 4.1; 7.2) and implies that such had visited the church at Ephesus but had not won a hearing (*Eph* 9.1).[16]

Inevitably this raised the question of legitimation and necessitated the testing of itinerant preachers. Although letters of recommendation were used by some Christians when travelling (Rom 16.1f.), they may not have always seemed appropriate or adequate for those who claimed a God-given authority to teach and they are not mentioned in the *Didache*. One form of self-legitimation which was to prove unreliable was the possession of charismatic gifts such as is claimed by Paul's opponents in 2 Cor 12.12 and still commands respect in the *Didache*, 'Do not test or examine any prophet who is speaking in a spirit.'[17] More enduring were tests of behaviour or doctrine. The passage just quoted continues, 'But not everyone who speaks in a spirit is a prophet, unless he has the behaviour of the Lord.... Every prophet who teaches the truth, if he does not do what he teaches, is a false prophet', and prolonged stays or the request for money are also seen as evidence of a false prophet (11.8–10, cf.11.5–6). It is easy to imagine that here, as in Paul's

---

[16] See Lake, 'Der Strijd'. The anathema of Gal 1.9 is more likely to be spiritual condemnation than ecclesiastical censure.

[17] *Didache* 11.7. Testing of spirits or of false prophets is also implied, in a different context, by Mt 7.19; 1 Thess 5.21; cf. Hermas, *Mand* XI.

reaction to his opponents, different forms of legitimation could come into conflict.[18]

The doctrinal test is also given in the *Didache* in words we have already cited in relation to 2 Jn 10–11, that one who comes and teaches the things already mentioned is to be received, but the purveyor of an alien and destructive doctrine is to be ignored (*Didache* 11.1–2). Correct teaching would, as here, be defined by the church imposing the test and in the absence of fixed creeds to which to appeal there must have been an ongoing need to express the norm and considerable variation in the definitions received.[19] Christianity in Asia Minor in particular must have taken a number of forms if the Pauline Epistles, Revelation, the Johannine literature and Ignatius are all witnesses to the area, both in what they teach and in what they oppose. A simple and clear division between orthodoxy and heresy would be anachronistic; there was a wide range of interpretations and a number of what in retrospect might be called fringe or heterodox groups. The process of definition and drawing boundaries did not take place overnight or without dispute.[20]

The need to test visitors put the onus on the local community, and would focus on the offer or denial of hospitality which

[18] See G. Theissen, 'Legitimation and Subsistence: An Essay on the Sociology of Early Christian Missionaries', in *The Social Setting of Pauline Christianity*, Edinburgh 1982, 27–67 who distinguishes between the charismatic legitimation claimed by the itinerants of Palestinian origin and the functional legitimation claimed by Paul as organiser of a community; while Theissen's reconstruction rests on a particular understanding of the role of conflict, it seems clear that in Corinth different criteria for legitimation did come into conflict.

[19] Thus both 2 Jn 10 and *Didache* 11.1 speak of the teaching already defined; *Clem. Recog.* IV.34.5–35.5 has a similar, probably anti-Pauline, injunction in terms of James's teaching.

[20] If we were to set the Johannine literature in Syria, the same diversity would be found; on the slow process of drawing boundaries see Ehrhardt, 'Christianity before the Apostles' Creed', 103–8.

would betoken either approval and support or rejection. Like hospitality, the testing of visitors is the responsibility of the whole community (Rev 2.2; Ignatius, *Eph* 9.1f.; *Didache* 11), an extension of it being the task of the whole community to exercise discipline over its members (2 Thess 3.6,11; 1 Cor 5.1). In the Pastoral Epistles we find the not unexpected development which makes hospitality the particular duty of bishops and widows (1 Tim 3.2; 5.10) and dealing with false teachers the perogative of the bishop or leader of the community (Tit 1.9,13). Presumably, however, it would have been the heads of households who would have been in a particular position to offer hospitality and this would have given them considerable influence whether or not they held recognised positions of leadership in the community.

The role of households within the life and development of the early church was undoubtedly of central importance although much can only be inferred by implication from the sources.[21] The letters of Paul and of Ignatius imply the possibility of addressing, and therefore presumably the meeting of, all Christians in any one place—in Roms 16.23 Gaius is described as the host of 'the whole church'. However, Paul's missionary strategy was to start with households (1 Cor 1.16; cf.Acts 16.15,34 etc.), and no doubt the same was true of other bearers of the Christian message. Where a whole household had been 'converted' they would virtually constitute a community in themselves, while household relationships and loyalties inevitably continued to loom large.[22] As such they would have allowed a degree of diversity within the church and could even become a focus for division. One of the points at issue between Paul and the church at Corinth had been whether an Apostle

[21] See F.V. Filson, 'The Significance of the Early House Churches', *JBL* 58 (1939) 105–12; Stuhlmacher, *Philemon*, 70–75 with brief bibliography.

[22] G. Delling, 'Zur Taufe von "Häusern" im Urchristentum', *NT* 7 (1965) 285–311, 305–7; see above n. 21.

should require financial support (1 Cor 9.18; 2 Cor 11.7f.; 12.13) and this may imply that the 'apostles' he opposes had claimed and found such support in some households which would then become the centres of parties within the community.[23] The letters of Ignatius imply the existence of fringe groups on the edge of what Ignatius recognised as the church, with some holding eucharists without the bishop, while from Nag Hammadi we know of a gnostic élite continuing within a church whose ecclesiastical structures they rejected; all this would have been made possible and even encouraged by the pattern of meeting in homes.[24]

Although it would be natural to assume that the leaders in the church would be householders—and the Pastorals may support such an assumption (1 Tim 3.4)—this was probably not always the pattern nor would every householder have held a structured role of authority. The tensions to which this could also lead are easy to envisage.

It is against this background that warnings against love of prestige and preeminence become significant. This is a recurring theme in a number of contexts, and reflects the fact that the problem of authority in the early church was more than the question of different types of legally instituted leadership. A number of factors may lead to the exercise and recognition of power or influence and often rationalisation or theological interpretation of that power develop subsequent to its use, if they appear at all.[25] Already in this discussion we have met the

[23] So Theissen, 'Legitimation and Subsistence', 55–6.

[24] Note the call to unity in Ignatius's letters and see C.K. Barrett, 'Jews and Judaisers in the Epistles of Ignatius', in *Jews, Greeks and Christians*, ed. R. Hamerton-Kelly and R. Scroggs, Leiden 1976, 220–44, esp. 234–5; W. Schoedel, 'Theological Norms and Social Perspectives in Ignatius of Antioch', in *Jewish and Christian Self-Definition*, ed. Sanders, I, 30–56; for a comparable situation in the Nag Hammadi literature see *Interpretation of Knowledge* (N.H. XI.1) and K. Koschorke, *Die Polemik der Gnostiker gegen das kirchliche Christentum*, Leiden 1978.

[25] See B. Holmberg, *Paul and Power*, Lund 1978.

power exercised by the early prophets and teachers based on charismatic gifts, lifestyle, teaching or calling, that of the householder which would reflect his social standing, and that of the leadership defined by appointment or 'ordination'; we may add that proper to those older in years or in the faith.[26] The tensions which might arise between these have already been implied by *Didache* 15.2. Moreover, problems will arise when the development and acquisition of power are not accompanied by a developing theological understanding of authority. Some would see such a situation behind Mt 23.6–10 with its condemnation of those who desire chief seats or titles of honour, ostensibly the scribes and Pharisees but perhaps with the leadership of Matthew's own church in mind.[27] Among Gnostic sects it appears that hierarchical structures could be associated with the demiurge, to be rejected by those with full spiritual knowledge, so that to be called bishop or deacon is a sign of subjection to the demiurge.[28] On the other hand, love of chief place can also be condemned in those who capitalise on the influence given them by their charismatic gifts (Hermas, *Mand* XI.12).[29] The danger of false pride is one which may befall any in authority (Ignatius, *Smyrn* 6.1, 'Let not office exalt anyone'; Hermas, *Vis* III.9.7) and the desire to be a teacher may reflect an

---

[26] See *1 Clement* for tensions over the proper respect due to those of seniority and for hospitality as a 'weapon' in this context; for a discussion see H. Chadwick, 'Justification by Faith and Hospitality', *Studia Patristica* IV, TU 79, Berlin 1961, 281–5.

[27] See A. Ehrhardt, 'Christianity before the Apostles' Creed', 90, n. 53; R. Brown and J. Meier, *Antioch and Rome*, London 1983, 70; H. Frankemölle, 'Amtskritik im Matthäus-Evangelium?', *Bib* 54 (1973) 247–62.

[28] In *Apocalypse of Peter* (*N.H.* VII.3) 79.22f. there is a polemic against those who let themselves be called bishops or deacons; see E. Pagels, ' "The Demiurge and His Archons" —A Gnostic View of Bishops and Presbyters?', *HThR* 69 (1976) 301–24.

[29] Reiling, *Hermas*, 51 doubts whether 'πρωτοκαθεδρία' here refers to an official position of leadership. For self-recommendation by false prophets see Origen, *C. Celsum* VII.9 (see n. 14).

unmerited pursuit of prestige (Hermas, *Sim* IX.22.1–3). While such reserve about positions of authority may often have been justified, it may equally often reflect fundamental tensions in the development of authority structures.

It is against this background that we must set both 2 and 3 John. Here too we have the problem of travelling teachers—missionaries in 3 John. In 2 John they are to be tested by the tradition of the community, and those who fail are not to be shown hospitality, 'received into the house', whether that be a private home or the meeting place of the church. In 3 John both Gaius and Diotrephes are in a position to offer or refuse hospitality. Diotrephes has refused it and the implications of this are not lost on the Elder—for by what standards have they failed the test? Tensions over power and influence are inescapably present; Diotrephes appears to act with the support of the majority of his congregation and in giving it the name 'church' the Elder apparently acknowledges that Diotrephes was more than host to a group of the main church meeting in his home. The Elder too expects to wield influence although on a different, less tangible basis from that of Diotrephes. We are observing a war of words with little appeal to uncontested grounds for authority, and all this fits well into the struggles for power and influence that might arise from the situation we have sketched out and need not reflect conflict between different patterns of recognised ministry. However, in this case these struggles were probably the ultimate outcome of tendencies within the Johannine tradition and can only be understood in the light of the Johannine understanding of authority and of true membership of the community.

The Johannine Background

If 2 and 3 John share certain fundamental issues with a wide spectrum of the early church, the nature of their particular response must reflect the theological tendencies of the Johannine tradition from which they stem. The issues which have been highlighted both by our exegesis and by our survey of hospitality and wandering teachers in the early church are those of the structure of the church and authority within it, openness to outsiders, whether other forms of Christianity or 'the world', and the definition of the boundaries of the elect community and of what might be taught within it.

(a) Church and Authority

The Johannine understanding of the church is a topic which has provoked much study with little final consensus, for the Gospel is notoriously susceptible to diametrically opposed interpretations and there has been found in it both a strong ecclesiastical structure and yet also a 'free spirituality' with a 'horror of all hierarchical organistion'.[30] In part this is because, in the words of R. Schnackenburg, 'the Church did not constitute the dominant theme of the gospel, even though it was one of its constant perspectives'[31]—although it is precisely in the meaning of the word 'Church' here that the problem lies. The Gospel and First Epistle lack much of the terminology which from the rest of the New Testament we might see as the technical language of the church, and yet it is obvious that their primary interest and goal are the life and experience of the community for whom they were written; it is the relationship between these two aspects of the Gospel which fires the debate.

There is general agreement that Jesus's disciples play a dual role; they are his original closest followers who were with him during his ministry (14.9; 17.12) and as such have a unique role

[30] See D. Moody Smith, 'Johannine Christianity: Some Reflections on its Character and Delineation', NTS 21 (1975) 222–48. R. Schnackenburg, The Gospel according to St John (New York 1982) III, 204; the quotations come from Campenhausen, Ecclesiastical Authority, 136.

[31] Schnackenburg, Gospel, 217.

(15.27). However, the term which is most frequently used is 'disciple' (μαθητής), a term which is fluid and can extend from these close companions through to his adherents, some of whom fall away or show limited faith (6.60ff.; cf. 19.38). At its most fundamental level to be truly a disciple is simply to continue in Jesus's word (8.31). Thus the Farewell Discourses are addressed to his 'disciples' (13.5,22; 16.17,29); some of them are specifically named (Simon Peter, Thomas, Philip), and yet, in contrast to the Synoptic Last Supper accounts, the time and place are only loosely defined, and it would appear that what is said is equally addressed to all future believers who are marked as 'disciples' by their mutual love in faithfulness to Jesus's comands and by their 'bearing fruit' (13.35; 14.21; 15.8,14). It is easy to believe that these chapters arise from and are understood as words addressed to all 'who believe' (17.20), who are 'disciples', and who are also commanded to love and promised the spirit (14.16) as well as persecution (16.2).[32] In a similar way the role of eyewitness by the original disciples is crucial (15.27; 19.35) and yet it would seem that the Johannine church did continue to use eyewitness language of itself (1.14).[33]

It is in accord with this that the 'Twelve' as we meet them in the Synoptic Gospels play a very muted role in John—they are not listed nor sent out in pairs[34]—and inasmuch as continuity with the later church lies in being 'disciples' there can be no suggestion that the 'Twelve' have a particular or authoritative function to be inherited by a further particular group or ministry within the community.

Within this general paradigmatic role of the disciples in John two figures are more clearly portrayed—Simon Peter and the

[32] The sense that the Farewell Discourses are directed to all (Johannine) believers has led many to see behind them 'sermons' from the Johannine church; see B. Lindars, *The Gospel of John*, London 1972, 465–9.

[33] See Hoskyns, *Fourth Gospel*, 86–95 and below, p. 144.

[34] The 'Twelve' as such are only mentioned in Jn 6.67,70f.; 20.24.

Beloved Disciple, who would seem to be set in contrast to each other. As so often noted, while Peter denies that he is a disciple (18.17,25ff.), it is the Beloved Disciple who remains by the cross and is entrusted with the care of Mary (19.26f.); it is he whom Peter must request to ascertain from Jesus the identity of the betrayer, for he is lying 'in the bosom' of Jesus (13.23) even as Jesus is 'in the bosom' of the Father (1.18). It is the Beloved Disciple who outruns Peter to the tomb on Easter morning and believes (20.3–8), and some would argue that it is he who can bring Peter into the courtyard of the High Priest's residence during Jesus's trial (18.15f.).[35] In John 21 Peter is indeed given pastoral care of the flock and his martyr's death is foretold (21.15–19), but the Beloved Disciple, who had been the first to recognise the risen Lord (21.7), has a different calling which is not for Peter to question (21.20–22), even if Jesus wills that 'he remain until I come'. It is with this disciple that there is associated the witness of the Fourth Gospel itself (21.24).

The significance of this contrast has been much explored as the key to the Gospel. What here has been spoken of as contrast many have seen as conflict, and if the Beloved Disciple is unlikely to be purely a historical figure but must have some representative role, then so must Peter. The growing, albeit posthumous, importance of Peter towards the end of the first century is well known and so, for some, he must represent the developing ecclesiastical leadership of the church over against which is set a different sort of ministry represented by the Beloved Disciple. For others Peter stands for a group within the church or even the 'main-line' church separated from which is the (Johannine) community in the Beloved Disciple.[36]

[35] This seems unlikely as it is hard to account for the failure to identify him; see also below n. 39.

[36] See Kragerud, *Der Lieblingsjünger*; G.F. Snyder, 'John 13:16 and the Anti-Petrinism of the Johannine Tradition', *Biblical Research* 16 (1971) 5–15; T. Lorenzen, *Der Lieblingsjünger im Johannesevangelium*, Stuttgart 1971; Kragerud

However, while the contrast between the two figures is undoubtedly there, we can hardly speak of explicit rivalry or conflict. Against seeing here a conflict of ministries we must note that the Beloved Disciple is no more the recipient of the Spirit or of any other gift or task than are all the disciples, including Peter, and that it is only in the possibly redactional ch. 21 that Peter is recognised as leader;[37] against a conflict of church groups, even if the Beloved Disciple does represent Johannine Christianity, he makes no confession of faith which sets him above Peter and the others.[38] The Beloved Disciple first appears for certain in the Farewell Discourses (13.23—'one of his disciples . . . , whom Jesus loved') and while this may have historical grounds it is surely significant that it is in these chapters supremely that we are led to think not only of the first disciples but also of later believers. Supremely what is said about him is that he is the *'disciple'* whom Jesus *'loved'*; his importance is his relationship with Jesus and this remains true wherever he appears.[39] That in some sense he is an ideal of that faith and dependence on Jesus which gives a unity with Jesus and his purposes not even shown by Peter seems inescapable.[40] If accurately representing the original intention of the Gospel,

discusses previous interpretations before presenting his own. R. Brown, *The Community of the Beloved Disciple*, New York and London 1979, 82–8.

[37] It is a crucial part of Kragerud's thesis that Jn 21 is integral to the Gospel (*Der Lieblingsjünger*, 15–19).

[38] See F. Mussner, *The Historical Jesus in the Gospel of John*, Freiberg and London 1967, 56f. Brown, *Community*, 85 has to interpret Thomas's confession in 20.28 as that which the author *hopes* the non-Johannine 'Apostolic' Christians will make.

[39] Thus it is unlikely that the Beloved Disciple stands behind the anonymous disciples of 1.35–40 or 18.15f.

[40] Kragerud, *Der Lieblingsjünger*, 50 argues that the Beloved Disciple cannot represent an ideal because this would not give Peter a constrasting role and because he shares the ignorance of the other disciples at 13.28 and 20.9; however, these points do not really disqualify the interpretation suggested here.

21.24f. also imply that his testimony, the Johannine testimony as enshrined in the Gospel, is as valid, necessary and permanent as the pastoral ministry undoubtedly exercised and represented by Peter. Through the Beloved Disciple the Gospel would seem to be making its own claims, giving them at least equal rank to the very different claims that must have been assumed for Peter.

The limited role of the Beloved Disciple hardly gives us leave to see behind these claims different church groups in conflict; it may be that we should think of different understandings of faithfulness to Jesus, of what is the test of discipleship and of membership of the church, a question which would involve attitudes to ministry and authority. If this be so then Peter's pastoral calling is acknowledged but it is given no priority over that supreme calling of being a 'disciple'.

Theories which see the Beloved Disciple as representing a pattern of ministry have frequently joined hands with those which emphasise the role of the Holy Spirit, the Paraclete, in the Fourth Gospel. Here, chiefly in the Farewell Discourses again, the Spirit is given the tasks of convicting the world of sin, righteousness and judgement, of leading the disciples into all truth, of proclaiming the things to come and of reminding them of Jesus's words (14.26; 15.26; 16.8–11,13), but supremely of being 'another' Paraclete, of continuing the work of Jesus within the Church (14.16; 16.14). This, it is argued, points to the importance of the Spirit, and hence of prophecy, in the Johannine church; if the Gospel reflects no interest in the sort of ecclesiastical leadership which might be represented by Peter, then the form of ministry it does defend is surely a prophetic or charismatic ministry.[41] In support of this, the exodus of 'false prophets' in 1 Jn 4.1f. has been seen as the result of the unrestrained charismatic activity of these prophets, while

[41] So G. Johnston, *The Spirit-Paraclete in the Gospel of John*, SNTSMS 12, Cambridge 1970.

Revelation, probably in some sense Johannine, points to the importance of the prophetic witness.[42] Some have sought more precisely to identify this prophetic ministry, the ministry supposedly more particularly represented by the Beloved Disciple, with that of the wandering prophets and ascetics whom we have already met.[43] In this case we should think of the Johannine literature as reflecting the self-awareness of this particular group or pattern of Christian living as opposed to the picture of a narrower, 'prophetic' leadership (the Johannine 'school') within a wider Johannine 'community'.[44]

On the surface this is a very neat theory: Johannine Christianity finds its *Sitz im Leben* in circles of, or led by, prophets or wandering charismatics; as one such the Elder defends that pattern of ministry against the developing institutionalised leadership of the wider church in 3 John, and a similar battle is fought in John 21.[45] Unfortunately the theory does not stand up to closer scrutiny. We have already seen that to see the Beloved Disciple as representing a pattern of ministry in conflict gives too much interpretative priority to ch. 21 and ignores his role in the wider theology of the Gospel. That the Paraclete has the tasks of revelation, teaching and witness cannot without other support justify identifying here the self-consciousness of (itinerant) charismatics; this support is not

[42] See Moody Smith, 'Johannine Christianity', 232–3, 243–4; Kretschmar, 'frühchristlicher Askese', 43f.

[43] See above pp. 126ff.; this position is particularly represented by Kragerud.

[44] Thus Johnston, *Spirit-Paraclete* and M. Boring, 'The Influence of Christian Prophecy on the Johannine Portrayal of the Paraclete and Jesus', *NTS* 25 (1978–9) 113–23 speak of the Johannine church as led by prophetic figures while Kragerud speaks of the Johannine circle as one of the wandering charismatics; the terminology of 'school' and 'community' and the relation between them is often confused in discussions of the Johannine background, see Brown, *Community*, 101–2.

[45] See Kragerud, *Der Lieblingsjünger*, 104–12; Jn 21 is also related to 3 John by H. Thyen, 'Entwicklungen', 296ff.

forthcoming for the Elder of 2 and 3 John makes no claim to spiritual authority,[46] while the Gospel lacks those traditions which in the Synoptics have been seen as reflecting the experience of the wandering prophets.[47] The language of 'false prophets' in 1 Jn 4.1 owes more to traditional depictions of eschatological opponents than to their real character, while generally the functions of the Spirit in the Gospel and 1 John have more to do with teaching than with prophecy.[48]

The promise of the Spirit to all disciples in the Gospel and the absence of any suggestion of diversity of gifts of the Spirit speaks against the picture of a particular prophetic ministry within the community; so too in 1 Jn 2.27 all believers possess an 'anointing' and so have no need of a teacher.[49] In this sense there is truth in the position which sees Johannine 'authority' as that experienced by each individual who in his own right is a disciple, is called to the appropriate pattern of trust, faithfulness and being loved (Jn 14.21) which is that of the Beloved Disciple, possesses the Spirit, and is related to Jesus without mediation of ministry or sacraments. Yet, although we can speak of the individualism of Johannine theology, this is not a free spirituality which has no loyalty but the individual's awareness of the Spirit's movement, nor a charismatic enthusiasm which

[46] See further below, pp. 154f. and contrast Campenhausen, *Ecclesiastical Authority*, 122 cited at n. 81.

[47] See above p. 127 and n. 6; Theissen, *First Followers*, 24–30 argues that the Synoptic Son of Man Christology, with its dialectic of suffering and glory, reflected and interpreted for the wandering prophets their own experience of rejection and homelessness; John's use of the Son of Man traditions is very different although it too may reflect the experiences of the community, see W. Meeks, 'The Man from Heaven in Johannine Sectarianism', *JBL* 91 (1972) 44–72.

[48] See D. Hill, *New Testament Prophecy*, London 1979, 146–52.

[49] Whatever the meaning of the 'anointing' the connection with teaching is important. W. Bousset, *Kyrios Christos*, 220f. argues that John is no longer familiar with pneumatic enthusiasm and sees the Spirit as 'the Spirit of the sacrament, the Spirit of the office and of the confession', but this is equally unjustified.

rejects the shackles or tradition and institution; as we shall see, in John possession of the Spirit goes hand in hand with faithfulness to the words or commands of Jesus, while the theme of discipleship is tightly linked to that of eyewitness just as in 1 John the insight each believer possesses goes hand in hand with a strong emphasis on what was 'from the beginning'.[50] Thus, if there were authority structures in Johannine Christianity—and how can there have been none?—we would expect them to be related to that line of witness which authenticates the tradition. Yet even here the evidence is ambiguous as the author of 1 John well illustrates.

Only when explaining why he is writing does the author use the first person singular 'I' (2.1,7,8,12–14,21,26; 5.13); otherwise the letter is characterised by its use of 'we', linking the author with his readers or with other believers.[51] The only apparent exception to this comes in the opening verses, 'That which was from the beginning, that which we have heard . . . concerning the word of life . . . that which we have seen and heard we proclaim also to you, that you may have fellowship with us' (1.1–4). Here the vivid language of physical witness and the contrast between 'we' and 'you' invite talk of the authority of witnesses, and if not of eyewitnesses then of a group who felt themselves to be the heirs of that first witness to the physical life and death and resurrection of Jesus, a group with whose authority the writer speaks.[52] And yet the language of this passage is notoriously indirect, with its neuter '*that* which was from the beginning, which we have heard', and the loosely attached '*concerning* the word of life', language which seems more likely to refer to the Gospel message than to the incarnate

[50] See below ch. 5, pp. 174–7. Note also the tight cohesiveness implied by Meeks, 'Man from Heaven'.
[51] For a full discussion see Harnack, 'Das "Wir" '. E.g. 1 Jn 1.6–10; 2.2–3 etc.
[52] See Schnackenburg, *Johannesbriefe*, 52–8; Brown, *Epistles*, 158–61.

life of Jesus. More significantly, later in the Epistle similar language can be used apparently of all believers; in 1 Jn 4.12–16 it is said that if *we* love one another, God abides in *us* and his love is made complete in *us*, something witnessed to by the gift of the Spirit to *us*; 'and *we* have seen and bear witness that the Father sent his Son as Saviour of the world. Whoever confesses that Jesus is the Son of God, God abides in him and he in God. And *we* have known and believed the love which God has for *us*'. The same 'we' must be those who love, who experience divine indwelling, who have seen and bear witness, who have known and believed the love God has for them.[53] The language of witness can be used of the whole community, rooted in their experience of God's love and gifts, although presumably only possible because some did physically see and believe. In the same way, although the author addresses his readers as 'children' (2.1 etc.), i.e. in the language of teacher to pupils, he must acknowledge that they have no need of a teacher (2.27). With whatever authority the writer may speak, it allows him to say little that cannot equally be said of or for his readers, who have the authority given by belief and life within the community; indeed, given the probable stress on the Gospel message or tradition of the community as that which was 'from the beginning' in the opening verses of the letter, it is likely that the authority with which the writer speaks as 'we' in those verses is ultimately the authority of that tradition and community life.[54]

Clearly there were influential figures in Johannine history who could claim to be particularly part of the witness tradition—the 'we' of Jn 21.24 who published the Gospel and the original witness whose testimony is enshrined in the Gospel—but there is no clear hint that that influence was

---

[53] So Harnack, 'Das "Wir" '.

[54] See K. Weiss, 'Orthodoxie und Heterodoxie im 1 Johannesbrief', *ZNW* 58 (1967) 247–55, 249–50; see further below ch. 5, pp. 173–6 on the importance of tradition of 1 John.

theologically articulated or institutionalised. Alongside it firmly stands the independence and experience of the whole community with its supreme embodiment of the witness in the Gospel or the tradition of the community. The tension between these two poles may well hold the key to the Johannine understanding of authority and perhaps to 2 and 3 John.

(b) *The Limits of the Community*

The strong community sense of the Johannine church of which we have here begun to become aware is a commonplace in modern scholarship; it is marked by a clear awareness of the boundaries of the community, of the difference between being 'in' or 'out', and by a growing alienation from those outside. All this has been described from a variety of perspectives which we may for the moment leave for later discussion.[55] For our purposes here it is enough to illustrate this from the thought of the Gospel and First Epistle and to consider the implications for the sort of situation envisaged by 2 and 3 John.

The exclusivism of Johannine thought is signalled by the sharp contrast between light and darkness, between believing and not believing (Jn 3.16–21), between God and the world (15.18f.), a contrast which is marked by hate and judgement and which would serve to separate believers from all others with no possibility of compromise. Along with this is the strong doctrine of election (6.44) which might seem to leave little room for struggle or progress, or for welcoming new insights from outsiders. The entire initiative is God's, and those who are chosen are sharply divorced from those who are not and from the world (17.9,14f.). The other side of this alienation from those outside is the binding together of the community by the

---

[55] See below ch. 5, pp. 180–7. This picture of the Johannine community has been well drawn by Meeks, 'Man from Heaven', but not all share his picture of a totally isolated community: see ch. 5, n. 42.

command to love one another, as opposed to the Synoptic love of neighbour; this would both encourage a church in a hostile environment which needed to reinforce its self-identity and also make it hesitant towards unknown or unaccredited visitors.[56] The realised eschatology of the Gospel, eternal life as a present possession,[57] and the 'egalitarian' individualism which we have already noted, belong to the same pattern of thought. These characteristics are even more sharply present in I John; there the awareness of election finds expression in statements of assurance such as 'We know that we are of God and the whole world lies under the evil one' (5.19). The world is the source of hatred and is to be avoided (2.15–17; 3.13); apparently it is not the place for mission, and the success of the 'antichrists' there is an indication of their true character (4.1,5). They belong to the world and no appeal is made to them nor even any prayer for them.[58] Those who are within are secure in being 'of God' and in the fullness of their knowledge (2.20f.,27); and yet there is a sense that the world may be invading the community and language which in the Gospel defines unbelief ('to have sin' Jn 9.41; 15.22,24) is now used of those within the community who, in spite of their claims to the contrary, are not true members of the elect (I Jn 1.8).[59] The community is bound together not only by the command to mutual love but equally by faithfulness to the tradition of the community.

Undoubtedly this could become a caricature and in the Gospel presents only one side of a theology which can also stress

[56] See above ch. 3, pp. 73–4 and nn. 66–69.

[57] See below ch. 5, p. 194.

[58] See above ch. 3, pp. 97–8 and note the contrast with Ignatius in his letter to the church of Smyrna.

[59] This is part of a wider shift in the Epistle towards a focusing on the community; see below ch. 5, pp. 205ff. and note the caution there against assuming that the Epistle follows the Gospel—our language here of 'shift' may need modifying.

the responsibility of the individual for his or her response and retain at least some universalistic-sounding sentiments.[60] Yet it is these characteristics which have earned Johannine Christianity the description as a sect, a description which, notwithstanding the problems of precise definition in using that term, has proved useful in exploring the thought of Gospel and Epistles.[61] In this context analyses of sectarian development may help us reflect on what we have found in 2 and 3 John, as, for example, an account of a more modern 'sect': 'The sect had acquired a sense of sacredness about its own values which was derived more from the sense of separateness and community-identity than from the actual intrinsic manifestation of sacredness of life and practice. The growing convergence of the ideals of separation and sanctity—a sect already in the heavenly state—was evident.'[62] 2 John, in the address to the community as 'the elect lady', already witnesses to the concentration on the heavenly state rather than the historical form of the church. Furthermore, while the expulsion of those who contravene standards of faith, behaviour or organisation is often the natural consequence of the exclusive demand for commitment characteristic of a sect, it is significant that the church to which the above sect belonged had already practised the sanctions of refusal of fellowship not only against those who held false views but also against other communities who, while themselves sound, had remained in

[60] Ch. 5, pp. 195–6.
[61] Brown, *Community*, 14–7, 88–91 uses the term with caution because he believes that the Johannine community was still open to other 'Apostolic' Christians; Meeks, 'Man from Heaven', 70f. uses the term to explore the Johannine community's inner dynamic. See also R. Scroggs, 'The Sociological Interpretation of the New Testament: the Present State of Research', *NTS* 26 (1980) 164–79.
[62] B.R. Wilson, 'The Exclusive Brethren: A Case Study in the Evolution of a Sectarian Ideology', in *Patterns of Sectarianism*, London 1967, 287–337, 301 describing a group (the 'New Lumpists') within the Exclusive Brethren in the 1870s.

fellowship with the former.[63]

Before we too quickly move on to draw conclusions for 2 and 3 John, there is one further factor which emerges from the problem of 'the world outside' in 1 John. As we have seen, 'the world' is beginning to invade the community; the 'false prophets' are of the world (4.5) and yet presumably this would not have been made manifest if they had not actually left the community (2.19). 'Not all are of us'! This is why the spirits must be tested (4.1) lest there are still some 'of the world' within the community. This hints at a mood of suspicion and internal distrust which we do not meet in the Gospel, even with its plea for unity in ch. 17. While the relationship between the authorship and also between the destination of the three Epistles may remain uncertain, we can probably only understand 2 and 3 John if we bear in mind the effect of such a mood of suspicion against the background of the Johannine attitudes to authority and to the community which we have explored.

The Outcome in 2 and 3 John

The route we have taken would seem to lead naturally to our destination in 2 John. In our exegesis of that letter we have already had cause to speak of an appeal to loyalty to the community's origins (vv. 5–6), of a concentration on the teaching which characterises true or false claimants to Christian (Johannine) status (v. 7), and of tradition as that which defines

[63] Ibid., 299, 'It was wrong to remain in fellowship with those who held false views, and further, it was wrong not to excommunicate even those who remained in fellowship with those who held wrong views, even though the former were themselves doctrinally sound' (referring to communities not individuals). There are of course enormous difficulties in comparing a New Testament writing with a group whose sense of 'orthodoxy' presupposes the whole development of the emphasis on testable right belief within the Christian church; the parallel is drawn here only as a heuristic device.

both true and false Christian living. The strong sense of the election of the community belongs to the same trend, and in this context the denial of hospitality to those with an alien and false interpretation of the Christian message, which we have seen to be the primary function of the letter, appears as the inevitable consequence of the development Johannine thought has taken. Characterised as the irredeemable opponents of God, there is no hint of the licence of the *Didache* which allowed them to prove themselves before being judged and gave initial respect to charismatic gifts.

So too, the description of the false teachers is a caricature and belongs to no single identifiable heresy. The tenor and structure of the letter imply that the sanctions of v. 10f. are in practice directed against any visitor who does not belong to the recognised Johannine tradition; it is the Johannine tradition which is the truth. Is this then the rejection of any non-Johannine form of Christianity and perhaps of any attempt by others to bring the various communities together as the church in one place, united to churches elsewhere through travelling teachers and delegates? Inevitably this question leads to the issue of such teachers in the early church and more particularly to the situation of 3 John.

To a substantial degree 2 John makes good sense in terms of the pattern of Johannine theology witnessed to by the Gospel and First Epistle. 3 John presents many more problems, although, perversely, it is its ordinariness of language, in contrast to the idiosyncratic vocabulary and thought of the rest of the Johannine corpus, which constitutes a major part of the enigma. Perhaps, then, it is not surprising that in the history of interpretation of the minor Johannine Epistles during the last one hundred years 2 John has received little attention, being seen as an echo of 1 John. Debate has centred on 3 John, and primarily on the relative positions of Diotrephes and the Elder, and on the precise nature of the point at issue between them.

While a detailed study of the debate would not be appropriate here,[64] a brief resumé of the major lines of approach will be useful in exploring the factors to be considered and the pitfalls which beset any attempt at reconstruction.

The dominant approach has been to see the conflict as a matter of church authority. Most frequently, the Elder, whether or not identified with the Apostle John or one of Papias's Elders, has been seen as exercising a wide sphere of authority, while Diotrephes belongs to the local community and is fighting for some form of autonomy. The least specific solution merely ascribes to Diotrephes an excess of personal ambition.[65] Attempts at clearer definition have made Diotrephes if not a monarchical bishop then at least an embryonic one, so that 3 John reflects the assertion of independence by the local community and office against an earlier, wider form of authority, although it is in defining this latter that views begin to diverge.

The interpretation according to which the Elder, especially when identified with the Apostle John, could be described as an 'Over-bishop' now has little currency, for the historical evidence for and parallels to such a position are lacking.[66] Now those who argue for a wider authority are more generally agreed in seeing it not as of an 'institutional' kind so much as 'patriarchal'. For some this is the type of authority which would naturally be attached to an apostle or member of the primitive community,[67] but most see more than this.

[64] It is well summarised by Haenchen, 'Neue Literatur', 267–82.

[65] Westcott, *Epistles*, lvi.

[66] This was suggested by J.E. Belser, *Die Briefe des Heiligen Johannes*, Freiburg im Breisgau 1906; see also Chapman, 'Historical Setting'—John had been asked by Paul to take control of Asia. For a discussion of the evidence for the provincial organisation of the early church see A. v. Harnack, *The Expansion of Christianity in the First Three Centuries*, London 1904–5, II, 64–94.

[67] So in the 1st edition, R. Schnackenburg, *Die Johannesbriefe*; Westcott, loc. cit.

Again it is the writings of A. v. Harnack which have most influenced the debate. In his study of 3 John he identified the author with Papias's 'presbyter John', as one who had patriarchal authority over the whole of Asia Minor and who was superintendent of a missionary organisation whose members regularly reported to him.[68] The conflict could be seen as that between such a provincial organisation and the local community now growing in independence, or, from another angle, as an example of the tension between the church as a creation of a 'missionary or apostle, whose work it remained' and its status as an independent local community.[69] The influence of the picture drawn from the *Didache* is seen when the Elder is said to represent 'the patriarchal-universal and enthusiastic organisation'.[70]

Appeal, if not specifically to the Elder John, at least to Papias's elders has been repeatedly made, and particularly to their role as representatives of the apostolic tradition.[71] Many scholars, however, have preferred to develop the link with the argument for a class of wandering preachers in the early church; thus the Elder is to be seen as a prophet or teacher of the early period and his conflict with Diotrephes as that between the itinerant ministry and the local community.[72] As we have seen, this non-institutional or 'spiritual' authority has been found reflected elsewhere in the Johannine literature as the dominant or only form of authority recognised in that tradition. Several scholars

---

[68] *dritten Johannesbrief.*

[69] Ibid., 21, 'es ist der Kampf der alten patriarchalischen und provinzialen Missionsorganisation gegen die sich konsolidierende Einzelgemeinde, die zum Zweck ihrer Konsolidierung und strengen Abschliessung nach aussen den monarchischen Episkopat und ihre Mitte hervortreibt'; the second perspective comes from *Expansion* II, 94.

[70] *dritten Johannesbrief*, 26.

[71] Bultmann, *Epistles*, 95; Dodd, *Epistles*, 155; Houlden, *Epistles*, 4f.

[72] Goguel, *L'Église Primitive*, 136–7; Kretschmar, 'frühchristlicher Askese', 43f.; Kragerud, *Lieblingsjünger*, 104f.

combine this with an appeal to Papias's Elders as disciples of the apostles and guarantors of tradition—which implies a modification of the 'prophet-teacher' model—or simply as representatives of such itinerant charismatics.[73]

In all these approaches the issue is of a wider, personal authority in opposition to a local one, whether that be institutional—Diotrephes as a monarchical bishop—or merely based on ambition.[74] Even attempts to escape this framework seem unable to succeed. Thus E. Haenchen saw both the Elder and Diotrephes as leading Elders (*praeses presbyterii*) of neighbouring communities, but still appealed to 'presbyter' as a bearer of tradition in Irenaeus and Papias to explain the author's reference to himself as 'The Elder'.[75] K. Donfried, while rejecting Papias's evidence as too obscure, also interprets the Elder as holding an ecclesiastical office as 'monarchical elder' but reverts to Harnack's idea of a regional missionary organisation—he is '*the* most important presbyter in a regional network of churches; and further . . . he directed and controlled the missionary activity in this region'.[76]

With greater sensitivity to the fact that 3 John survived in the company of 2 and later 1 John, there has been more of a tendency recently to interpret the title 'the Elder' as of one who

[73] Bornkamm, 'πρέσβυς', 671f. who argues that the wildness of the traditions reported by the 'Elders' might lead to the discrediting of the appeal to apostolic tradition and hence also to the discrediting of the Elder of 2 and 3 John; E. Gaugler, 'Die Bedeutung der Kirche in den johanneischen Shriften', *IKZ* 15 (1925) 27–42, 37; Campenhausen, *Ecclesiastical Authority*, 121–3. Harnack was less explicit: he associates the Catholic Epistles with his 'apostles' (*Expansion* I, 428) and also identifies the missionary brethren of 3 John with them (ibid., 436), but the Elder was not one of the brethren (*dritten Johannesbrief*, 19); nonetheless, 3 John is an example of the conflict between local management of the church and the 'apostles' (*Expansion*, II, 95).

[74] Houlden, *Epistles*, 8, 153 sees him as a bishop or monarchical elder; Brooke, *Epistles*, lxxxix sees him as a man of great personal ambition, the type against whom the episcopate was introduced as a safeguard.

[75] 'Neue Literatur', 288–9; see above ch. 3, p. 54.

[76] 'Ecclesiastical Authority', 328.

saw himself as the guarantor of *Johannine* tradition with the right to address and visit other churches of the 'Johannine' communion; Diotrephes and his church may be desiring greater independence, either in defence against competing claims to represent the 'mother' church after the schism implied by 1 John, or in (over-)zealous response to an injunction such as that of 2 John, if not 2 John itself.[77]

The derivative role of 2 and 3 John within the Johannine tradition makes it difficult to identify the Elder with the Apostle John, even if the latter could be confidently associated directly with any part of that tradition; the enormity of Diotrephes's action, apparently with substantial support, and the hesitancy of the Elder's response also speak against the author being someone of such stature.[78] We have already seen that appeal to Papias's Elders founders on our real lack of knowledge about them and their role, and certainly that what we do know offers no grounds at all for attributing to them an 'itinerant', 'patriarchal' or 'charismatic' ministry.[79]

Indeed, the idea of a 'patriarchal' authority is hard to establish from other sources or from the Epistles themselves. The author of Revelation's relationship with the seven churches cannot be cited as a parallel, because he speaks not on his own authority but as the bearer of God's word to these communities.[80] Moreover, it is reading more into the exchange of greetings and promises of visits in 2 and 3 John than these epistolary conventionalities merit, to base on them a picture of the Elder with a pastoral authority over a large area. It is true that in 2 John he writes to a sister community of the one from which he

---

[77] Grayston, *Epistles*, 160f.; Brown, *Epistles*, 738.

[78] So Käsemann, 'Ketzer und Zeuge', 295, 301 against the identification of the author with one of Papias's Elders. The question partly depends on one's, or the author's, view of the meaning of being an Apostle.

[79] See above ch. 3, pp. 59–60.

[80] The parallel is drawn by Donfried, 'Ecclesiastical Authority', 331–2.

speaks, but the self-conscious structure of that letter makes it hazardous to base any reconstruction of his historical position on it, while in 3 John itself the reference to the brethren, whom may only have been two in number, can hardly establish the author as the head of a missionary organisation.[81]

Equally insubstantial is the appeal to the 'wandering prophets', especially if they are not to be found in or behind the Fourth Gospel. There is certainly no evidence from 2 and 3 John themselves that the Elder appealed to the Spirit or to the 'living authority endowed by "the truth"' and that he might thus be called 'a prophet or teacher of the early type'.[82] Inasmuch as even Harnack found our only 'certain proof' of a conflict between the two forms of ministry in 3 John, the assumption of a local non-charismatic and a wandering charismatic ministry coming into conflict should not be so easily made as it so often is.[83] It seems probable that the contrast between institutionalised ecclesiastical authority and the freer guidance of the Spirit is a modern one as anachronistic and over-rigid when applied to the early church as is the 'orthodoxy v. heresy' model.

Too many of these reconstructions have failed to relate the conflict behind 3 John to the rest of the Johannine tradition. That has in part been recognised by those who have either seen the problem in the light of the situation following the 'schism' of 1 John, or who have sought to discover the conflict over patterns of ministry as already reflected in the Gospel. The attempt to bring 3 John even closer to the other Epistles and to

[81] See above ch. 3, p. 99 and n. 123. Contrast Campenhausen, *Ecclesiastical Authority*, 122, 'His followers are known to one another, and enjoy mutual fellowship. Whole congregations look to him as their spiritual father, or have members who enjoy his especial confidence, and who give hospitality to travelling brethren and evangelists.'

[82] Campenhausen, *Ecclesiastical Authority*, 123; see also Käsemann, 'Ketzer und Zeuge', 311, 'Er will nichts anderes sein als der Zeuge des Christus praesens.'

[83] Harnack, *Expansion* II, 94f. See also above pp. 127–8.

see the conflict as a doctrinal one stumbles on the objection that an author who could dictate the harsh injunction of 2 Jn 10, would hardly pass over the heresy of Diotrephes, if such there was, in silence. This objection can be made not only against those who have seeen Diotrephes as a heretic,[84] but equally against Käsemann's inversion of that thesis. His argument was that it is the Elder who was the heretic in the church's and in Diotrephes's eyes and who had been excommunicated by his opponent for the 'gnostic' views such as are contained in his Gospel (John).[85] If, as we shall argue, we deny that the Elder was the author also of the Fourth Gospel, we can hardly ascribe to him the appeal to the Spirit and to the witness to and encounter with the 'Christus praesens' which for Käsemann characterises Johannine theology (and therefore that of the Elder) in contrast to the appeal to the continuity of the church and office made by Early Catholicism and Diotrephes.[86] More fundamentally, the author of 2 John would surely have never recognised the justness of his own excommunication but would have branded its perpetrator as, if not the antichrist, then at least one to be avoided at all costs. Yet the recognition that Diotrephes's treatment of the brethren and their supporters parallels that advocated in 2 John against teachers of suspect doctrines is a valid one and a fundamental contribution to the debate. This insight must surely be retained and, assuming 3 John is not totally *de novo*, included in any attempt to relate the letter both to the Johannine tradition of which it is in some way a part and

---

[84] H.H. Wendt, 'Zum zweiten und dritten Johannesbriefe'; W. Bauer, *Orthodoxy and Heresy in Earliest Christianity*, Philadelphia 1971, 91–3.

[85] 'Ketzer und Zeuge'; J. Heise, *BLEIBEN: Menein in den johanneischen Schriften*, Tübingen 1967, 164f. accepts the thesis in modified form. While rejecting Käsemann's thesis as it stands Bultmann and Houlden accept that doctrinal issues may be involved; see also Strecker, 'Die Anfänge', 38.

[86] Although later recognising that the Presbyter was not the author of the Gospel, Käsemann felt his central thesis could be retained.

to those conflicts in the early church of which we do have ample evidence.

At first sight 3 John appears something of an anomaly in its apparent divergence from Johannine ways of language and thought. There is less explicit theologising and such as there is seems to follow a different direction from the thought of 2 John. The Elder commends the travelling brethren without any demonstration of the acceptability of their doctrine, surely a necessary measure in the light of 2 John. His support of missionary work (3 Jn 8) is far more positive than the thought of 1 John generally and hence involves the use of language more typical of the Pauline corpus than the Johannine. His condemnation of Diotrephes has equally little theological grounding, a phenomenon which, as we have just seen, can not be ascribed to his own heretical status. Reflecting all this is the number of non-Johannine elements in the Epistle, particularly striking when we contrast the parasitical relationship between the Elder's other letter, 2 John, and the First Epistle.

On the other hand, 3 John does make sense when it is seen as bringing together the two trajectories studied earlier, that of wandering teachers and the structure of the early church and that of the development of Johannine thought. The former implies that we are in the sphere not of defined forms of institutional authority but of power and influence which have not been adequately theologically or institutionally interpreted. That such a problem should arise within the Johannine tradition is readily understandable, with its lack of articulation about authority and the possible tensions between structured ministry and the importance of the Johannine witness. In that setting rival candidates for power, different forms of influence, as well as the claims of a structured ministry could easily be examined and found wanting in Johannine terms and be understood purely non-theologically as a wrong desire for first place; Jn 13.12–17 in particular might reflect such a judgement or act as a presupposition for one.[87] Defence of existing or growing power or influence would be more difficult than its condemnation, and yet it is inevitable that power or influence there would be within the Johannine tradition. As we have seen, there were the influential figures of the Johannine tradition, but in particular the experience of schism we find reflected in 1 John could stimulate the emergence of those who could give guidance or support, while the practical justification of their existence would not so easily be matched by a theological justification in Johannine thought. Alternatively, the acceptance of differing patterns of discipleship and authority which may lie behind the figures of Peter and the Beloved Disciple in the Gospel might easily be upset by developments on either side and decline into suspicion and antipathy. Such precision, however, may be neither possible nor necessary. It is precisely the importance of our initial discussion of the early church background that it highlights the wide variety of contexts in which influence would actually be exercised and the consequent tensions between them as well as the problems of theological rationalisation.[88]

This means that the ambiguity of the relative positions of the Elder and Diotrephes lies at the heart not simply of our problem of interpretation, but of the original problem itself. His use of Johannine language (and possibly of 1 John) suggests that the Elder did claim to represent the Johannine tradition, although despite that claim it cannot be simply assumed that he did in fact stand in direct line with the most influential figures of the Johannine tradition going back to the original witnesses. The

---

[87] H. Thyen, 'Johannes 13 und die "kirchliche Redaction" des vierten Evangeliums', in *Tradition und Glaube*, ed. G. Jeremias et al., Göttingen 1971, 343–56, 354–5 associates Jn 13.20 with the Diotrephes incident.

[88] See above pp. 133–4; Malherbe, 'Inhospitality', 110 also argues that it is a matter of power rather than authority although he does not recognise the theological dimension of the conflict within a Johannine context.

preservation of 2 and 3 John probably indicates that his claim was eventually accepted as valid. His use of the epithet 'Elder', significant to his first readers although no longer so to us, and his address to the members of more than one congregation as (his) children also imply an assumption of authority and influence. It is an authority which he sees as rejected by Diotrephes's actions, although he can neither defend it nor ascribe to that rejection any theological significance. The importance of this is made clear when we contrast him, in different ways, with both Paul and Ignatius. For Paul rejection of himself means rejection of his proclamation of Christ and of his calling to be an Apostle, carrying a theological meaning far exceeding any personal affront (2 Cor 10–13).[89] For Ignatius there can be no membership of the church and no salvation without submission to the bishop (*Trall* 2; *Magn* 3.6–7; *Eph* 5). The author of 2 and 3 John has no such theological understanding of his rebuff, nor of the recognition he demands. He sees the opposition to him as the act of a tyrant and hopes to have opportunity to make his point and to reassert his position, but how he can do this remains unclear, perhaps to himself as well as to us. Even the more distinctively Johannine 2 John gains its authority not from the claim of the author to stand in line with the original eyewitnesses (cf. 1 Jn 1.1ff.) but through the use of a Pauline-type greeting.

Diotrephes's position is equally obscure, largely because we cannot hear his voice. The Elder's concern is only with how Diotrephes's behaviour affects himself, namely the exclusion of the brethren and the rejection of his own patronage of them. With the influence which, as we have seen, such teachers may have expected to exercise in any community they visited, it would not be surprising that they should become either victims

---

[89] Thus Campenhausen, *Ecclesiastical Authority*, 123 is wrong when he compares the Elder's reaction with that of Paul.

or weapons in a struggle for power. More specifically, in a Johannine context their exclusion could also reflect the self-assurance of a church which felt in no need of anyone to teach them (1 Jn 2.27) as well as the repulsion of any external influence from a tightly cohesive community. The severity of Diotrephes's action and his insults against the Elder together with the parallel in 2 Jn 10f. do suggest that this is more than simple dislike of outside influence, and that it is given a doctrinal rationale. However, the absence of any reference to doctrinal norms either in defence of the Elder or of the brethren, or in condemnation of Diotrephes suggests that the Elder is not aware of any serious theological dispute between himself and Diotrephes.

It would seem, therefore, that it is Diotrephes who is making theological judgements, the significance of which the Elder fails to understand. If Diotrephes condemns him and the brethren on doctrinal grounds, these are not so well defined and acknowledged for the Elder to see them as leading to his exclusion; for him this remains tyranny and an insult. We may find a not dissimilar situation behind *Smyrn* 5.2 where Ignatius dismisses the praise of those whose doctrine he found unacceptable—no doubt his spurned admirers did not see the doctrinal debate as so fundamentally divisive as did Ignatius.[90] Furthermore, in the case of 3 John, even if doctrinal norms are being sought and developed, at present the situation is still dominated by insult and argument.[91] In the absence of mutually recognised standards, conflict must appear personal, just as in the absence of a mutually recognised theological understanding of authority, the holding of power or influence must appear as secular ambition and tyranny.

[90] See Schoedel, 'Theological Norms', 35f.
[91] Ehrhardt, 'Christianity before the Apostles' Creed', 92f. sees a combination of personal bitterness and the desire for right doctrine as lying behind 3 John.

This leads us to the clue to the ambiguity of 3 John and the situation behind it, and therefore also to the importance of the letter for Johannine history. The limits of our knowledge reflect the limits of the author's interests. Only to a marginal extent does the Elder see the struggle in theological terms; far more it is for him a matter of parties or sides. On the one side we have the Elder, the brethren, Demetrius and even some members of Diotrephes's community; on the other stands Diotrephes, presumably with his own supporters although these receive no explicit mention. In practical terms the division between the parties is expressed by acceptance of the brethren on the one hand and by continuing membership of the church headed by Diotrephes on the other. Theologically, it is expressed by the Elder in the language of Johannine tradition as a matter of loyalty to the truth and of seeing or being 'of God', and in the language of the wider church as a matter of doing good or doing evil, of acting worthily of God and of being testified to. All this is language which gains its force not so much from its theological vitality as from its place in tradition; it is—and this is particularly true of the Johannine terms—'party' language. Quite possibly Diotrephes saw things in a similar way and both doctrine and forms of organisation may have been seen from this same 'party' perspective.

Yet if this is so, it is only a practical development and example of the tendency to exclusivism and introversion which we have traced as an element in Johannine thought throughout and as a particular point where 1 John speaks more sharply than the Gospel. It would not be surprising that this pattern of thought should lead to the exclusion of anyone not totally committed to the elect body together with an inability to enter into dialogue or theological exploration. In 3 John party lines are hardening even more clearly than in 1 John and we are no longer aware of theological factors as having primary importance in the drawing of those lines; rather it is elements of organisation, power and personalities which are the most visible factors. Thus the language which in the previous paragraph we have described as the theological expression of the division between the parties no longer has the real theological grounding and force of its earlier use. Instead it has become an expression of approval or calumny; 'truth' has become a slogan for what the author sees as genuinely Johannine and the exhortation to imitate good in 3 Jn 11 is not the theological platitude it may appear to be, but an appeal to Gaius to join the right side. The sense of belonging to a well-defined and elect group has swallowed up the dialectical structure of Johannine thought witnessed to by the Gospel—a claim we shall explore yet more fully in the next chapter; here in these Epistles dialogue is no longer a means of reaching the truth, instead—as so clearly also in 2 Jn 10f.—possessing or being of the truth rules out the need or possibility of dialogue.

Theologically 3 John does make good sense within the Johannine trajectory; historically it remains ambiguous and it may not be possible to be any more precise than we have been so far in this discussion. The following factors need to be brought into consideration. It is improbable that Johannine Christianity was the only or even the main representative of Christianity in the area. We should affirm that, even if we sit lightly to the traditional setting of the Gospel in Ephesus, firstly because it is difficult to find any convincing location where Johannine Christianity could be totally *geographically* isolated from other Christian groups, and secondly because 2 and 3 John do imply some links with the Pauline tradition while the question of links between the Gospel and Synoptic-type traditions remains an area of debate.[92] If, as seems probable, there is a complex history

---

[92] Egypt might be the only setting where we could argue for a *geographically* isolated Johannine group but this is only because of our general ignorance about Christianity there. See also Moody Smith, 'Johannine Christianity', 226–30, 237.

behind the Johannine tradition, this no doubt involved not only changes of geographical situation but also changing relationships with other Christian groups.[93] A self-identity which includes a strong sense of isolation, such as recent studies have rightly identified in the Gospel of John,[94] need not imply geographical isolation, nor perhaps exclude the Johannine community from having existed as a fringe group, a separate household community (or series of separate ones), to some extent sharing the life of the main church but with its main loyalties being to its own religious experience and tradition.

The letters of Ignatius imply that there was in the church at large a movement towards monarchical episcopacy and towards more precise definition of membership of the church and of doctrinal formulation. However, the sense that at times Ignatius is hard-pressed to plead his cause suggests that not all saw it as he did, and it would be a long time before standards of membership and of organisation were so clearly demarcated as we might at first assume. However, if in Ignatius submission to the bishop could be seen as equally as valid a sign of belonging to the church as is true doctrine (*Smyrn* 8), the existing tendencies to introversion and self-sufficiency within the Johannine tradition would have pulled in the opposite direction.

This could lead us to construct a picture by which Diotrephes is the representative of the dominant church group, sharing some of the views we find in Ignatius, no longer content with the independence of the Johannine fringe group and perhaps questioning its doctrines.[95] The more rigid drawing of boundaries, itself a reflection of a tendency towards fixing

[93] This much can be stated without following any particular reconstruction of Johannine history.

[94] E.g. Meeks, 'Man from Heaven'; see below ch. 5, p. 187.

[95] So G. Richter, 'Zum gemeindebildenden Element in den johanneischen Schriften', in *Studien zum Johannesevangelium*, ed. J. Hainz, Regensburg 1977, 383–414, 412f.

norms and towards standardisation in the first to second century,[96] has led to the expulsion of 'Christians' whom the Johannine group at least supported and sponsored, while, even apart from the doctrinal question, the authority assumed by the Elder cannot be accommodated. Demetrius and Gaius may also have groups of Christians meeting in their houses and the crucial question is how they will align themselves.

An alternative reconstruction would be to suggest that Diotrephes and the Elder represent a split within Johannine Christianity, whether or not related to the schism of 1 John. Both hold positions of influence not directly justified by the Gospel but both claim to be Johannine. Neither accepts the other's assumption of power nor the particular way it is being exercised. Diotrephes may, possibly with reason, have found the Elder doctrinally suspect in Johannine terms (because of the latter's non-Johannine links?), and he may represent the continuation of the independence and antipathy to mission of 1 John. It is a hole-in-the-corner affair, far removed from the momentous conflicts described in earlier interpretations of 3 John, and significant to us only because of the theological dimension already explored.

Ultimately any attempt at a confident reconstruction must founder on those silences of the letter whose significance we have already suggested and on our ignorance about the constitution and self-identity of the first Christian groups. How far distinctive theological formulations represent distinctive groups, or how far apparently inconsistent attempts at formulating the Christian faith could be found side by side within one community, possibly through the medium of house churches, will remain something of an enigma.

To see the conflict as one within Johannine Christianity may

---

[96] See J.M. Robinson and H Koester, *Trajectories through Early Christianity*, Philadelphia 1971, 15; also the three volumes of *Jewish and Christian Self-definition*, ed. E.P. Sanders et al.

explain the 'peculiarities' of 3 John—its distinctive, non-Johannine vocabulary, its firmer links with secular conventions and language and the signs of its independent history within the growth of the canon. 3 John would express how the Elder wrote naturally, thus betraying that Johannine language had become something of a code to be adopted as appropriate but not consituting the author's habitual way of thinking; when he must defend his 'Johannine' status and claim the Johannine mantel he does so in 2 John by adopting and adapting the forms of 1 John, not without indications that this is not an entirely natural guise. It is the need to write for the community in the idiosyncratic language which will be recognised as their own which has created 2 John.[97]

Small wonder then that 3 John might not be preserved on the same terms as its 'sister' Epistle. Its significance may have been as the 'foundation document' of the community—perhaps of Gaius's—and as a reminder of the origins and calling of that community, but primarily for internal use.[98] 2 John is a directive for behaviour to be used or appealed to as the situation it envisages arose. Although heavily dependent on 1 John, its function was to give directions on wandering teachers who do not follow the Johannine norm as conceived by the Elder; 1 John had not covered this because it did not think of the community as taking the initiative, it was the 'false prophets' who had 'gone out from us' (1 Jn 2.19). It is possible that it was the experience of rejection behind 3 John which led to a reinforcement of boundaries against all comers and acted as a catalyst for the intensification of the refusal of dialogue. To some degree the Elder is turning the tables against Diotrephes in

[97] This is probably preferable to seeing 2 John as pseudonymous without any obvious purpose or explanation of this particular pseudonym; Heise, *BLEIBEN*, 164ff. argues for pseudonymity as does Bultmann, *Epistles*, 107–8; see also Schunack, *Briefe*, 108–9.

[98] So Brown, *Epistles*, 732.

using 1 John to this purpose—particularly if Diotrephes claimed to stand within that same tradition. For the same reason 2 John might eventually have been appended to 1 John in an attempt to bring its circulation beyond the original community and in recognition that 1 John, now being more widely read, was its god-parent.

Yet 2 John also joins hands with that tendency which may itself have led to the exclusion of the 'brethren', namely the growth of the idea of a received body of tradition to be preserved against innovation, and the more rigid definition of the boundaries of the church (cf. 1 Tim 1.10; 2 Tim 4.3; Tit 1.9; 2.1; Jude 3; 1 Clement 7.2).[99] From this we might expect the further isolation of Johannine Christianity and perhaps too the reduction of numbers caused by the divisions which had split the community. Perhaps to all this we may attribute the apparently restricted circulation of the Gospel in its early history.[100] However, that, despite this, not only the Gospel but also these two remnants of past conflicts together with 1 John found a way to acceptance by the wider church within its canon of Scripture remains one of those enigmatic ironies which must continue to stretch the imagination of both historian and theologian.

[99] See E. Schweizer, Church Order, §6.
[100] Cf. W. Loewenich, Das Johannes-Verständnis im zweiten Jahrhundert, BZNW 13, Giessen 1932; J.N. Sanders, The Fourth Gospel in the Early Church, Cambridge 1943.

Chapter Five

THE JOHANNINE 'GOSPEL'?

The use of the term 'Johannine tradition' needs little apology; in what has gone before it has been impossible to avoid speaking of the Johannine community and of seeing that community's history and tradition as traced through the Gospel and Epistles. There is nothing new in this—literary studies of the relation between the Gospel and First Epistle, studies of the redaction of the Gospel and attempts to reconstruct behind the Gospel a history of the community prior to its writing have in turn contributed to the confidence with which 'Johannine community' or 'Johannine Christianity' are discussed in modern scholarship.[1]

That consensus is surely a valid one, but less valid is the tendency to consign 2 and 3 John to supporting footnotes or to a final appendix or stage of a history whose essential contours and direction have already been determined by the analysis of the Gospel first and then of 1 John. Rather it is in these two Epistles, despite their brevity, that we have a clear contact with known issues and controversies in the early church and hence it is they which can provide a proper starting point for analysing the nature and causes of the Johannine response. Yet it is precisely by taking this starting point that we are then forced to ask wider questions of the Gospel and First Epistle about Johannine thought than those which we have already begun to explore in the previous chapter. The outcome in 2 and 3 John inevitably raises the question how far the theological and historical picture they paint was the unavoidable consequence of the theology of the Johannine tradition and particularly of that expression of it which we find in the Fourth Gospel.

[1] See below nn. 91, 97.

166

This means that our primary concern is not with how far stages in the prior history of the Johannine community or in its consequent history can be traced through analysis of the construction or redaction of the Gospel—although these issues cannot be totally avoided. Rather, what are the patterns of Johannine theology and what responses does it offer to particular problems and issues? That we can discern changing— to avoid the loaded term 'developing'—responses has already become clear in our discussion so far, and that the Gospel must be assigned a certain priority has been suggested by our study of the love command tradition. However, in recognising that the Johannine tradition involves change we must not make the common mistake of tracing a linear progression through the Gospel and Epistles supposing that this directly reflects the history of the tradition and the community. Even if the Gospel is rooted in a community and in a tradition, it seems unlikely that its purpose was to record directly that community's history, neither need the Evangelist simply have been repeating his community's tradition—he was no doubt using it but also reinterpreting it, perhaps critically and certainly stamping it with the marks of his own individuality.[2] Similarly, even if it can be shown that 1 John is dependent on the Gospel, this need not mean that the author has understood or followed it fully nor deny that where he differs, rather than showing a development from the Gospel he may be continuing the original thought of the community or developing an independent reflection on it.[3]

[2] Cf. F. Wisse's caution about arguing from document to community in 'Prolegomena to the Study of the New Testament and Gnosis', in *The New Testament and Gnosis*, ed. A Logan and A. Wedderburn, Edinburgh 1983, 138–45, 144; however, acceptance of different authors within the Johannine corpus demands some historical reconstruction.

[3] This may account for many of the difficulties of ascribing priority to the Gospel noted by Grayston, *Epistles*, 12f. See below pp. 209ff. and nn. 94–5 for further caution about assuming the Epistle is directly dependent on the Gospel, although there are equal difficulties in assigning priority to 1 John.

It is of course true that neither the Gospel nor the Epistles were written 'in abstract' but in particular contexts and situations. This observation is often used to account for the differences between them. Thus, for example, in the Epistles the situation is one of internal division and conflict while in the Gospel we are more aware of the external conflict with unbelief epitomised by the Jews; the conclusion can then be drawn that the Gospel was written in the context of dialogue with the Synagogue, a dialogue which is over by the time of the Epistles where the community is on the defensive, erecting barriers against internal dissent—a change of context which may explain the changes in theology such as the new emphasis on 'believing *that*'.[4] In response, it is doubtful whether the relation between historical situation and theology is such a simple one; the characteristic dialectic of the Gospel is too deeply embedded in its theology to be purely a reflection of historical dialogue— indeed dialectic and dialogue are not the same—while historically it seems probable that the community is no longer in dialogue with the Synagogue by the time of the writing of the Gospel.[5] So too the characteristic absence of dialogue from the Epistles, far from being a result of their historical context, may have gone a long way towards creating it. However, this appeal to differences of context has frequently been fundamentally a defensive one rooted in the desire to maintain common authorship of Gospel and Epistles (or at least 1 John). That question is not our primary consideration here—rather we are concerned to explore patterns of theology in the Johannine tradition under the stimulus of 2 and 3 John.

[4] This is frequently asserted; see R. Whitacre, *Johannine Polemic*, SBLDS 67, Chico 1982 for a detailed working out of this position. See further below pp. 212–3.

[5] See M. de Jonge, 'Jewish Expectations about the "Messiah" according to the Fourth Gospel', *NTS* 19 (1972–3) 246–70, 264–5; below p. 212, and nn. 40, 103.

As has just been implied, the earlier debate on the relationship between the Gospel and First Epistle focused on the question whether they shared common authorship—with the onus of proof being on those who would question this *datum* of tradition. The balancing of similarities and differences of style, language and theology led to much debate but to no consensus so that in retrospect even a fundamental article by C.H. Dodd in 1937 and the responses it provoked seem to have made little progress beyond earlier discussions by A.E. Brooke, R. Law and, even earlier, by H.J. Holtzmann.[6] If this approach has lost its vitality, it is only part of a wider realisation of the inconclusive nature of such methods in discussing the authenticity of New Testament writings—for statistics rarely produce conviction—and a corresponding move to reconstruct the presuppositions and life-situation of the literature under debate. Yet before we too quickly draw comparisons with, for example, discussions of the Pauline authorship of Ephesians, it must be emphasised that there is no internal claim within the Johannine literature to common authorship of the Gospel and the First Epistle and/or Second and Third Epistles. The external evidence would seem to be dependent on the ascription of all the Johannine writings to the Apostle John, an ascription that cannot be traced with certainty before the time of Irenaeus and which in the case of the minor Epistles took considerable time to

---

[6] C.H. Dodd, 'The First Epistle of John and the Fourth Gospel', *JRLB* 21 (1937) 129–56; idem, *Epistles*, xlvii–lvi; he was answered by W.F. Howard, 'The Common Authorship of the Johannine Gospel and Epistles', *JThS* 48 (1947) 12–25; W.G. Wilson, 'An Examination of the Linguistic Evidence Adduced against the Unity of Authorship of the First Epistle of John and the Fourth Gospel', *JThS* 49 (1948) 147–56; A.P. Salom, 'Some Aspects of the Grammatical Style of 1 John', *JBL* 74 (1955) 96–102. For earlier discussions see Brooke, *Epistles*, i–xxvii; R. Law, *The Tests of Life*, Edinburgh 1909, 339–63; H.J. Holtzmann, 'Das Problem des ersten johanneischen Briefes in seinem Verhältnis zum Evangelium', *Jahrbücher für protestantische Theologie* 7 (1881) 690–712; 8 (1882) 128–52, 316–42, 460–85; Moffatt, *Introduction*, 590–3. See Haenchen, 'Neue Literatur', 4–8.

be established; ironically, Revelation, perhaps the first to be ascribed to the Apostle, was in due course distinguished from the Gospel and Epistles by its language and thought, and *therefore* removed from the responsibility of the Apostle.[7] In all, this might suggest that the onus of proof should be as much on those who assert common authorship, frequently while denying that that author was the Apostle.

That the Gospel and Epistles share a great range of common words, phrases and metaphors, many not to be found outside these writings, needs no proving; it is apparent on even a cursory reading and can be substantiated by study of lists of the parallels which are readily available in the introductions of commentaries and in the studies mentioned earlier. However, the way these common concepts and language are handled in each of the writings is as important as the differences of language and style which are equally well documented. At the same time differences in language and style need treating with caution; style is always related both to length and to form of literature, to the demands of a paraenetic letter or of a Gospel, while language must be determined by subject matter—the omission of 'fruit' (καρπός) from the Epistle is hardly significant despite the fact that it comes twelve times in the Gospel, since ten of these are in the passage about the Vine (15.1–10).[8] Nevertheless, even with this caution and with the recognition that books acknowledged to be by the same author can differ widely in style and

[7] See ch. 1 esp. pp. 11–12.

[8] Failure to observe this is a weakness in Dodd's arguments; so also 'προσκυνεῖν': 1 Jn 0x, Jn 11x but 9 of these come in 4.20–24; see further Howard, 'Common Authorship', 18–9. The absence of 'πέμπειν' in 1 John may be because it is only used for certain moods and tenses in John, the others being supplied by 'ἀποστέλλειν'; only the 'ἀποστέλλειν' moods and tenses occur in 1 John; see Howard, ibid. and C. Tarelli, 'Johannine Synonyms', *JThS* 47 (1948) 175–7. More problematic is 'κύριος' (of Jesus): 1 Jn 0x, Jn 41x; 31 of the Gospel uses are in the vocative and 9 of the others in ch. 20–1, but 1 John, like Jn 20–1, is post-resurrection.

vocabulary,[9] the evidence of language and style must be of some importance in reflecting the interests and concerns of the author and his mode of expressing those concerns. For these reasons it is still important to analyse and examine points of vocabulary and style.

In the discussion that follows, therefore, two lines of approach will be brought together. The questions which we shall ask of the Gospel and Epistles must in part be prompted by those theological concerns which have arisen so far, but to avoid charges of arbitrariness or of choosing such questions as will predetermine the overall conclusion reached the evidence of the stylistic and literary comparison of the Gospel and Epistles must also be given full weight. In this way we are not seeking to give a comprehensive account of the theology of Gospel or Epistles but to make a few soundings to determine whether they are hewn from a common rock to a common pattern, and to suggest where further explorations may be made.

1. Tradition and the Spirit

The role of the received tradition of the community will make a good starting point inasmuch as our own analysis, confirming earlier studies,[10] has highlighted this as an important element in the Johannine 'trajectory'.

Tradition *qua* tradition clearly does act as a focus of loyalty and as an interpretative key in 2 John; in terms of vocabulary this is signalled by the use of 'teaching' in v. 9, a word which does not occur in 1 John. We can see the significance of this when we note that whereas here possession of Father and Son is dependent on 'abiding in the teaching', in 1 Jn 2.22 the

[9] E.g. 'σώζειν' (cited by Dodd in his support): 1 Jn 0x, Jn 6x but Rom 8x, 1 Cor 9x, Gal 0x.

[10] Conzelmann, 'Anfang'; Bergmeier, 'Verfasserproblem'.

condition is true confession while 'abiding' is in 'him'.[11] The appeal to the love command in 2 Jn 5–6 is an appeal to the tradition of the community 'from the beginning', and the false confession of the antichrist in v. 7 is determined by traditional language taken from 1 Jn 4.2 and possibly from the Gospel's description of Jesus as 'he who comes into the world'.[12] 'Truth', whose marked increase in 2 and 3 John is notable, is frequently used as a catchword characterising the true believer ('in truth'), and in some sense seems to signify the exclusive characteristic or possession of the community—and here 3 John agrees with the Second Epistle, although we have remarked on the apparent convergence with secular usage.[13]

Whereas 1 Jn 4.1ff., on which 2 Jn 7 is dependent, introduces the false confession of the antichrist within the context of the discernment of spirits and speaks of 'false prophets' and of the 'spirit of error', 2 John (as also 3 John) lacks any reference to the spirit or to prophets, false or true. There is nothing in either Epistle to suggest that 'the spirit' is seen as part of the problem, whether or not in tension with tradition, and no evidence to interpret the conflict between the Elder and Diotrephes in 3 John as one between the 'Spirit' and 'Tradition'.[14]

It is tempting to draw parallels with the Pastoral Epistles or with Jude in this emphasis on tradition,[15] but there are important differences. 2 and 3 John make no use of the language of transmission and succession, even though this could have been useful in their different polemics, and it is by the use of particular

---

[11] See ch. 3, pp. 93–5.

[12] Ch. 3, pp. 76,86.

[13] Ch. 3, p. 70 and n. 58.

[14] Johnston, *Spirit-Paraclete*, 149 sees Diotrephes as the charismatic while for Kragerud, *Lieblingsjünger*, it is the Elder who is the man of the Spirit! See further ch. 4, pp. 140–2.

[15] As does Bergmeier, 'Verfasserproblem', while Conzelmann, 'Anfang' sees 1 John in these terms. For the concern with tradition as a mark of the Pastorals see also above ch. 4, p. 165.

'Johannine' terms and phrases rather than by the use of the technical vocabulary of tradition that the author marks his interest in that which was 'from the beginning', showing little interest in how it reached the present or might be authenticated.

2 John is undoubtedly dependent on the First Epistle, but its emphasis on tradition is not simply a repetition of what is to be found there. Certainly tradition is important for 1 John; the love command, whose significance is marked by the frequency of associated vocabulary, already plays a constitutive role in this respect as 'from the beginning', and there is a strong call to abide by what you have heard from the beginning (2.24). 'To believe' is 'to believe that', 'πιστεύειν' being used like 'ὁμολογεῖν' (to confess) followed by a confessional formula, in contrast to the Gospel's 'believe in' or absolute 'believe';[16] what matters now is conformity with particular statements of belief rather than eschatological decision. A comparison of the opening verses of 1 John with the Prologue of the Gospel is instructive here:

Jn 1.1,14	1 Jn 1.1f.
ἐν ἀρχῇ ἦν ὁ λόγος, καὶ ὁ λόγος ἦν πρὸς τὸν θεόν, καὶ θεὸς ἦν ὁ λόγος. ... καὶ ὁ λόγος σὰρξ ἐγένετο καὶ ἐσκήνωσεν ἐν ἡμῖν, καὶ ἐθεασάμεθα τὴν δόξαν αὐτοῦ, ...	ὃ ἦν ἀπ' ἀρχῆς, ὃ ἀκηκόαμεν, ὃ ἑωράκαμεν ... περὶ τοῦ λόγου τῆς ζωῆς, ... ἥτις ἦν πρὸς τὸν πατέρα καὶ ἐφανερώθη ἡμῖν, ...

That the two passages are related is suggested by the unusual 'was *with* God/the Father' using the preposition 'πρός'. Yet whereas in the Gospel 'word' (λόγος) refers to the pre-existent, divine Logos who was incarnate in the historical figure of Jesus, in 1 John the loose connection between 'that (*neuter*) which was

---

[16] For all that follows reference should be made to the Tables in Appendix I; not all the information given there will be discussed in this chapter although much of it could be used to fill out the picture. 'πιστεύειν': Jn 98x, 1 Jn 9x; 'ὁμολογεῖν': Jn 4x, 1 Jn 5x; note the importance of confessional formulae in 1 Jn 2.22; 4.2,15; 5.1,5.

from the beginning' and 'concerning the word (*masc.*) of life' suggests that the latter refers not to the incarnation but to the Gospel message.[17] Although at first sight an apparent echo of the 'in the beginning' of the Gospel prologue, in 1 John 'from the beginning' is a characteristic phrase which, as we have already observed, looks back to the beginning of Christian or the community's experience. The interest here is now in the proclamation which makes known the original experience of faith. It is now this which can become the object of the claim 'we have seen', as the testimony of the original eyewitnesses is appropriated; again there is no appeal to any succession through whom this claim is mediated, for, as we have seen,[18] the same language of direct witness can also be used by the community (4.14). However, what is 'from the beginning' is to be proclaimed and heard (1.3,5; 2.7) and in this as in the absence of 'teaching' (see above) 1 John has a more kerygmatic understanding of tradition than does the Second Epistle.

In similar contrast to 2 John, faithfulness to 'his commands' and right confession are in the First Epistle set in a context of experience of the Spirit (3.23–4.5); however this would seem to do little to modify or influence the Epistle's interest in tradition—and we have already had to reject attempts to see in 1 John a representative of the Spirit or prophetic circles in implicit opposition to growing ecclesiastical structures or tradition.[19] It is true that each Christian possesses 'an anointing' (χρίσμα) which gives him full, independent knowledge (2.20,27), but even if the term suggests an association with the

---

[17] See Dodd, *Epistles*, 3–5; Schnackenburg, *Johannesbriefe*, 61–3; J. Héring, 'Y-a-t-il des Aramaïsmes dans la Première Épître Johannique?', *RHPhR* 36 (1956) 113–21 wishes to see 'ὅ' as a mistranslation of the Aramaic indeclinable relative ' ד ' which should have been rendered 'ὅν' (masc.), but an Aramaic background to 1 John is unlikely.

[18] See ch. 4, p. 144.

[19] Ch. 4, pp. 142f..

Spirit,[20] the failure to make this explicit is significant. Instead there is a close link if not identification with teaching,[21] and just as 'the anointing' is to 'remain in you' (2.27), so also must 'what you have heard from the beginning' (2.24).

In fact, far from being characterised by the Spirit, 1 John has little idea where to place it on the theological map. Possession of God's Spirit is indeed the sign and seal of true confession and love, and is an expression of God's indwelling in the believer (3.23f.; 4.13), but the Spirit has no independent character or function and can even be understood on a level with other spirits—the spirit of error—if only to be distinguished from them (4.1–6). Here again an apparent echo of the Gospel hides a deeper difference. 'The spirit of truth' is also to be found in the Gospel (Jn 14.17; 15.26; 16.13), but the contrast with 'the spirit of error' peculiar to 1 John indicates both a different understanding of the spirit and a different use of the genitive 'of truth'. For 1 John truth is part of a dualist framework and is defined in part by the contrast with error; in the Gospel the Spirit is the one who communicates the divine revelation which is *the* truth. While it is true that for the Epistle to call Jesus a Paraclete (2.1) is not incompatible with the description of the Spirit as 'another Paraclete' in John (14.17), the difference points to different conceptions of the role of the Spirit as well as a different use of the 'Johannine' term 'Paraclete'.[22]

[20] It is a matter of debate whether we should see a link between 'anointing' as a rite belonging to initiation and baptism even if anointng with oil was not yet part of the baptismal ceremony; see Nauck, *Tradition und Charakter*, 147–82 and the criticism by Schnackenburg, *Johannesbriefe*, 152–3; a reference to the Holy Spirit, given in baptism, might then be implied. Note also that Jesus as 'the Anointed One' (χριστός) was 'anointed' by the Holy Spirit at his baptism.

[21] So Dodd, *Epistles*, 58–63; Houlden, *Epistles*, 79.

[22] See further Dodd, 'First Epistle and Fourth Gospel', 146–8; Moffatt, *Introduction*, 592. Ctr. Jn 16.13 'ἐκεῖνος τὸ πνεῦμα' (masc.) with 1 Jn 5.6, 'τὸ πνεῦμα τὸ μαρτυροῦν' (neut.). The Spirit is in no sense 'another Paraclete' in 1 John while Jesus's role as 'Paraclete' is primarily associated with forgiveness of sins, not reminding, leading into truth etc.

We may say that for the Johannine Epistles an appeal to the tradition 'which is from the beginning' is fundamental for understanding what it means to be a Christian in the present. Quite how tradition is experienced and passed on is not made clear, but certainly it is not seen in terms of the Spirit. In 1 John tradition does include some practical content in the command of mutual love, but even so its role as tradition is never forgotten; in the same way the author stresses that right christological confession is essential, but makes little attempt to relate its content to his doctrinal teaching.[23] In 2 John the process would seem to have gone a stage further yet only highlights what is already true of 1 John—we can only witness the original witness and there is no new expression of truth for a new situation.

Set against this background how does the Gospel appear? The very act of consigning the traditions of faith to writing in Gospel form is presumably significant, although would not of itself either preclude other continuing development of those traditions or imply a claim to final authority, as the Gnostic writings make clear.[24] A step towards such a claim is made in the editorial addition in Jn 21.24–25 where the witness of the Gospel is acknowledged in terms of tradition as being faithful. However, a reading of the Gospel itself implies that 'witness' is not being understood as merely the repetition of the past, for alongside recollection there is equally clearly interpretation. It seems likely that the Fourth Evangelist must have seen his contribution as part of the witness of the Paraclete with and through the witness of the disciples as promised in 15.26–27, and this implies that the Spirit-Paraclete provides at least one context for dealing with the problem of tradition, the continuing witness of and to the past, in the church.

Thus the Spirit will bring to the minds of the disciples all that

[23] See below pp. 198–200.
[24] Contrast D. Bruce Woll, *Johannine Christianity in Conflict*, SBLDS 60, Chico 1981, 126.

Jesus has told them (14.26), a 'remembering' which the Gospel sees as consequent on Jesus's glorification (2.22; 12.16), itself the precondition of the gift of the Spirit (7.39; 16.7); yet this 'remembering' clearly involves new understanding and leads to faith (2.22), so the Spirit can be said to 'guide' the disciples in all truth (16.13).[25] Yet this guidance is no free and independent activity; the Spirit does not only witness about Jesus (15.26), and yet, even if he is the source of new insights, these are in fact only what 'he hears' (reading 'ἀκούει' in the present tense)[26] from Jesus (16.13), so that there is a unity between the 'remembered' words of the earthly Jesus and the teaching of the Spirit as the organ of the risen Jesus. It is not only the distinctiveness and creativity of the Gospel which suggests that it is the fruit of such an understanding of the witness of disciples and Spirit; just as the incomplete understanding of the disciples can be looked back upon in the light of fuller insight now received (2.22; 20.9), so too the day when Jesus (16.25) or the Spirit (16.12–13) can go beyond the limitations of the earthly ministry to more open speech is surely now present in the Gospel. Of course nowhere in any of the Gospels do we find mere repetition of the words of Jesus—if nothing else, the experience of the resurrection made this impossible—and a contrast between the Synoptics and John in these terms is false; yet it is in the Fourth Gospel that we find this sensitivity to the question of how the church can address its present context while remaining faithful to the past event of the incarnation. The problem is answered and the reality of new interpretation is met by seeing the ongoing work of the Spirit as actuating and reaffirming tradition, and, beyond that, by understanding both tradition and Spirit christocentrically. Just

[25] Jn 16.13 'ἐν τῇ ἀληθεια πασῃ' ℵ D W Θ *al*

εἰς την ἀληθειαν πασαν A B *pc*

While the difference in meaning is slight the reading of ℵ etc. may put the emphasis on guidance *in the sphere* of truth.

[26] With ℵ L 33 b e against 'ἀκουσει' (fut) read by B D W *al* vg; 'ἀκουσῃ' A 𝔐.

as the Spirit speaks the words of Jesus and so glorifies Jesus (16.14), so also it is not the tradition which is regulative for the community but Jesus who as revealer spoke and still speaks; it is not tradition which is the object of hearing and believing but Jesus.[27]

A natural consequence of this is the use of language in the Gospel which can sound static or dogmatic, and which remains in unresolved tension with the recognition of the incomplete understanding of the disciples during Jesus's earthly ministry. It is because Jesus is the source of all understanding that the disciples believe from the start (1.41,45; 2.11,17); there is little ethical teaching and apparently no room for striving because the Christian has no further to go than to abide in Jesus and his word (8.31; 15.4–10).[28] Jesus's work as Revealer is a unity and complete; there can be no further revelation. Jesus does not reveal a body of material which is identifiable as 'Tradition'; it is often said that he reveals only that he is revealer or that his word is identical with himself,[29] but the emphasis is more that he is the revealer of God (ch. 17). There is no other way to God and knowledge of him than through Jesus and his word (14.7), and yet the Gospel itself bears witness to the certainty that Jesus and his word can be heard through the tradition or preaching (and therefore through the Spirit) in every situation and age.

The call to discipleship therefore is a call to abide in Jesus's word (8.31) or to keep his word (8.51f.). In the Farewell Discourses 'keeping Jesus's word' (14.23,24 (words); cf. 15.20) is used in parallel to 'keeping Jesus's commands' (14.15,21; 15.10),

[27] See Käsemann, Testament, 38, 40.

[28] Note that abiding here is in Jesus (ctr. 2 Jn 9). On this aspect of Johannine thought see E. Schweizer, 'The Concept of the Church in the Gospel and Epistles of St. John', in New Testament Essays in Memory of T.W. Manson, ed. A.J.B. Higgins, Manchester 1959, 230–45, 237; also N. Dahl, Das Volk Gottes, Oslo 1941, 167–74.

[29] R. Bultmann, Theology of the New Testament, London 1952–5, II.63f.; Käsemann, Testament, 46f.

but more than obedience to specific injunctions is in mind; 'his word' is inseparable from Jesus himself and the totality of his revelation. Jesus's word is God's word (14.24; cf. 12.49), and thus is the agent of both judgement and life (12.48–50); to keep it is to experience life and divine indwelling (8.51f.; 14.23), just as Jesus's unity with the Father is expressed by his keeping God's word or commands (8.55; 15.10)—neither may we forget that Jesus is himself the Word.[30] Although 1 John shares with John (and Revelation but not 2 or 3 John) the language of 'keeping his word' or 'commands', the element of obedience to a known injunction has come to the fore as 'Word' has lost its christological overtones (1 Jn 1.1)[31] and as the theme is brought into closer connection with the command of mutual love (3.23–24; 5.2–3; cf. 2.3–8). Keeping his word comes only once (2.5) and there is greater stress on keeping his commands with 'his' as often as not referring to God (3.22,24; 5.3; ?2.3,4).

There are anomalies in the Gospel's presentation; in chapter 17 the Spirit does not appear at all in the exploration of unity and the disciples are said to have kept God's word (17.6). The keeping of Jesus's commands and the command of mutual love are beginning to come together in 15.1–17, thus leading to the oscillation between singular and plural commands found only here in John and regularly in the Epistles. Are these signs of later redaction reflecting some of the same concerns as the Epistles, to be put on one side if we are to grasp the real thought of the Fourth Evangelist,[32] or are they essential parts of the Gospel which 1 John has taken further? This is an issue to which we will

[30] On love as entailing the keeping of Jesus's words see F. Segovia, 'Love and Hatred of Jesus and Johannine Sectarianism', *CBQ* 42 (1981) 258–72. 'παραλαμβάνειν' is used in Jn 1.11 of accepting Jesus while in the rest of the New Testament it is used of accepting a body of teaching. On Jesus's word as agent of judgement and life in 12.48ff. see Barrett, *Gospel*, 434.

[31] See above p. 174. On John's and 1 John's use of 'τηρεῖν' see above ch. 3, p. 78 and Appendix I, Table E.

[32] See Becker, 'Abschiedsreden'.

have to return more than once. There is not space here for the analysis and exegesis necessary to discuss arguments about redactional material, except to point out that we have already argued that in John the love command is 'new' and is looked back upon by I John where it is also 'old' and 'from the beginning'.[33] We should not too easily seek to uncover layers of redaction supposedly reflecting stages in a development which can be reconstructed as if the Gospel and Epistles constituted an archaeological site; originality in concept and originality in time are not coterminous, while the 'later' ideas of the Epistles may reflect the original or continuing ideas of the community or any part of it. The Gospel as we have it reflects a variety of responses to the idea of tradition and faithfulness to the past; while in I John we have noted both the absence of a strong doctrine of the Spirit and a stress on teaching or tradition as fact or as something given and regulative in its own right, the Gospel is marked by a christocentricity and by a focusing on Jesus as revealer which hold together potentially conflicting stresses on faithfulness to the word, to the witness based on seeing, and on openness to the things to come which the Spirit will announce. Why is this focus missing in I John; has it been lost or was it the Evangelist's purpose to introduce it in order to supplement the understanding of his community? Perhaps even more intractable—what pattern of faith, practice and leadership in a church might reflect such a tightly drawn theology?

2. The Community in History and the World

If the community looks back to its own tradition, how does it view the wider spectrum of the past and of the world? What is the community's attitude to the broader context in which it is

[33] See above ch. 3, pp. 74–6.

placed? That 2 and 3 John reflect and are a not surprising outcome of tendencies towards exclusivism, towards an emphasis on election and towards a concentration on membership of the community as sign and guarantee of 'being of God', has already become clear. This is manifested in 2 John's refusal of hospitality to visitors not bearing the true doctrine, for such 'heretics' are more surely the representatives of the world than would be unconverted pagans; 3 John admittedly supports missionary work and thus signals its distance from the rest of the Johannine corpus by the vocabulary associated with this, yet since such work is by, or in aid of, 'the truth' (3 Jn 8), an element of party spirit is not lost.

1 John provides us with a more detailed picture. There, as we have seen, the past is the past of the community; it is tradition, 'that which was from the beginning', 'the beginning' being the community's beginning not the world's. Thus the community is not set in the wider context of God's dealings with his people; 1 John is marked by the absence of any use of the Old Testament or of terms such as 'writing' or 'law' which in the Gospel are used to express the fulfilment of Israel's religious experience in Jesus. The only possible exception, the reference to Cain and Abel as an ethical example (1 Jn 3.12), is a common one and probably comes from a tradition of Christian catechesis rather than from independent use of the Old Testament.[34] Inasmuch as in the New Testament only 2 and 3 John and Philemon share this failure to use the Old Testament it can hardly be attributed to the possibility that the community to which the Epistle was written was gentile, and in view of the Jewish background often posited for the letter it is particularly striking. In line with this is

---

[34] For Cain in the New Testament see Heb 11.4; Jude 11. On his role in Jewish tradition see G. Vermes, 'The Targumic Versions of Genesis 4:3–16', in *Post-Biblical Jewish Studies*, Leiden 1975, 92–126. See also M. Wilcox, 'On investigating the use of the Old Testament in the New Testament', in *Text and Interpretation*, ed. E. Best and R. McL. Wilson, Cambridge 1979, 231–43, 240.

the absence of any of the epithets traditionally applied to Israel and then reapplied to the Christian church elsewhere in the New Testament; the community is not understood as part of the continuing activity of God in history and the world.[35]

Just as there is no witness from 'salvation history', so the only witness is the internal one experienced by the community or individual (5.10); tradition too is important in that *we* express it and witness to it and find it true in ourselves (2.8), with no historical sense of how 'we' come to be heirs of that tradition and witness. So too there is no looking foward to a future history of the community, no striving or growth but just continuing as we are until 'his manifestation' (3.2) when we shall be like him.

This does not mean that there is no understanding of history in 1 John, but rather that history is only understood in relation to the church. The present is the era of light, the darkness belongs to the past and is passing away (2.8), but this light is limited to the church. The language and framework of eschatology are being applied to the history of the community; this is equally true when the fulfilment of the 'last hour' is seen in the historical appearance of the 'false prophets' (2.18).[36] Yet this is not a true historicising for it only serves to mark the contrast between the church and the world or darkness and no other elements of the historical sequence are given theological significance.

With this centring of all interest on the community it comes as no surprise that 1 John makes no reference to any mission to the world carried out by the community and never suggests that such proclamation is an essential part of Christian living.

[35] The contrast here with Hebrews (e.g. ch. 11) militates against seeing Hebrews and the Johannine literature as coming from a common or related circle as argued by O. Cullmann, *The Johannine Circle*, London 1976, 54–5.
[36] See ch. 3, p. 80; G. Klein, 'Das wahre Licht scheint schon', *ZThK* 68 (1971) 261–326.

Instead, it is the schismatics who have 'gone out into the world', where their apparent success—the world listens to them—only serves for the author to prove that they belong to the world and not to God (4.4–6). There is here more than the jealous resentment of a community whose own attempts at mission had proved ineffective, for it reflects a fundamentally negative attitude to the world and the church's role there. The world stands in opposition to believers—like the darkness it is passing away (2.8,17); just as it failed to recognise Jesus, so it fails to recognise believers as children of God (3.1). Instead its attitude to the community is one of hatred (3.13), and, in response, love for the world is impossible for any member of the community—such love would be incompatible with love for God (2.15f.). God and the world are thus brought into direct opposition and so too are believers and the world (4.4f.; 5.19); there appears no possibility of bridging that opposition or of establishing any form of communication.

Because of this gulf between the two camps it comes as no surprise that the love of God is seen as primarily directed towards the believer (*us*: 3.1,16; 4.9,16; cf. 5.1f.). The two references to God's saving purpose for the world (2.2; 4.14) sound like statements which have survived in tradition and they have no effect on the theology of the immediate context or of the Epistle as a whole. In fact the contexts show that although Jesus is described as Saviour of the world, this is only applied to the company of believers. 2.2 comes at the end of a section concerned with the fact of *our* sinning while 4.14 comes in the middle of a celebration of God's love for *us* and *our* experience of his abiding in *us*. God indeed sent his Son *into* the world but it was so that *we* might live through him (4.9); in contrast to Jn 3.16 the world here is only the location and not the object of God's love and God's salvation.[37] A failure to grapple

[37] See L. Schottroff, *Der Glaubende und die feindliche Welt*, Neukirchen-Vluyn 1970, 285ff.

theologically with the meaning of God's love for the world, like the failure to recognise God's dealings with humanity or with the Jews in the past, could easily be coupled with an absence of any sense of responsibility towards the world through the proclamation of the Christian Gospel. If the community is the bearer of the light now shining, that light does not illuminate the darkness but only reveals the impenetrability of that darkness.

This negative attitude to the world should be distinguished from the gnostic rejection of the world and all matter. 1 John reflects no doctrine of a fall or of the intrinsic evil of the material world which stands eternally opposed to the divine light. Rather than cosmological theory the theological conviction of the community's election combined with the probable historical situation and experience of the community have produced this 'dualism'. The theological conviction would mean that schism (1 Jn 2.19), clearly a traumatic experience, would have to be seen as demonstrating that the heretics had never been members of the elect body, otherwise the reality of that election would be undermined. In the light of such an experience, boundaries would have to be reinforced, the community would come to see itself as a citadel in which dwell the elect who possess the truth. Impulses to self-preservation and the preservation of the truth are in the ascendant and the assurance that God works, and has worked, in and for the community alone would exclude the possibility of looking for evidences of his presence elsewhere, perhaps even in other forms of Christianity.

That in the Fourth Gospel we also find reflected a community aware of its separation from the world, perhaps including other forms of Christianity, is a commonplace of Johannine scholarship. What is significant here is how this sense of otherness is articulated in the Gospel. There the world—which is not inanimate but comprises the world of men and women—

lies open to God through whose Word it came into being. It is both the sphere and the goal of God's saving purpose. Jesus's authority and mission extend to all, he comes into the world (1.9; 3.19; 6.14; 9.39; 11.27; 12.46; 16.28; 18.37), he is, potentially, Saviour of the world (3.16; 4.26; 8.12; 17.2), and in one sense 'his own' to whom he comes are all people (1.10,11). Anyone (τις) and everyone (πᾶς) can respond in faith and through faith have eternal life (1.7–9; 3.16; 6.40,51; 7.37). So too the disciples must, like Jesus, have a mission and the world must be its sphere (4.38; 17.18f.; 20.21);[38] so too although the world cannot receive the Spirit (14.17), the Spirit must operate in and on the world (16.8–11).

But the freedom to believe is also the freedom not to believe; when it rejects Jesus the world remains 'world' and does not become disciples or children of God. When the opportunity for transformation is refused the world remains over against God and thus *becomes* a sphere to be viewed negatively; the world can then be restricted as 'this world' (ὁ κόσμος οὗτος) (8.23; 12.25,31; 13.1; 16.11; 18.36) with the implied eschatological contrast with the world to come. The world then becomes the representative of all opposition to Jesus (7.7) and to those who follow him (15.18), and in this opposition finds itself judged (16.8f.,33; 12.31).[39] When in 15.18–16.4 the hatred of the world is manifested in putting the disciples out of the synagogue this probably indicates not that for John the 'world' only refers to the Jews of his own time as well as of Jesus's, but that the 'Jews' of the Gospel have become more than the contemporaries of Jesus, they are a specific symbol of the world in its rejection of

---

[38] See J. Kuhl, *Die Sendung Jesu und der Kirche nach dem Johannes-Evangelium*, Kaldenkirchen 1967, although he overstates the case when he says that for John the church is a thoroughly missionary entity; see also M. de Jonge, 'The Son of God and the Children of God', in *Jesus: Stranger from Heaven and Son of God*, Missoula 1977, 141–68, 156.

[39] See de Jonge, 'Son of God', 157–8.

God's Son.[40] If negative statements about the world predominate in the Farewell Discourses in contrast to the more positive ones of earlier chapters this is because the world's rejection of Jesus in the cross is now viewed as accomplished and the world has established its identity in opposition to God.[41] Yet even in ch. 17 where there is the greatest concentration of statements contrasting Jesus and his disciples with *the* world (and not just *this* world as in 8.23), they are still sent *into* the world (17.18).

Inevitably this means that neither Jesus nor his disciples are 'of the world' (8.22f.; 17.4; 15.18). Firstly this is because as Saviour and Revealer Jesus cannot be of the world, he is 'from above' and comes into the world (3.31; 8.23); secondly, the disciples, because they do believe, cannot be 'of the world' which rejects Jesus. In following Jesus they have left the sphere of the world to enter a new existence; this is 'birth from *above*' (γεννηθῆναι ἄνωθεν) even as Jesus is he who comes from *above* (3.3f.,31). Three points need to be made here. Firstly salvation becomes the gathering of those who believe so that they become, like the disciples, not of this world. Such an understanding of salvation does not deny mission but it does modify its interpretation.[42] Secondly, the believer's existence as not being of the world is not inherent in him or herself—the believer is not already *by nature* not of this world, but only in dependence on Jesus as the

[40] See E. Grässer, 'Die antijudische Polemik im Johannesevangelium', *NTS* 11 (1964–5) 74–90; ctr. Segovia 'Love and Hatred' who denies that 'the world' is wider than the Jews. We should probably use the Farewell Discourses to interpret the earlier part of the Gospel although even there the Jews are not 'live' participants in the debate, see W. Meeks, 'Am I a Jew?', in *Christianity, Judaism and Other Graeco-Roman Cults*, ed. J. Neusner, Leiden 1975, I, 163–86.

[41] See T. Onuki, *Gemeinde und Welt im Johannesevangelium*, WMANT 56, Neukirchen-Vluyn 1984.

[42] See Hahn, *Mission*, 160 and above n. 37; Onuki, *Gemeinde und Welt* denies Meek's ('Man from Heaven') picture of a totally isolated community and argues that Johannine dualism allows the community to cope with the fact of unbelief and hence to continue in the world.

one who comes from above as Revealer. Thirdly, the Fourth Gospel uses a complex of 'in-group' language which draws together Jesus and believers in their separateness from all others; terms like the 'going' of Jesus (7.34f.; 8.21), 'birth from above' (3.3f.), the 'descending' bread of life which is Jesus's flesh (6.17–65), both express their 'otherness' and reinforce it by being only fully comprehensible to those who belong to the community. For the outsider, like Nicodemus, they remain a puzzle, and indeed an obstacle, while those who can say 'we know and believe' (3.11; 6.68f.) are already brought within the circle of meaning.[43]

No doubt this sense of 'otherness' reflects the actual experiences of the community. It understands itself as living in theological and sociological isolation from 'the world'. The relative priority of, and the interaction between, the theological interpretation of isolation and a specific historical experience of being isolated, such as exclusion from the Synagogue (9.22; 12.42; 16.2) is a complex question.[44] From our standpoint it is hard to distinguish between those theological claims which may have led to such exclusion and those which have been used to justify the consequent isolation; did the Johannine community's christology lead to the break with the Synagogue or does it serve to reaffirm the community in the light of that break?[45]

---

[43] This characteristic of the Fourth Gospel has been richly explored by Meeks, 'Man from Heaven', de Jonge, 'Jewish Expectations', H. Leroy, *Rätsel und Missverständnis. Ein Beitrag zur Formgeschichte des Johannesevangeliums*, Bonn 1968.

[44] The references in 9.22 etc. and John's hostility against the Jews undoubtedly imply the bitterness of the conflict even if it is impossible to identify that conflict with any known historical incident such as the *Birkath-ha-Minim*; see the rather tendentious article by R. Kimelman, '*Birkat-Ha-Minim* and the Lack of Evidence for Anti-Christian Jewish Prayer in Late Antiquity', in *Jewish and Christian Self-Definition*, ed. Sanders, II, 226–244.

[45] Meeks, 'Man from Heaven' is rather more finely nuanced than J.L. Martyn, *History and Theology in the Fourth Gospel*, 2nd edition, New York 1979.

However, what is clear is that the problem of the world is understood by John eschatologically and, because the eschatological event is the coming of Jesus, christocentrically. It is the coming of Jesus which establishes both the lostness of the world when it rejects him and the identity of the believer as 'not of the world' in responding to him. Again superficial similarities mask a deep difference from both the gnostic devaluation of the material world and from I John. As to the former we may note the very limited interest in the origins of the world's unbelief despite 8.44 and references to the prince of this world (12.31; 14.30; 16.11); as to the latter we should observe that the Gospel never makes explicit the contrast between 'of God' and 'of the world' such as we find in I John, while the Epistle lacks entirely all that vocabulary which in the Gospel expresses the true origin and belonging of Jesus and hence of believers away from the world (e.g. to ascend and descend ἀναβαίνειν, καταβαίνειν, (from) above ἄνω, ἄνωθεν, and even 'from' παρά).[46] All these underline that for John everything turns on the response to Jesus and the decision for or against faith.

The same is true of John's attitude to history, for history finds its meaning and fulfilment in pointing to Jesus. On the one hand this means that past history can be affirmed; the primary figures and features of Jewish religious experience do bear witness to Jesus. Abraham rejoiced to see Jesus's day (8.56), Moses wrote about him (5.46f.), the Scriptures witness to him (5.39), as, more recently, did John the Baptist (1.19–34; 5.33ff.). More generally, in Jesus and his ministry the Old Testament and its imagery find fulfilment, so that even if none of the terminology of 'the true Israel' is used of the church, the idea is firmly present that it is those who believe in Jesus and not the 'Jews' who are the true

---

[46] Also 'to lift up' (ὑψοῦν), 'glory' (δόξα), 'to glorify' (δοξάζειν), all of which are part of what Leroy, *Rätsel und Missverständnis* describes as the Gospel's 'Sondersprache'. On the contrast between God and the world in I John as part of a comprehensive scheme see Lindars, 'Persecution', 67f.

heirs of God's people, the true seed of Abraham, who are incorporated in the true vine, receive the bread from heaven or belong to the good shepherd.[47]

Yet there is not in John a 'salvation history' as that term is usually understood. God's continuing self-revelation and saving activity are not traced through, there is no progression of witness and the past is not seen as a time of growth or of preparation.[48] Instead all history centres on Jesus and the only true perspective is a christocentric one; 'Before Abraham was I am' (8.58). In the incarnate Jesus we see the eternal Word who was 'in the beginning' and through whom was creation itself. The only value of the past is that it points to Jesus and for this reason the author can use the imagery of the Hellenistic world as readily as that of the Jewish; Jesus fulfills all the aspirations and religious ideals of both Jew and Greek.

Thus the alienation of Jesus and his disciples from the world does not lead to an alienation from the past, for the past can be seen to find its true meaning in Jesus, and in Jesus alone. This means that history and past experience are never self-explanatory; the Scriptures are in vain if it is supposed that there is life in them independent of Jesus (5.39), and in failing to see their true import the Jews are repudiating and are repudiated by their own past (5.39,45–47; 7.19–24).[49]

So too, although there is for believers a future, a time of doing greater things (14.12) and of being led in all truth and being told of what is to come by the Spirit (14.26; 15.26), the experience of the future never goes beyond Jesus's revelation which is itself complete (14.7,26; 17.6f.).[50]

[47] See P. Borgen, *Bread from Heaven*, NT.S 10, Leiden 1965; C.K. Barrett, 'The Old Testament in the Fourth Gospel', *JThS* 48 (1949) 155–69.

[48] See Bultmann, *Theology*, II, 8.

[49] See M. de Jonge, 'Jewish Expectations', 260, 'If Scripture is not read and interpreted with the centre of Johannine theology as starting-point, one will never discover the truth revealed by God.'

[50] See further pp. 177–8.

We must say again that it is not easy to see how this strong sense of the separateness of the community found actual expression; it must clearly have been a response to their historical experiences and yet neither the difficulties of positing geographical isolation nor the evidence of links with other Christian traditions and the more positive references to mission can be ignored.[51] However, it is striking that this common theme of separateness is expressed differently in the Gospel and in 1 John in a way which cannot be attributed simply to changes of context. It is not only the experience of internal schism which has made 1 John cast the world in such a thoroughly negative role while John keeps open the door for converts from the world to enter the community. Instead it is the underlying theological impulse which is different; for John the world receives its meaning from the coming of Jesus in which there is both the possibility of salvation and yet also the judgement of the world in its refusal to believe; in 1 John the world is separated from those who believe not by the decision for faith but by their antithetical and irreconcilable origins.

3. The Believer and the Community

All that has been said so far points to a concentration on the believer and the community. In 2 and 3 John membership of the community is the focus both of tradition and of truth, while the absence of dialogue together with the use of party language has suggested to us that for these Epistles being a Christian has virtually become a matter of the group that one belongs to, and is only genuinely found within that group. In one sense this

[51] See above nn. 38, 42; R. Brown, ' "Other sheep not of this fold". The Johannine Perspective on Christian Diversity in the Late First Century', *JBL* 97 (1978) 5–22.

could be said of the whole Johannine corpus,[52] but again we are concerned with the expression of this theme in the Epistles and the Gospel.

In the previous two sections we have already discovered that in 1 John it is impossible to speak of either tradition or God's saving activity outside the framework of the community addressed. This is evident in the contrast between 'us' and 'them', between being 'of God' or 'of the world', for that contrast is made manifest in the response to the tradition of the community. *Because* they deny the tradition their departure proved that the schismatics had never belonged to the elect, to 'us'; it is therefore not apostasy (as in Heb 6.4–6) but the revealing of their true colours. Faith is understood in terms of confession rather than as the existential commitment of the believer to Jesus—hence, as often noted, 'to believe' is used alongside 'to confess' in 1 John in contrast to John's use of 'to believe in me/him' or simply 'to believe'.[53] Thus there can be both true and false confession and confession is given an institutional significance which brings faith within the same framework as tradition.[54]

In this way tradition, community, faith and election come together as totally interdependent. Christian belief and election without membership of *this* community are inconceivable, so that even if the language of ecclesiology such as we are familiar with elsewhere in the New Testament is lacking in 1 John, yet the community is always presupposed. The church is more than the sum total of believers for it is the place where the age to come is already manifest, it is here that the light is already

[52] See A. Correll, *Consummatum Est*, London 1958; de Jonge, 'Jewish Expectations', 263.

[53] See above n. 16.

[54] P. Bonnard, 'La première Épître de Jean est-elle johannique?', in *L'Évangile de Jean*, ed. M. de Jonge, 301–5, 303: confession has 'une valeur institutionelle'.

shining while the world, like the darkness, is passing away (2.8,17).

If, then, the community is the place of election, the individual shares in that election more as a status than as an event. God's love is seen in that 'we' are, and are called, children of God (3.1); believers are those who are born—the perfect tense—of God (2.29; 3.9; 4.7; 5.1,4,18). There is no reference to when or how that status was given and little to support the suggestion that the thought of baptism is dominant.[55] The interest is rather in the possession of a status, a status which appears both static and irreversible—once born that birth cannot be denied or undone. The theme is thus used in the service of giving assurance and not—as would be possible (cf. Heb 5.12–14; 1 Cor 3.1f.)—in the service of a call to strive and grow to maturity. Election is a present reality, the blessings of the age to come are experienced here and now. The believer conquers (present) the world (5.4), has passed from death to life (3.14), has eternal life (5.12), and even cannot sin (3.9)—a claim which creates its own problems (cf. 1.8f.), but which is rooted in the certainty that believers possess the benefits of the age to come, one of which must be sinlessness.[56]

This may seem to contradict the statement often made that 1 John exhibits a return to the future eschatology of the primitive church in its references to 'his coming' (2.28; 3.2) and to the day of judgement (4.17).[57] In fact these references, despite their apparent contrast with the Gospel, show no interest in the

[55] Ctr. Nauck, *Tradition und Charakter.*

[56] On this see J.L. Bogart, *Orthodox and Heretical Perfectionism in the Johannine Community as Evident in the first Epistle of John*, SBLDS 33, Missoula 1977, 66–91; see below p. 193.

[57] Dodd, *Epistles*, liii; C.F.D. Moule, 'A neglected Factor in the Interpretation of Johannine Eschatology', in *Studies in John*, NT.S 24, Leiden 1970, 155–60 argues that the Gospel's realised eschatology is appropriate to its individualism while the future eschatology of 1 John is more appropriate to the community; however, in 1 Jn 3.2 the emphasis is on the transformation of the individual.

usual themes of the cosmic significance of the Parousia, of the final vindication of the righteous and of the punishment of sinners, or of the joy of being taken to be with Christ. When he appears 'we' shall be like *him* because we shall see *him* as he is, but this will be no unprecedented transformation inasmuch as we are already God's children—the thought is fluid and might almost seem to point to *God*'s appearing (2.28–3.3).[58] The 'day of judgement' brings no terror because we are already in the sphere of divine love and beyond that of judgement (4.17).[59] Although in 3.2–3 the hope of future transformation exerts some ethical force, the future references do not modify the understanding of present Christian experience as if it were but a foretaste, a 'seeing through the glass darkly', rather they only set a seal on the reality of what is now known and thus reinforce the believer's assurance.

Such an understanding could and did create problems, notably an inability to affirm the reality of sin in believers' lives and their consequent need for forgiveness (1.8ff.).[60] The vocabulary related to sin thus looms larger in 1 John than in the Gospel as the author combats this divorce between Christian experience and the realities of daily living (1.7–2.2; 2.4,9–11), but in the end he fails so to modify his theology as to render impossible such an interpretation. His stress on obedience to the commands—namely the command to mutual love which does have some content in ch. 3—never realises its full potential for accommodating the ethical dimension of the Christian life, and we are left with the impression that his certainty of the election of believers could not easily make room for a moral imperative.[61]

[58] Unless 'ἐὰν φανερωθῇ' should be translated 'if/when it is manifested' although this seems less likely; see the commentaries.

[59] This would seem to be the sense of a difficult passage; see especially Gaugler, *Johannesbriefe*, 247.

[60] See Houlden, *Epistles*, 88–97.

[61] See Lieu, 'Authority to become children of God', 223–4.

It is equally clear that the Fourth Gospel was written for and presupposes the community as created by Jesus and as the locus of truth. A similar strong sense of election is expressed through language which can imply that the elect are predetermined, language which has to be balanced against the more universalist statements. Believers are 'of God' or 'of the truth' (8.47; 18.37), they are the sheep who hear his voice, or 'his own', the proper possession of Jesus (10.3,14,26; 13.1), and it is only because they *are* his own that they can respond to his call. On the other hand those who are not of the truth reject Jesus because they *cannot* respond (8.43–47). This belongs to a wider dualism, to the division between light and darkness, between being 'of the truth' or 'not of the truth', which is neither a moral dualism nor always subsequent to the decision for faith, but which sometimes seems to be responsible for that decision (3.19–21). Although there may be a fundamental difference in conception (see below), there are many echoes of the language of gnosticism,[62] and these statements stand in tension with those that speak more positively of the openness of the world to God and his love.

This sense of election is again reinforced by the realised eschatology of the Gospel. Already the believer has eternal life (3.16f.; 6.47) and has left the realm of death (5.24f.); already Jesus has given them the glory which God had given him (17.22), albeit his glory was expressed through suffering and death. So full assurance is given the believer both of the security of his election (6.37; 10.28) and of the completeness of Jesus's revelation (14.7; 17.6f.), leaving apparently little room for progress or striving.

However, the superficially similar ethos of the Gospel and

---

[62] E.g. *Gospel of Truth* (*N.H.* I.3) 21.25, 'Those whose name he knew in advance he called at the end'; 22.2, 'if one has knowledge, he is from above. If he is called he hears, he answers, and he turns to him who is calling him'. See J.M. Lieu, 'Gnosticism and the Gospel of John', *ET* 90 (1979) 233–7.

First Epistle obscures fundamental differences when it is seen that the Gospel adds other important elements to the picture:

(a) For John election is never the possession of believers but is always an act of God in Jesus. It is because the elect are the gift of God to Jesus (17.6) and not through any inherent status of their own that they enjoy safety. No-one can come to Jesus unless the Father draw him but neither will Jesus turn away or lose any whom God does so draw (6.44,37). The disciples did not choose Jesus but Jesus chose them (13.18; 15.16). There is no ontological relationship between believers and their Redeemer which others do not share so as to make them a predetermined élite; the relationship is a created one and its creator is God.

(b) Language which implies two predestined classes of those who do or who cannot respond is balanced by that which stresses that no-one has a natural propensity towards God. Being chosen involves a complete change of nature, it demands being born again or from above; it is this radical transformation rather than any interest in the status thus achieved which is the primary interest of the Gospel (3.3–8; 1.12–13). Hence, in contrast to 1 John, the Gospel only once (1.13) speaks of being born 'of God', a concept which could lead to ideas of a divine nature (cf. 1 Jn 3.9), and instead speaks of being born again or from above (3.3,7) or of (water and) the Spirit (3.5,6,8). Such language emphasises that the decision for faith is not made on a worldy basis but is the surrender of self to God; it is not a matter of one's nature (φύσις), although in retrospect it may be said that the decision is a reflection of one's identity, whether one is of God or not.[63] Having said this, a passage like 3.19–21 with its implication that some already love darkness rather than light and so will not come to the light, or 8.47 'you cannot hear because you are not of God', cannot be ignored. Similar predeterminist language can be found in Paul (1 Cor 1.18; Rom

[63] See Bultmann, *Theology* II, 23.

8.28–30) and also whenever Christians have sought to emphasise the priority of God in the work of salvation and have pushed that priority back into God's eternal plan or foreknowledge.[64]

(c) Yet decision is necessary and each person is responsible for their own decision. The declarations that the offer of salvation was for the world, for all, show that no-one can have as an excuse for the failure to believe, that the call to faith was not made to him. When such universalist statements are immediately followed by more 'predeterminist' ones this only preserves the primacy of God even in the decision to believe (3.16–21). Decision is fundamental for it is of eschatological significance; it is in the call to faith and in response to that call that judgement lies (3.16f.,36; 6.47), for Jesus is both Judge and Saviour. In this sense John has preserved the eschatological call to repentance of traditional eschatology, while the absence of this theme in 1 John is marked by the absence of the language of 'judgement' (other than the rather different 'day of judgement' in 1 Jn 4.17).

(d) Within this framework the question of apostasy can be dealt with. Jesus can say 'Did I not chose you twelve and yet one of you is a devil?' (6.70). 'In the very nature of Revelation— because it rouses man's resistance—there lies the possibility for the apostasy even of a disciple'.[65] Judas's desertion comes even after the foot-washing in which the disciples are brought into the benefits of Jesus's death and so he remains a prime example of the falling away even from those Jesus had chosen. Neither are the scattering of the disciples before the crucifixion (16.32) or Peter's denial forgotten. It seems possible that John's community had already known schism (6.60–71) and the evangelist has to cope with those whose faith ultimately proves

[64] See H. Conzelmann, *An Outline of the Theology of the New Testament*, London 1969, 252–4.

[65] Bultmann, *Theology* II,43.

inadequate by Johannine standards (8.31ff.); such apostasy never takes Jesus by surprise yet the very attempt to deal with the problem without denying them the epithet 'disciples' points to a recognition of the tension between the two certainties of God's free action and human free response.[66]

The eschatology of the Gospel also emphasises that election has its source and life outside the believer. The ultimate nature of the call to faith is made plain through the realised eschatology, for just as the rejection of Jesus carries with it judgement, so the decision to believe, whose reverse side is election, brings the gifts of the new age. However, even when the decision is made, the believer does not possess life in himself; only God has life in himself and the Son to whom God has given that right (5.26). The few passages of future eschatology are therefore of real theological significance and not simply to be attributed to a redactor's failure or unwillingness to understand the Gospel. The believer is not autonomous through any rebirth, inherent nature, existential act of faith, mysticism or sacramentalism, but still needs to be raised up and this raising up remains an act of Jesus (6.39f.,54; 12.48).[67]

In this way the presence of the eschatological age is not tied to the believer or to the community but to Jesus; it is in Jesus that the new age has come and only in relation to Jesus that it is experienced. The assurance of believers is also christocentrically determined, determined by Jesus's coming and his obedience to his Father (17.1–26). Therefore sin in the Gospel refers to unbelief and as such finds its meaning in relation to Jesus (9.41; 15.22,24), but is not an issue for the believer, whereas in 1 John the 'Johannine' phrase 'to have sin' belongs to the debate about the possibility of sin by would-be members of the community.[68]

---

[66] See further below pp. 212–3.

[67] See Barrett, *Gospel*, 67–70.

[68] So also in 1 Jn 3.8–10 those who sin are said to be children of the devil while this is said of the unbelieving Jews in Jn. 8.44 (cf. the use of

For John it is only in believing in and abiding in Jesus that the believer knows freedom and the gifts of the new age (8.31–35), and there is no talk of the assurance of faith apart from unity with him.

4. The Role of Jesus

Each of the 'soundings' we have made has directed us to this further probe, the attitude to Jesus. Linguistic analysis also points to this as a crucial issue. 3 John is striking for its failure, alone in the New Testament, to make any explicit reference to 'Jesus' or 'Christ'; 'Son' is also absent as are 'Father' and 'Lord', so that only 'God' is used and even here the references are within traditional idioms (v. 11).[69] Although 2 John uses a wider range of vocabulary about Jesus and God, the reference to Jesus Christ the Son in the greeting comes from the traditions of the wider church, possessing both Father and Son in v. 9 echoes 1 John as does the coming of Jesus Christ in flesh in v. 7; the 'teaching of Christ' (v. 9) seems to mean 'our Christian teaching', while it is significant that in v. 4 it is the Father from whom we have received the commandment—it is not rooted in the earthly ministry of Jesus. We are left with a somewhat enigmatic picture of the significance of Jesus for these two Epistles.

Turning to 1 John we are struck by the tension between the oft-noted theocentricity of the Epistle and its stress on the necessity of right belief in Jesus. The believer knows God (4.6–8; 5.20) (but can also claim to *have known* Jesus (2.3–4; 3.6 etc.)),[70] he has fellowship with God (1.3,6), is born of God and is a child of God (2.29; 3.9; 4.7; 5.1,4,18; 3.1,2,10; 5.2) and is therefore 'of

ἀνθρωποκτόνος [murderer] in both contexts, 1 Jn 3.15; Jn 8.44); in 1 Jn 2.29; 3.7,10 righteousness is to be 'done', while in Jn 16.8,10 it is that of which the world is convicted. However, on perfectionism in John see Bogart, *Orthodox and Heretical Perfectionism*, 83–155.

[69] See ch. 3, pp. 107,116.

[70] Although only in the phrase 'known *him*', on which see below.

God' (3.10; 4.4,6; 5.19). Abiding too can be 'in God' and God abides 'in us' (4.12,15,16). The religious imagery is largely that of the Gospel but there is at least a difference in emphasis in that in the Gospel 'abiding' is in Jesus (Jn 6.56; 15.4–7) and knowledge of God is dependent on knowledge of Jesus and his revelation (14.7; 17.3). Similarly in 1 Jn 1.5 God is light while this is said of Jesus in John (1.5ff.; 3.19; 8.12 etc.).[71] The picture is complicated by 1 John's prediliction for the pronoun 'he' (αὐτός), so that abiding is 'in him', knowledge is 'of him', and the commandments are 'his', and while the context sometimes clearly indicates whether 'he' is Jesus (3.6) or God (3.22–4; 5.2,3), most frequently the reference is ambiguous often with arguments from sense contradicting those based on context (2.3–6; 2.27–28; 3.1; 4.13,21).[72] This need not mean that Jesus is being assimilated to the status of God so much as that there is a lack of precision about Jesus's role. This is confirmed by what else is and is not said about Jesus.

That Jesus is the Christ or the Son of God—the two are used as equivalents[73]—and that belief in him as such is essential is the recurring theme of the Epistle (2.22–23; 3.23f.; 4.1–3,15; 5.1,5,10–13). Yet why this should be so and what it means is not clear. Jesus is not linked to the believer's new birth, although he is also the one born of God (5.18),[74] neither is he the giver of

[71] See further Moffatt, *Introduction*, 591; Law, *Tests of Life*, 355–7; Lieu, 'Authority to become children of God', 221–2.

[72] In 2.3–6 the explicit 'love of *God*' may suggest 'he/him' refers to Jesus although in 2.6 Jesus is designated by 'ἐκεῖνος'; in 2.28 '*his* coming' might seem to determine that 'he' in the section is Jesus but 2.29 speaks of having been 'born from *him*' where the reference must be to God (cf. 5.1); the same is true of 3.1 which is inseparable from the problem of 3.2–3, on which see p. 193 and n. 58 above; the emphasis on God in 4.11–16 probably means that 'he' in v. 13 is also God, while the commandment 'from him' in 4.21 may well, in the light of 3.22–4 (?2.3–6), be God.

[73] See de Jonge, 'Variety and Development in Johannine Christology', *Stranger from Heaven*, 193–222, 201–3.

[74] As in the Gospel Jesus is 'υἱός' (son) while disciples/believers are 'τέκνα' (children); ctr. Rom 8.29.

eternal life; that he is not the revealer is signified by the absence in 1 John of the complex of vocabulary which expresses this theme in the Gospel (ascending, descending etc.).[75] His death is efficacious for *our* sins (1.7; 2.2), and he is also our advocate when we confess our sins (2.1), but these themes are not related to each other or given any theological grounding; rather they reflect the particular demands of the Epistle's background. The confessional statements may be important precisely as such: commitment is not so much to the person as to the Christian message which includes such statements about Jesus. The use of the present tense and of the emphatic pronoun 'that one' (ἐκεῖνος) when speaking of Jesus may suggest that it is his present role within the tradition or teaching of the community as an example which is more certain for the author than his historical significance (2.6; 3.3,5,7,16; 4.17).[76]

This should make us hesitate before seeing 1 John as primarily a piece of antidocetic polemic concerned about a proper evaluation of Jesus's incarnate life, death, and resurrection. In fact there is no reference to the major historical moments of his life and no mention of the resurrection. The Epistle has none of the sense which we found in the Gospel that the church still lives now in relation to the events of the life of Jesus, neither does it use the Spirit as a way of understanding the believer's relationship with the risen Jesus. In all, Jesus's role in the life of believers is a remarkably muted one and this is the reverse side of the fundamentally theocentric expression of Christian experience.

It would seem that the relationship with God requires no reflection except for the question of the moral consequences— and even so the main thrust of the letter is the assurance of the reality of that relationship. The individual believer and the community as a whole are determined in the present through

---

[75] See above p. 188 and n. 46.
[76] See Braun, 'Literar-Analyse', 282.

their relationship with God. It is this relationship which is the very meaning of their existence as believers. Jesus, the object of tradition and the means of forgiveness, stands at the beginning of that Christian existence but it is God who inspires its continuity.

The Gospel does of course intend to retell the life of Jesus, but it is not this alone which leads to its greater christocentricity, for through the Gospel form is expressed a conviction, which could also have been expressed in an Epistle, that in Jesus the world was and is confronted with God, even beyond the limits of Jesus's incarnate life, in and beyond the Gospel.[77]

This conviction is expressed first of all in the depiction of Jesus as bringer of salvation. The images of Jesus as light, life, shepherd, resurrection, way and truth together with the reiteration that it is to Jesus that men must come (6.37), his flesh and blood that they must partake of (6.54), in him that they must abide (15.1–10), to the implicit exclusion of all others, these all point to Jesus as the centre of the experience of God. Through his coming and through his death Jesus brings salvation (6.51; 10.15,17f.; 11.50).

Yet this cannot be understood apart from the fact that Jesus reveals and provides a way to the Father (14.6); only by seeing or knowing Jesus is it possible to see or know the Father (8.19; 12.44; 14.7–9). The description of Jesus as the one who comes from and goes to the Father, the ascending-descending group of terms, and the theme of the glory of Jesus—all of which are missing from 1 John—present Jesus as the one true revealer of God.[78] In this way Jesus has a mediating role—as Jesus is related to the Father so is the believer related to Jesus and only through Jesus to God (14.20). The christocentricity of the Gospel points beyond itself to God whom Jesus reveals and makes accessible. It

[77] See also E. Schwiezer, 'Jesus der Zeuge Gottes', in *Studies in John*, 161–8, 168.

[78] Above p. 188 and n. 46.

is here that we find the paradox of equality and subordination which marks John's portrayal of Jesus's relationship to the Father. Jesus's work is God's work, which can lead to language of equality (5.17–18; 10.30), and yet because Jesus's sole purpose is to do *God*'s work there must be an element of subordination (14.28).[79]

However, this does not mean that Jesus's significance comes to an end once he has revealed God to the believer. Abiding in Jesus and his word is always the real essence of the believer's life (8.31; 15.1–10), the believer's life is dependent on Jesus's living (14.19) and the believer can only abide in or be in Jesus, not in God (6.56; 14.20; 15.1–10; but cf. 14.23). In the future, just as during his ministry, there is no merging of Jesus with God. The Gospel thus projects into eternity the work of Christ as revealer so that even beyond the limitations of his earthly ministry Jesus remains the mediator of knowledge and of experience of God.

This is of course the function of the Gospel as a whole as it seeks to answer the problem of how the church should continue to live in relation to the events of the incarnate life of Jesus. It is expressed more specifically through the concept of the Spirit-Paraclete. We have seen how the Spirit, although dependent on Jesus's departure, establishes a continuity with the work of Jesus, being ascribed the same activities, reminding the disciples of Jesus's words, and, by proclaiming what Jesus still says, directing the community to Jesus.[80] Although the Spirit does not figure at all in Jn 17 there is the same note of continuing dependence on Jesus as he prays to the Father both for his disciples and for future

[79] See C.K. Barrett, 'Christocentric or Theocentric? Observations on the Theological Method of the Fourth Gospel', in *La Notion Biblique de Dieu*, ed. J. Coppens, Gembloux 1976, 361–76; idem, ' "The Father is greater than I" (Jo 14,28): Subordinationist Christology in the New Testament', in *Neues Testament und Kirche*, ed. J. Gnilka, Freiburg 1974, 144–59.

[80] See above p. 177; note how both the Paraclete and Jesus are sent, 'convict' the world or men's sin (3.20; 16.8), do not speak 'ἀφ' ἑαυτοῦ', bear witness etc.; cf. Boring, 'Influence of Christian Prophecy'.

generations of believers, although here the completeness of Jesus's task of revelation looms larger. Elsewhere in the Farewell Discourses Jesus talks of his coming again alone (14.19) or with the Father (14.23), to the disciples, in language which appears to go beyond both the resurrection appearances and the coming of the Spirit.[81] Thus the community lives in a dialectical situation of knowing, because of the fullness and finality of Jesus's revelation, and yet still being dependent on the revealer.

In another way the Gospel expresses this by not limiting the meaning of the incarnate life of Jesus to the time of the incarnation. The Gospel can be read on two levels, reflecting the life of Jesus and the experience of the community, so that the story of Jesus as rejected and hated by the world, listened to by the few, gives meaning to the community who, like Jesus, are not of the world and share those same experiences.[82] So too, the Johannine Christ speaks the language of the Johannine kerygma—the historical boundaries have merged without destroying the past. Jesus still speaks and is heard and believed in the kerygma.[83]

Discipleship too belongs not just to Jesus's followers during his earthly ministry but is the pattern for all believers. Peter is called to follow Jesus not at the beginning of the ministry but at its end when he is entrusted with the care of the flock (21.19–22). Following means not just sharing Jesus's destiny here on earth but also sharing in the place he has prepared for them (13.36–14.3) and in his glory (17.24). Because discipleship is, as we have seen, faithfulness to Jesus's word (8.31), every generation of believers is faced with the same demand and the same possibilities as was the first.[84] Moving in a different

[81] See Barrett, *Gospel*, 466, 491f.
[82] However, this can be over-stressed, see below pp. 213–5 and nn. 107ff.
[83] This theme is developed by Mussner, *Historical Jesus*.
[84] See ch. 4, p. 137; see further A. Schulz, *Nachfolgen und Nachahmen: Studien über das Verhältnis der neutestamentlichen Jüngerschaft zur urchristlichen Vorbildethik*, Munich 1962, 161–70.

direction, ch. 17 faces the problem of the unity of the church equally within a christocentric theological framework.[85] The unity of the church is rooted in Jesus' unity with the Father (17.21); ultimately that is a unity which is expressed in love, God's pre-eternal love for Jesus (17.23–26) which extends also to the disciples. Elsewhere in the Gospel there is the Father's love for his Son (3.35; 5.20 etc.), Jesus's love for the Father (14.31), God's love for the disciples (16.27; 14.21,23) as also Jesus's love for them (13.1,34 etc.), and their love for Jesus (14.15,21–24,28), but not their love for God. In this context the command for the disciples to love one another (13.34f.; 15.12,17) belongs to this reciprocal complex of love, the focal point of which is Jesus and which expresses the continuing life of the community and its members in their relationship with God through Jesus.[86] Again we are brought back to a contrast with 1 John where love for each other is given content (1 Jn 3.11–18), is contrasted with love for the world (2.15), and is seen as evidence for, or a corollary of, love for God (4.20–5.2). There God's love for believers is seen in the giving of his Son, for God is love (4.8,16), but Jesus does not play an active or central role in that reciprocal love between God and believers which is at the heart of religious experience (4.7–5.2).

John's own attempt to hold together the reality and significance of the earthly life of Jesus and the continuing presence of the risen Son in the community has led to those tensions which have allowed his picture of Jesus to be labelled both docetic and antidocetic. Jesus is truly human, he can weep and be tired, yet he is almost transparently divine, knowing and speaking of his unity with the Father and facing death not with

---

[85] See Käsemann, *Testament* esp. 56–73.

[86] So also M. Dibelius, 'John 15[13]. Eine Studie zum Traditionsproblem des Johannesevangeliums', in *Festgabe für A. Deissmann*, Tübingen 1927, 168–86; M. Lattke, *Einheit im Wort*, Munich 1975,—Love is 'Ausdruck einer wesentlichen Einheit zwischen Vater, Sohn und den Seinen' (169).

the agony of a Gethsemane but with the words 'Now I am coming to you'. That this picture could be interpreted docetically has often been demonstrated, whether or not it was in the history of the Johannine community.[87] Its origin surely lies in the attempt to keep Jesus at the centre of the continuing life of the community as well as of the story of his earthly ministry.

Conclusion

What then are the results of our soundings? Are the Gospel and Epistles hewn from a common rock to a common pattern, and what can be said about the composition and nature of that rock? Clearly the Gospel and Epistles do have in common not merely a wide range of vocabulary and preferred theological modes of expression, but also a distinctive view of the community and of its members and their relations with those outside. A strong sense of election, of the present possession of the gifts of the age to come, of exclusivism and of alienation from the 'world' outside provides the hallmarks of that distinctive view. These could, and elsewhere have, been given more detail by reference to the consequent understanding of authority, of love and so on. It is equally clear that there is a significant shift of focus between the Gospel and Epistles—and even these latter do not present a complete unity.

It would be possible but wrong to understand this shift simply as the development, but one-sided development, by the First Epistle of the thought of the Gospel.[88] Possible because the Gospel balances realised eschatology with more traditional statements of future hope, a strong sense of election with an emphasis on the individual's responsibility to respond,

[87] See Käsemann, *Testament*.
[88] See further below pp. 207–8 and n. 90.

predeterminism with the universal scope of God's salvation, the world as opposition with the world as the sphere and goal of the mission of the Son, tradition with the creativity of the Spirit, God as the one whom Jesus makes known with Jesus as the only way by which God can be known. In each case it might seem that 1 John holds on to the first member of those partnerships far more firmly than he does the second, that a creative dialectic has been surrendered in the interests of the security of dogmatism and exclusivism. Yet it would be wrong to see the relationship purely in these terms because the fundamental issue to which each of our soundings has led us is that of the christocentricity of the Gospel. Each of the tensions in the Gospel to which we have just referred is held together by the person of Jesus, so that tradition, Spirit, election, response, the world and eschatology have all been seen to receive their definition by reference to Jesus. For John Jesus is not simply the historical figure who stood at the beginning of the tradition, of faith, of knowledge of God or of the eschatological age; tradition is Jesus's word, in one sense Jesus himself, spoken directly to each situation, faith is always centred on Jesus who is alone the way to God, and the eschatological age is experienced only where Jesus is present and is experienced. This focal role is not filled by Jesus in 1 John; rather, it seems to be played by the idea of the community[89]— the community possesses and guarantees the tradition, the community is the sphere of election and also the locus of the eschatological age, faith affirms the tradition of the community, and the world is by definition outside this charmed circle, excluded from mission and from dialogue. This community-centred approach is equally, if not more so, true of the Second

[89] Note how in Jn 16.33 Jesus says he has conquered the world (ἐγὼ νενίκηκα τὸν κόσμον); in 1 Jn 5.4,5 this is said of 'our faith' or of the one who holds the right faith, and in 1 Jn 4.4 it is said 'you have conquered (νενικήκατε) them'. Similarly in Jn 8.35 it is the Son who remains for ever (in 12.34 the Christ) while in 1 Jn 2.17 he who does the will of God remains for ever; it is this sort of difference which makes lists of parallels of language and concept misleading.

and Third Epistles and undoubtedly issued in the situation there reflected.

The common ground with which we started this section suggests that the self-understanding and probably the general context of the community were fundamentally the same throughout; that situation and self-understanding have been sufficiently discussed here and elsewhere not to need detailed repetition at this point. However, if the Johannine Christians did thus have a strong sense of the individual but shared a tightly cohesive self-consciousness, stimulated by or provoking a sense of isolation and rejection, real or imagined, then their theological exponents responded to this context in significantly different ways. We may move from the theological rationale to the probable sociological context being interpreted but we cannot move the opposite way as if only a single theological rationale were possible given a particular sociological setting. Hence a sociological description is important, but it is not a total description. For while the fourth Evangelist builds his theology within an understanding of reality centred on Christ, 1 John makes his response using the community and the believer's experience as his theological interpretative key.

If this fundamental difference of theological focus means that 1 John cannot be interpreted as a (one-sided) development of the theology of the Gospel, neither need it be the next stage in the history of the Johannine community following the Gospel. It has become standard to see the Epistles as subsequent to the Gospel and as carrying the history of the Johannine Christians a step further. Often this means that the conflict and schism reflected in 1 John are traced back to the thought of the Gospel; it is argued that the schismatics developed the 'high' christology of the Gospel so as to lose all touch with the humanity of Jesus, that they pushed the language of realised eschatology and of sinlessness so far that they no longer had any sense of the fact of sin, of moral obligation or of the hope yet to be fulfilled.

Whether this is to be seen as a possible or as a fundamentally mistaken interpretation of the Gospel, the author of 1 John is said to refute them by an appeal to other aspects of the Gospel buttressed by a conservative reaction visible in his future eschatology, his appeal to what was 'from the beginning' and his evaluation of the work and example of Jesus.[90] His silence about the Spirit-Paraclete, always a problem for those who see a close dependence of 1 John on the Gospel, can then be explained by the schismatics' claim to possess that Spirit and by the author's inability to deny that element in the Johannine tradition or to supplement it with alternative understandings of authority. One development of this approach sees the 'high' christology which the schismatics pushed too far not as one aspect of the thought of the Gospel but as the final stage of the christological development of the thought of the Johannine community as it can be traced in the Gospel—history does not begin with the finished Gospel but is visible behind it. To this some would want to add the possibility that the reaction against the heretics is also to be found in redactional additions to the Gospel, namely in the antidocetic, 'ecclesiastical' or 'sacramental' passages (e.g. 1.14; 5.28f.; 6.51b–58).[91]

[90] Bogart, *Orthodox and Heretical Perfectionism*, 135 sees the opponents as misusing the thought of the Gospel while Brown, *Community*, 107 is less willing to commit himself. For the argument generally see Smalley, *1, 2, 3 John*, xxvi–xxx; Houlden, *Epistles*, 11–20 and the articles cited in n. 91.

[91] E.g. U.B. Müller, *Die Geschichte der Christologie in der johanneischen Gemeinde*, Stuttgart 1977; G. Richter, 'Präsentische und futurische Eschatologie im 4 Evangelium', in *Gegenwart und kommendes Reich*, ed. P. Fiedler and D. Zeller, Stuttgart 1975, 117–52; idem, 'Die Fleischwerdung des Logos im Johannesevangelium', *NT* 13 (1971) 81–126; 14 (1972) 257–76. Müller's reconstruction is more complex than that of Richter and whereas the latter sees Jn 1.14 as part of the antidocetic reaction he sees it as stemming from those who stressed the divinity of Jesus as preexistent Son of God. For a summary of Richter's views see A.J. Mattill, jr., 'Johannine Communities behind the Fourth Gospel', *TS* 38 (1977) 294–315; for a different view of the development of Johannine eschatology see M.-É. Boismard, 'L'Évolution du Thème Eschatologique dans les Traditions Johanniques', *RB* 68 (1961) 507–24.

Our analysis suggests that the problem is by no means so simple. There is the obvious danger of reconstructing the views of the heretics from the language and the silences of the Epistles and then using that reconstruction to explain both the language and the silences. We have seen reason to question whether the schismatics made a particular claim to be spirit-filled or held a clearly docetic christology which we are in a position to reconstruct;[92] the same might be said of their eschatology or attitudes to sinlessness, about which the author speaks only in terms of 'he who says' or 'if *we* say'.[93] Yet if we cannot reconstruct the heretics from the Epistle, neither can we then relate them to the Gospel. Moreover the author's own attitude to the significance of Jesus, to the possibility of sinlessness and to ways in which a realised eschatology is to be qualified is at the least ambivalent. In addition, the apparent total lack of impact which the Gospel's teaching about the Spirit-Paraclete and its thorough christocentricity have made on the thought of the Epistle remains a major problem for those who see the two in simple continuity. Leaving aside the question of the nature and origin of the views of the schismatics, K. Grayston has some grounds for suggesting that the First Epistle can be read as a first attempt at a response, with the Gospel as a more polished and creative answer.[94]

Yet there are points at which it does seem that the thought of I John is closely related to and even secondary to if not derived from that of the Gospel. The 'old—yet new-ness' in 1 Jn 2.7–8 of what in Jn 13.34 is a 'new' commandment is a prime example. Can 1 John's use of 'word' and 'from the beginning', especially in 1.1–4, be understood without reference to the language and thought of the Gospel's prologue despite the shift in meaning?

[92] See above ch. 3, pp. 80–2.

[93] On this and what follows see Lieu, 'Authority to become children of God'.

[94] Grayston, *Epistles*, 9–14.

The same might be asked of the other parallels in language, of the use of 'world' (κόσμος), or of the theme of 'having sin'.[95] Perhaps our problem is that the shifts in meaning, some of which are fundamental matters of perspective, combined with the close similarities in language and concept, are on any account difficult to explain, and we are often guided by preconceived ideas as to whether the more limited outlook of 1 John is to be portrayed as decline or as a preparatory stage.

Part of the answer—and of the problem—must lie in the acknowledged complexity of the origins and development of the Gospel. On the simplest level we may ask whether the links 1 John has with the Gospel are not in reality links with the community traditions behind the Gospel, some of which no doubt continued concurrent with the Gospel. An examination of hypotheses suggesting a relationship between redactional passages in the Gospel and the Epistles or their setting further illustrates the complexity of Johannine tradition.

As already mentioned, some have seen in the so-called antidocetic or sacramental passages of the Gospel signs of a redactor's hand, editing the Gospel in opposition to the heretics we meet behind 1 John, who had developed their views from the Gospel.[96] Other scholars have taken this approach further and have seen within the Gospel evidence of more substantial redaction or of consecutive layers of tradition; literary distinctiveness and new theological interests, often showing affinity with the thought of the Epistles, are held to indicate a new hand and a new context from that of the rest of the Gospel.[97] It is the Farewell Discourses which have proved the most fertile ground for such analysis, containing as they do clear

---

[95] See above pp. 146,197, and the comment above at n. 89.

[96] Above n. 91; see also Donfried, 'Ecclesiastical Authority', 333.

[97] J. Becker, 'Abschiedsreden'; idem, 'Aufbau, Schichtung und theologiegeschichtliche Stellung des Gebets in Joh 17', *ZNW* 60 (1969) 56–83; H. Thyen, 'Entwicklungen'; idem, 'Johannes 13'; J.L. Boyle, 'The Last

signs of a composite origin (14.31), although both these and the affinities with 1 John may be attributable to the origin of the Farewell Discourses in addresses to the community.

Upon examination many of the supposed parallels with the thought of the Epistles hide fundamental differences of approach. Certainly 1 John need not be interpreted as antidocetic, it has little interest in the sacraments, and the vocabulary of its future expectation is different from that of the Gospel, giving us no grounds for identifying the redaction of the Gospel with the concerns of the Epistles.[98] We have already seen that the interest in the command of mutual love in Jn 15 and 13.34f., although peculiar to these passages in the Gospel, cannot be assigned, as has been suggested, to a redactor *on the basis of* the importance of the theme in 1 John, because the Epistle presupposes and develops that theme as part of the tradition of the community.[99] Jn 17 and 15.18–16.15 have been characterised as redactional on the grounds that they share with 1 John an orientation towards the fact of salvation and towards

Discourses (Jn.13,31–16,33) and Prayer (Jn.17): Some observations on their Unity and Development', *Bib.* 56 (1975) 210–22; J. Painter, 'The Farewell Discourses and the History of Johannine Christianity', *NTS* 27 (1981) 525–43.

[98] So rightly Klein, 'Das wahre Licht' sees that the different eschatological terminology prohibits identifying the redactor of the Gospel with the author of 1 John (ctr. Becker, 'Aufbau', 82–3). 1 Jn 5.6f. is not unambiguous evidence for a sacramental interest in 1 John and may be dependent on Jn 19.34–5 rather than evidence that this passage is directed to the same situation and hence is redactional (ctr. Thyen, 'Entwicklungen', 286–8); unlike Jn 20.19–21; 21 there is no interest in the college of the 12 in 1 John and the means of forgiveness is viewed differently (ctr. Thyen, 'Entwicklungen', 291f.). Neither can the eyewitness theme of 1 John be associated with that theme and the associated theme of the Beloved Disciple in the Gospel so as to establish their place there as redactional (so Thyen, 'Entwicklungen', 274, 285ff.; M. de Jonge, 'The Beloved Disciple and the date of the Gospel of John', in *Tradition and Interpretation*, ed. Best and McL. Wilson, 99–114); there is no echo of the Beloved Disciple in 1 John.

[99] See above pp. 74–5 and ctr. Thyen, 'Johannes 13', 354; Becker, 'Abschiedsreden', 220, 233–4.

the revelation brought by Jesus which can be designated by 'truth';[100] but this is to ignore both the dualistic use of 'truth' in I John and the absence of Jesus's role as Revealer there, indeed to ignore that christocentricity which is a continuing theme even in these passages of the Gospel but which is absent from the Epistle.[101] Thus if there are redactional passages in John, or clear signs of subsequent layers of tradition, these can only be established on internal literary and theological grounds and not by appeal to supposed parallels with the Epistles.[102] Yet if this can be done—and some of the arguments for the distinctiveness of these passages may still stand— it will only illustrate the complexity and multiformity of the Johannine tradition and the history behind it.

That I John stands later in this tradition is often argued on the grounds that it is born out of a schism within the community of which the Gospel knows nothing; in contrast, the Gospel is said to face an external opposition rooted in the conflict with the Synagogue, a conflict which has left no traces in the Epistle. Yet while the hostility shown towards 'the Jews' in the Gospel undoubtedly reflects past conflict with the Synagogue, that conflict has by the time of the writing of the Gospel become the subject of reflection and interpretation.[103] Moreover, the Gospel does manifest a concern for unity (ch. 17) and does recognise the problem of apostasy and of inadequate belief (6.60f.,66; 8.31ff.). Yet even here we may ask whether 6.66 reflects a particular moment within the history of Johannine Christianity, and, if so, does it describe internal schism or the much earlier separation by

[100] So Becker, 'Abschiedsreden', 235f., 239–41; idem, 'Aufbau' 79, 81.

[101] On truth see above p. 69; on Jesus as Revealer see above pp. 200–1.

[102] This is by no means an easy task: note the sharply conflicting interpretations of Jn 1.14 epitomised by Müller and Richter (above n. 91); on Jn 6.51ff. see J. Dunn, 'John VI—A Eucharistic Discourse?', NTS 17 (1970–71) 328–38.

[103] See above nn. 5, 40. The assimilation of the Jews to 'the world' and the lack of reality in the dialogue suggest this.

or from non-Johannine Christians which helped constitute the distinctive Johannine community?[104] In part the answer depends on how far the hand of a redactor is seen in the sacramental teaching of the end of the chapter and also on a prior assumption about the representative role of the Apostles.[105] It may also be that the passage is not to be read purely in a historical-retrospective sense; what is crucial is that those who fall away number among Jesus's disciples; coming to Jesus is dependent on the gift of the Father (6.65), and yet even among the twelve who have been chosen by Jesus one is a devil (6.70). Here the question of apostasy is recognised as a mystery and even for the chosen, the disciples, there is no ultimate safety, at least not in themselves nor in their right belief (6.69, 'We have believed').[106] Once again, it is the fundamental difference of approach of the Gospel from that of 1 John which prevents relating them to each other simply in a chronological framework.

There are wider implications here for the attempt to trace the history of the Johannine community behind the Fourth Gospel. It has become popular to 'excavate' the Gospel in order to trace the community's origins in and eventual break with or exclusion from the Synagogue, to detect the influence of other ('Hellenist') forms of Christianity, the subsequent development of its own theology and its attitude to other Christian or 'semi-Christian' groups. The telling of the Gospel narrative thus becomes a mirror of the community's history, particularly

[104] Thus Brown, *Community*, 74f. sees 6.66f. as referring to Jewish Christians 'who are no longer to be considered true believers because they do not share John's view of the eucharist'; contrast K. Matsunaga, 'Is John's Gospel Anti-Sacramental?', *NTS* 27 (1981) 516–24 who refers the situation to a division within the Johannine church.

[105] Brown, loc. cit., n. 131 defends his interpretation because ch. 6 deals with 'the Jews' and 'the Twelve' whom he sees as representing 'outsider' groups; however, this depends on a particular interpretation of the role of the Twelve which is not without difficulties (see above ch. 4, n. 38).

[106] See above pp. 196–7 and the discussion by E. Haenchen, *John*, Philadelphia 1984, I, 306–8.

where the Gospel deliberately modifies the actual story of Jesus's ministry as we know it from the Synoptics.[107] In the absence of any external 'control',[108] the approach must depend on intrinsic force of argument. Yet here fundamental questions arise: it is of course to be expected that the thought of the Gospel will reflect some of the traditions important to its community, although without determining how they came into it.[109] On the other hand, was the Gospel concerned, even at a subsidiary level, to explain the community's history? If, for example, in 6.66ff. a theological point is being made about the only security of faith lying in its God-givenness, can we draw any confident historical conclusions from the passage either about Jesus's own ministry or about an incident in the background of the Johannine community? This is not to deny that John does reflect the community's own circumstances; it is to question whether those circumstances or past history can be 'read off' directly from distinctively Johannine passages. How indeed are the distinctiveness and the theological tensions of the Gospel to be understood?[110]

When the Gospel is viewed as reflecting the historical development of the community, then apparently conflicting theologies are seen as historically consecutive, the old being

[107] For this as a guide see Brown, *Community*, 20f.; so for example the confession by John the Baptist (Jn 1.15,30), the incident in Samaria (4.4–42) etc.

[108] Much has been made of the identification of the expulsion from the synagogue in 9.22 with the *Birkath-ha-Minim* particularly by Martyn, *History and Theology*; however, this is extremely unlikely, see above n. 44.

[109] Thus Meeks, *Prophet King*, finds links between Samaritan thought and that of the Fourth Gospel.

[110] It might be asked how Martyn's (*History and Theology*, 38–62) 'historical' reading of Jn 9 relates to a purely 'literary' reading (as by J.L. Resseguie, 'John 9: A Literary-Critical Analysis', in *Literary Interpretations of Biblical Narratives*, ed. K. Gros Louis, Nashville 1982, 295–303) or to Haenchen's interpretation (*John II*, 41f.) which sees the author as considerably restricted by his source material.

interpreted by the new by an author who 'thought synthetically, not dialectically'.[111] On the other hand, those who argue for the thorough-going redaction of the Gospel are also responding to those same tensions or 'contradictions' in the thought of the Gospel, although with very different conclusions. Rather than seeing these tensions as reflecting the prehistory of the community, creatively absorbed into a new unity, they ascribe them to the later history of the Gospel, adding an alien note to its original coherent thought.[112] There would seem to be a tendency to expect a monolithic unity, a single coherent pattern of thought which can easily be defined and labelled 'Johannine'. When that is not found appeal is made to subsequent redaction or to prior historical development. The problem of working with such a concept of unity is highlighted when the redactor is dubbed the real Johannine theologian or when multiple redactors are found whose work itself has been subjected to further redaction.[113]

However, this may be to miss the real unity of the Gospel, a unity which is *created* by the tensions or dialectic in its thought and which only thus constitutes its creative theological achievement. The origins of those tensions and of the unity must here be left open for they belong to the detailed study of the Gospel. However, what has become clear from reading the Gospel in the light of the Epistles is that the theological creativity of its response to the situation and to the theological

[111] Brown, *Community*, 52.

[112] So Richter's account of Johannine Christianity (see above n. 91) is essentially a story of disunity both in theology and in fellowship.

[113] Becker (above n. 97) assigns Jn 15.1–17; 15.18–16.16 and 16.16–33 to different hands; 15.3,7 and 15.19b–20a may be later additions while 17.3,12b,16,20f. are subsequent additions to the redactional ch. 17. Thyen sees the 'redactor' as responsible for at least Jn 5.26–9; 6.48–58; 13.12–17,20–6,34–5; 15–17; 21 and the Beloved Disciple passages; thus he is the characteristic Johannine theologian who reinterpreted a homogeneous *Grundschrift* and who merits the title 'the Fourth Evangelist' ('Entwicklungen', 267).

traditions of the community lies in the dialectic of its thought and in the way that that dialectic is mediated through and finds its resolution in the person of Jesus.

If 1 John made a fundamentally different response, 2 and 3 John stand in its wake. Here, as we have seen, there can be little question of 2 John's dependence on the First Epistle if not also on 3 John. Both Epistles may also know the Gospel or at least some of the material within it, although they are not moulded by its theology.[114] Perhaps, indeed, not all understood the Fourth Gospel and it needed a seal of approval (21.24) even within its own community. They bear witness to how, when not controlled by being tightly tied to the presence of Christ, the fundamental tendencies of Johannine thought could develop in ways which would never be creative. We may not be able to exclude the possibility that *historically* with 2 and 3 John Johannine theology followed a 'no through road', although that is again to leave unanswered the question of the survival of the various members of the Johannine corpus and their eventual acceptance by the wider church. The historical conclusion demands theological reflection. Standing within the canon do not 2 and 3 John bear witness that the ultimate test of any theology, faith, authority or even of the canon itself is that they bear witness to Christ alone?

---

[114] On the possible influence of Jn 10.18 on 2 Jn 4 see above ch. 3, p. 72; on the relationship between Jn 21.24 and 3 Jn 12 see ch. 3, p. 120; little can be made of the use of 'παρά' by John and by 2 John but not by 1 John (although see above p. 188). The confession of 2 Jn 7 may be influenced by the Gospel's description of Jesus (see ch. 3, p. 86).

Appendix I

TABLES

(1) 2 and 3 John*

A. VOCABULARY OCCURRING IN 2 JOHN, NOT IN 1 OR 3 JOHN

Word	2 John	John	Notes
(a) From epistolary opening and conclusion			
κυρία	2	0	See pp. 42, 65–6.
ἐκλεκτός	2	(1.34, v.l. of Jesus)	Usually in plural of Christians but cf. Rom 16.13. See p. 67.
χάρτης	1	0	
ἀδελφή	1	6 (literal)	In N.T. used literally or of fellow Christians. See p. 99.
χάρις	1	1.14,16,17	N.B. use in Pauline greetings. (v.l. in 3 Jn 4. See Table C).
ἔλεος	1	0	N.B. use in greetings of 1, 2 Tim and Jude. See p. 46–7.
παρά	3	33	See p. 60.
(b) From the rest of the letter			
εὑρίσκω	1	19	
πλάνος	2	0	Mt 27.63; 2 Cor 6.8; N.B. 1 Tim 4.1 (adj.). See p. 83.
βλέπω	1	17	⎫
ἀπόλλυμι	1	10	⎬ *Reward.* See pp. 88–9.
μισθός	1	4.36	⎪
πλήρης	1	1.14	⎭
ἀπολαμβάνω	1	0	Mk: 1; Lk: 5; Paul: 3.
προάγω	1	0	See pp. 91–3. In N.T. with chronological or temporal priority.

*The following lists, excepting B(e), are comprehensive.

Word	2 John	John	Notes
διδαχή	3	7.16,17; 18.19	See pp. 94, 171.
φέρω	1	17	
οἰκία	1	5	
κοινωνέω	1	0	See p. 97 (cf. κοινωνία: Jn: 0; 1 Jn: 4; 2 and 3 Jn: 0).

The only word which 2 John shares with 1 John but which does not occur in John or 3 John is ἀντίχριστος—2 Jn 7; 1 Jn 2.18,22; 4.3. See p. 79.

B. VOCABULARY OCCURRING IN 3 JOHN, NOT IN 1 OR 2 JOHN

Word	3 John	John	Notes
(a) From epistolary framework			
εὔχομαι	1	0	Acts: 2, Paul: 3, Jas: 1. See p. 43.
εὐοδόομαι	2	0	Paul: 2. See p. 43, 102.
ὑγιαίνω	1	0	Lk: 3, Pastorals: 8. See p. 43.
καλῶς	1	4 (not 'please')	Common in N.T. See p. 40.
κάλαμος	1	0	Not meaning 'pen' in N.T.
(b) Ecclesiastical and missionary terms			
ἐκκλησία	3	0	Common in Paul and Acts, not in 1,2 Peter or Jude. See p. 105.
προπέμπω	1	0	Acts: 3, Paul: 4, Titus: 1. Only Polycarp in Apos. Fathers. See pp. 106–7.
συνεργός	1	0	Paul only (12). See p. 107.
ἐθνικός	1	0	Matthew only (3). See p. 108.
ξένος	1	0	Mt, Acts, Paul, Heb, 1 Peter.
ὑπολαμβάνω	1	0	Not meaning 'to help' in N.T.
τοιοῦτος	1	4.23; 9.16	Well distributed in N.T.
ἐκβάλλω	1	2.15; 6.37; 10.4; 12.31; N.B. 9.34f.	Often in Gospels of exorcisms; not 'to excommunicate'. See p. 114.

Word	3 John	John	Notes
κωλύω	1	0	Well distributed in N.T.
ἐπιδέχομαι	2	0	Hap. Leg. in N.T. and Apos. Fathers.
φιλοπρωτεύω	1	0	New word, noun in Plutarch. See p. 111.
φλυαρέω	1	0	Hap. Leg. in N.T., noun in 1 Tim 5.13.
φίλος	2	3.29; 11.11; 19.12; N.B. 15.13–15.	Esp. Luke–Acts. See pp. 42,122.

(c) Ethical terms

Word	3 John	John	Notes
ἀγαθός	1	1.46; 5.29; 7.12	Common in N.T. See p. 116–7.
ἀγαθοποιέω	1	0	Mk, Lk, 1 Peter. Use in 3 John is closest to 1 Peter. See p. 117.
κακός	1	18.23,30	Common in N.T. See p. 116–7.
κακοποιέω	1	0	Mk, Lk, 1 Peter. Always in contrast to ἀγαθοποιέω. See p. 117.
ἀξίως	1	0	Paul only (inc. Eph). For ἀξίως τοῦ θεοῦ see 1 Thess 2.12. See p. 107.
μιμέομαι	1	0	2 Thess 3.7,9; Heb 13.7. See p. 117.

(d) Others

Word	3 John	John	Notes
ἀρκέομαι (passive)	1	2 (active)	Not significant.
εὐθέως	1	3	Not significant.
μειζότερος	1	0	John uses μειζων. μειζότερος may be a sign of the vernacular.
ἐμός	1	37	Rest of N.T.: 35. Cf. B.D. §285 as Asia Minor Koine.
ὑπομιμνήσκω	1	14.26	Lk, Pastorals, 2 Peter, Jude.
θέλω	1	23	Not significant.
οὖν	1	194	Frequency in narrative in John may explain its absence from 1 John.

(e) *The following omissions should be noted*

Word	John	1 John	2 John	Notes
Ἰησοῦς	239	12	2	Only N.T. book not to have it.
Χριστός	19	9	3	See p. 107.
πατήρ	137 (God: 123)	14 (God: 12)	4	
υἱός	56 (Jesus: 43)	22	2	
ἀρχή	8	8	2	See pp. 75–6.
ἐντολή	11	14	4	See pp. 72–6.
μένω	40	23	3	

The only word 3 John shares with 1 John, which does not occur in John or 2 John is ἀγαπητός—1 John (6), 3 John (4).

C. VOCABULARY SHARED BY 2 AND 3 JOHN AND ABSENT FROM 1 JOHN

Word	2 Jn	3 Jn	John	Notes
πρεσβύτερος	1	1	(8.9)	In N.T. usually plural. See pp. 52–64.
εἰρήνη	1	1	14.27; 16.33; 20.19,21,26	N.B. use in Pauline greetings, see pp. 46–48.
χαίρω				
(i) to greet	2	0	(not 'to greet')	See Jas 1.1; Acts 15.23.
(ii) to rejoice	1	1		See Lk 23.8. See pp. 39–40.
μέλας	1	1		Only 2 Cor 3.3 meaning 'ink'. In parallel phrase in 2 and 3 John.
ἐλπίζω	1	1	5.45	Well distributed in N.T.
στόμα	2	2	19.29	In parallel phrases in 2 and 3 John.
ἀσπάζομαι	1	2		Epistolary use in Paul, Heb 13.24; 1 Pet 5.13f. See pp. 39,41–2.
ἐργάζομαι	1	1	8	See pp. 88–9 on use in 2 John.

Word	2 Jn	3 Jn	John	Notes
χάρις	1	(1)	1.14,16,17	N.B. use in Pauline greetings. See p. 104 (v. l. in 3 John.)

2 and 3 John share no vocabulary with 1 John which does not occur in John.

(2) John and the Epistles

D. SIGNIFICANT VOCABULARY IN JOHN MISSING FROM 1 JOHN

Word	John	1 Jn	2 Jn	3 Jn	Notes
παρά	24 + gen. 9 + dat.	0	3	0 + gen	1 John uses ἀπό. See p. 216.
(κρίσις	11	1	0	0)	Judgement. See p. 196.
κρίνειν	19	0	0	0	(N.B. κρίνειν Rom: 18, Gal: 1)
κρῖμα	1	0	0	0	
γράφειν*	10(21)	0(13)	0(2)	0(3)	Old Testament/Law. See p. 181–2.
γραφή	12	0	0	0	
νόμος	14	0	0	0	(N.B. νόμος Rom: 72, 2 Cor: 0).
ἀναβαίνειν*	5(16)	0	0	0	Mission of Jesus from Above. See p. 188
καταβαίνειν*	9(17)	0	0	0	
ἄνωθεν*	4(5)	0	0	0	
ἄνω*	1(3)	0	0	0	
οὐρανός	19	0	0	0	
ὑψοῦν	5	0	0	0	
δόξα	18	0	0	0	
δοξάζω	23	0	0	0	

*With theological significance; total use in brackets

E. VOCABULARY WITH CHANGING IMPORTANCE IN THE EPISTLES

Word	John	1 Jn	2 Jn	3 Jn	Notes
ἱλασμός	0	2	0	0	*Sin etc.* See p. 193. ἱλασμός is a hapax legomenon in N.T.
ἀνομία	0	2	0	0	
ἁμαρτία	17	17	0	0	
ἁμαρτάνειν	3	10	0	0	
δίκαιος ..	3	6	0	0	
δικαιοσύνη	2	3	0	0	
καθαρίζω	0	2	0	0	
ἁγνός	0	1	0	0	John uses ἅγιος and ἁγνίζω.
ψεύδομαι	0	1	0	0	*Falsehood and Truth.* See p. 69.
ψεῦδος	1	2	0	0	
ψεύστης	2	5	0	0	ψευδοπροφήτης Jn: 0, 1 Jn: 1, 2 Jn: 0.
ἀλήθεια	25(4)°	9(1)°	5(3)°	6(3)°	° ἐν ἀληθείᾳ.
ἀγάπη	7(6)*	18	2	1	*Love and the Love-command.* See pp. 72–8.
ἀγαπᾶν	36(25)*	28	2	1	
φιλεῖν	13(3)*	0	0	0	*Use in John 13–17.
ἀγαπητός	0	6	0	4	
φίλος	6(3)*	0	0	2	
ἐντολή	11(7)*	14	4	0	
τηρέω	18(12)†	7(6)†	0	0	†with λόγος, ἐντολή. Rev: 11.
φῶς	22	6	0	0	
σκοτία, σκότος	8, 1	6, 1	0	0	On dualism see p. 69.
πνεῦμα	23	12	0	0	See pp. 174–5.

Appendix II

TEXT AND PARALLELS

The text given is that of the Nestle-Aland 26th Edition (Stuttgart, 1979), and is arranged in the lefthand column along lines influenced by the discourse analysis of J.A.du Rand in *Studies in the Johannine Literature, Neotestamentica* 13 (1981). * indicates words occuring only here in the Johannine literature, while † indicates hapax legomena in the New Testament (including the Johannine literature).

In the second column parallels are given from the Gospel and other Epistles of John. Full discussion of these parallels may be found at the page references given. However, when they are seen in terms of the whole Epistle, the distinctive content of each becomes clear as does also the tension between similarity and difference within the 'parallels'. The overall effect is to stress the distinctive contribution made by 2 John as well as its imitative nature, while the independent content and vocabulary of 3 John is equally sharply highlighted.

2 John

1 ὁ πρεσβύτερος
ἐκλεκτῇ* κυρίᾳ† καὶ τοῖς τέκνοις αὐτῆς,
οὓς ἐγὼ ἀγαπῶ ἐν ἀληθείᾳ,
καὶ οὐκ ἐγὼ μόνος
ἀλλὰ καὶ πάντες οἱ ἐγνωκότες τὴν ἀλήθειαν,

ὁ πρεσβύτερος
Γαΐῳ....
ὃν ἐγὼ ἀγαπῶ ἐν ἀληθείᾳ. 3 Jn 1

(οὐκ)οἴδατε τὴν ἀλήθειαν ... 1 Jn 2.21
καὶ γνώσεσθε τὴν ἀλήθειαν, Jn 8.32 (p. 68)

2 διὰ τὴν ἀλήθειαν τὴν μένουσαν ἐν ἡμῖν
καὶ μεθ' ἡμῶν ἔσται εἰς τὸν αἰῶνα.

3 ἔσται μεθ' ἡμῶν χάρις ἔλεος* εἰρήνη
παρὰ θεοῦ πατρὸς
καὶ παρὰ Ἰησοῦ Χριστοῦ τοῦ υἱοῦ τοῦ πατρὸς
ἐν ἀληθείᾳ καὶ ἀγάπῃ.

4 ἐχάρην λίαν ὅτι
εὕρηκα ἐκ τῶν τέκνων σου περιπατοῦντας ἐν
ἀληθείᾳ,
καθὼς ἐντολὴν ἐλάβομεν παρὰ τοῦ πατρός.

ἐχάρην γὰρ λίαν ἐρχομένων ... 3 Jn 3
τὰ ἐμὰ τέκνα ἐν τῇ ἀληθείᾳ περιπατοῦντα 3 Jn 4
(p. 104)
καθὼς σὺ ἐν ἀληθείᾳ περιπατεῖς. 3 Jn 3
ταύτην τὴν ἐντολὴν ἔλαβον παρὰ τοῦ πατρός
μου. Jn 10.18 (pp. 72,77)

5   καὶ νῦν ἐρωτῶ σε, κυρία,†
οὐχ ὡς ἐντολὴν καινὴν γράφων σοι
ἀλλὰ ἣν εἴχομεν ἀπ' ἀρχῆς,
ἵνα ἀγαπῶμεν ἀλλήλους.

  οὐκ ἐντολὴν καινὴν γράφω ὑμῖν ἀλλ' ... ἣν
εἴχετε ἀπ' ἀρχῆς ... πάλιν ἐντολὴν καινὴν
γράφω ὑμῖν, 1 Jn 2.7–8 (p. 74–6)
ἵνα ἀγαπῶμεν ἀλλήλους, 1 Jn 3.11 (cf. 4.7)
ἵνα ἀγαπᾶτε ἀλλήλους, Jn 13.34 (pp. 73–4,77)

6   καὶ αὕτη ἐστὶν ἡ ἀγάπη,
ἵνα περιπατῶμεν κατὰ τὰς ἐντολὰς αὐτοῦ·
αὕτη ἡ ἐντολή ἐστιν,
καθὼς ἠκούσατε ἀπ' ἀρχῆς,
ἵνα ἐν αὐτῇ περιπατῆτε.

  αὕτη γάρ ἐστιν ἡ ἀγάπη τοῦ θεοῦ, ἵνα τὰς
ἐντολὰς αὐτοῦ τηρῶμεν, 1 Jn 5.3 (p. 76)

ἡ ἀγγελία ἣν ἠκούσατε ἀπ' ἀρχῆς, ἵνα ... (cf.
above). 1 Jn 3.11 (cf. 2.24) (pp. 75,174)

7   ὅτι πολλοὶ πλάνοι* ἐξῆλθον εἰς τὸν κόσμον,
οἱ μὴ ὁμολογοῦντες Ἰησοῦν Χριστὸν ἐρχόμενον
ἐν σαρκί·
οὗτός ἐστιν ὁ πλάνος* καὶ ὁ ἀντίχριστος

  ὅτι πολλοὶ ψευδοπροφῆται ἐξεληλύθασιν εἰς τὸν
κόσμον. 1 Jn 4.1
πᾶν πνεῦμα ὃ ὁμολογεῖ Ἰησοῦν Χριστὸν ἐν
σαρκὶ ἐληλυθότα ... ὃ μὴ ὁμολογεῖ τὸν
Ἰησοῦν ... 1 Jn 4.2–3
τοῦτό ἐστιν τὸ τοῦ ἀντιχρίστου, 1 Jn 4.3
οὗτός ἐστιν ὁ ἀντίχριστος, 1 Jn 2.22 (pp. 78–87)

8   βλέπετε ἑαυτούς,
ἵνα μὴ ἀπολέσητε ἃ εἰργασάμεθα
ἀλλὰ μισθὸν πλήρη ἀπολάβητε.*

9 πᾶς ὁ προάγων*
καὶ μὴ μένων ἐν τῇ διδαχῇ τοῦ Χριστοῦ θεὸν
οὐκ ἔχει·
ὁ μένων ἐν τῇ διδαχῇ,
οὗτος καὶ τὸν πατέρα καὶ τὸν υἱὸν ἔχει.

πᾶς ὁ ἀρνούμενος τὸν υἱὸν
οὐδὲ τὸν πατέρα ἔχει,
ὁ ὁμολογῶν τὸν υἱὸν
καὶ τὸν πατέρα ἔχει. 1 Jn 2.23 (pp. 90–1)

10 εἴ τις ἔρχεται πρὸς ὑμᾶς
καὶ ταύτην τὴν διδαχὴν οὐ φέρει,
μὴ λαμβάνετε αὐτὸν εἰς οἰκίαν
καὶ χαίρειν αὐτῷ μὴ λέγετε·

11 ὁ λέγων γὰρ αὐτῷ χαίρειν
κοινωνεῖ* τοῖς ἔργοις αὐτοῦ τοῖς πονηροῖς.

12 πολλὰ ἔχων ὑμῖν γράφειν
οὐκ ἐβουλήθην διὰ χάρτου† καὶ μέλανος,
ἀλλὰ ἐλπίζω γενέσθαι πρὸς ὑμᾶς
καὶ στόμα πρὸς στόμα λαλῆσαι,
ἵνα ἡ χαρὰ ἡμῶν πεπληρωμένη ᾖ.

πολλὰ εἶχον γράψαι σοι
ἀλλ᾽ οὐ θέλω διὰ μέλανος καὶ
καλάμου σοι γράφειν·
ἐλπίζω δὲ εὐθέως σε ἰδεῖν,
καὶ στόμα πρὸς στόμα λαλήσομεν. 3 Jn 13–14
(p. 41)
ἵνα ἡ χαρὰ ἡμῶν ᾖ πεπληρωμένη. 1 Jn 1.4
ἵνα ἡ χαρὰ ὑμῶν ᾖ πεπληρωμένη. Jn 16.24 (cf.
15.11, 17.13; 3.29) (p. 99)

13 ἀσπάζεταί σε τὰ τέκνα τῆς ἀδελφῆς σου τῆς
ἐκλεκτῆς.

ἀσπάζονταί σε οἱ φίλοι. 3 Jn 15 (pp. 41–2)

3 John

1 ὁ πρεσβύτερος   ὁ πρεσβύτερος
  Γαΐῳ τῷ ἀγαπητῷ,   ἐκλεκτῇ κυρίᾳ . . .
  ὃν ἐγὼ ἀγαπῶ ἐν ἀληθείᾳ.   οὓς ἐγὼ ἀγαπῶ ἐν ἀληθείᾳ, 2 Jn 1

2 ἀγαπητέ, περὶ πάντων εὔχομαί* σε
  εὐοδοῦσθαι* καὶ ὑγιαίνειν,*
  καθὼς εὐοδοῦταί* σου ἡ ψυχή.

3 ἐχάρην γὰρ λίαν   ἐχάρην λίαν ὅτι εὕρηκα . . . 2 Jn 4 (p. 39)
  ἐρχομένων ἀδελφῶν
  καὶ μαρτυρούντων σου τῇ ἀληθείᾳ,   περιπατοῦντας ἐν ἀληθείᾳ, (cf. below)
  καθὼς σὺ ἐν ἀληθείᾳ περιπατεῖς·

4 μειζοτέραν† τούτων οὐκ ἔχω χαράν,
  ἵνα ἀκούω
  τὰ ἐμὰ τέκνα ἐν τῇ ἀληθείᾳ περιπατοῦντα.   ἐκ τῶν τέκνων σου περιπατοῦντας ἐν ἀληθείᾳ,
      2 Jn 4 (p. 104)

5 ἀγαπητέ, πιστὸν ποιεῖς
  ὃ ἐὰν ἐργάσῃ εἰς τοὺς ἀδελφοὺς καὶ τοῦτο
   ξένους,*

227

6 οἳ ἐμαρτύρησάν σου τῇ ἀγάπῃ ἐνώπιον ἐκκλησίας,*
οὓς καλῶς ποιήσεις
προπέμψας* ἀξίως⁵ τοῦ θεοῦ.

7 ὑπὲρ γὰρ τοῦ ὀνόματος ἐξῆλθον
μηδὲν λαμβάνοντες ἀπὸ τῶν ἐθνικῶν.*

8 ἡμεῖς οὖν ὀφείλομεν ὑπολαμβάνειν* τοὺς τοιούτους,
ἵνα συνεργοὶ* γινόμεθα τῇ ἀληθείᾳ.

9 ἔγραψά τι τῇ ἐκκλησίᾳ*
ἀλλ᾽ ὁ φιλοπρωτεύων† αὐτῶν Διοτρέφης
οὐκ ἐπιδέχεται† ἡμᾶς.

10 διὰ τοῦτο, ἐὰν ἔλθω,
ὑπομνήσω αὐτοῦ τὰ ἔργα
ἃ ποιεῖ λόγοις πονηροῖς φλυαρῶν† ἡμᾶς,⁵
καὶ μὴ ἀρκούμενος ἐπὶ τούτοις
οὔτε αὐτὸς ἐπιδέχεται† τοὺς ἀδελφοὺς
καὶ τοὺς βουλομένους κωλύει*
καὶ ἐκ τῆς ἐκκλησίας* ἐκβάλλει.

11 ἀγαπητέ, μὴ μιμοῦ* τὸ κακὸν ἀλλὰ τὸ ἀγαθόν.
    ὁ ἀγαθοποιῶν* ἐκ τοῦ θεοῦ ἐστιν·
    ὁ κακοποιῶν* οὐχ ἑώρακεν τὸν θεόν.

    πᾶς ὁ ἁμαρτάνων οὐχ ἑώρακεν αὐτὸν οὐδὲ
    ἔγνωκεν αὐτόν ... ὁ ποιῶν τὴν δικαιοσύνην
    δίκαιός ἐστιν ... πᾶς ὁ μὴ ποιῶν δικαιοσύνην
    οὐκ ἔστιν ἐκ τοῦ θεοῦ ... 1 Jn 3.6,7,10 (p. 116)

12 Δημητρίῳ μεμαρτύρηται ὑπὸ πάντων καὶ ὑπὸ
    αὐτῆς τῆς ἀληθείας·
    καὶ ἡμεῖς δὲ μαρτυροῦμεν,
    καὶ οἴδας ὅτι
    ἡ μαρτυρία ἡμῶν ἀληθής ἐστιν.

    οὗτός ἐστιν ὁ μαθητὴς ὁ μαρτυρῶν περὶ τούτων
    καὶ ὁ γράψας ταῦτα, καὶ οἴδαμεν ὅτι ἀληθὴς
    αὐτοῦ ἡ μαρτυρία ἐστίν. Jn 21.24 (p. 120)

13 πολλὰ εἴχον γράψαι σοι
    ἀλλ᾽ οὐ θέλω διὰ μέλανος καὶ καλάμου* σοι
    γράφειν·

    πολλὰ ἔχων ὑμῖν γράφειν
    οὐκ ἐβουλήθην διὰ χάρτου καὶ μέλανος;

14 ἐλπίζω δὲ εὐθέως σε ἰδεῖν,
    καὶ στόμα πρὸς στόμα λαλήσομεν.

    ἀλλὰ ἐλπίζω γενέσθαι πρὸς ὑμᾶς καὶ στόμα πρὸς
    στόμα λαλῆσαι ... 2 Jn 12 (p. 41)

15 εἰρήνη σοι.
    ἀσπάζονταί σε οἱ φίλοι.
    ἀσπάζου τοὺς φίλους κατ᾽ ὄνομα.

    ἀσπάζεται σε τὰ τέκνα τῆς ἀδελφῆς σου ...
    2 Jn 13 (p. 41)

BIBLIOGRAPHY

1. TEXTS AND SOURCES

Note: In Chapter One full references are given to Patristic sources as many of these may be unfamiliar to readers; in subsequent chapters only sources being cited for the first time and those which are less easily accessible are given with details of edition etc. The index of Ancient Authors and Sources can be used to locate the first reference to any work. For the text of the New Testament and for the Apostolic Fathers the following editions have been used.

ed. K. Aland et al., *Novum Testamentum Graece* post Eberhard Nestle et Erwin Nestle, 26th edition, Stuttgart 1979. (This is the text cited.)

ed. H. v. Soden, *Die Schriften des Neuen Testaments*, I *Untersuchungen*, Berlin 1900–10, II *Texte*, Göttingen 1913.

ed. C. Tischendorf, *Novum Testamentum Graece*, editio octava critica maior, Leipzig 1869–94.

ed. B.F. Westcott and F.J. Hort, *The New Testament in the Original Greek*, Cambridge and London 1881.

ed. G. Horner, *The Coptic Version of the New Testament in the Southern Dialect*, vol. 7, *The Catholic Epistles and Apocalypse*, Oxford 1924.

ed. J. Gwynn, *Remnants of the Later Syriac Versions of the Bible*, London and Oxford 1909.

ed. W. Thiele, *Epistulae Catholicae, Vetus Latina: Die Reste der Altlateinischen Bibel* 26/1, Freiburg 1956–69.

J.B. Lightfoot, *The Apostolic Fathers*, revised edition, London 1889–90. (For Clement, Ignatius and Polycarp.)

ed. W. Rordorf and A. Tuilier, *La Doctrine des Douze Apôtres (Didachè)*, SC 248, Paris 1978.

ed. M. Whittaker, Hermas, *Pastor*, GCS 48², Berlin 1967.

2. SECONDARY WORKS

A. Works on the Gospel and Epistles of John
Abbott, E.A., *Johannine Grammar*, London 1906.

Barrett, C.K., 'The Old Testament in the Fourth Gospel', *JThS* 48 (1947) 155–69.

——, ' "The Father is greater than I" (Jo 14,28): Subordinationist Christology in the New Testament', in *Neues Testament und Kirche* (für R. Schnackenburg), ed. J. Gnilka, Freiburg 1974, 144–59.

——, 'Christocentric or Theocentric? Observations on the Theological Method of the Fourth Gospel', in *La Notion biblique de Dieu*, ed. J. Coppens, Bibliotheca Ephemeridum Theologicarum Lovaniensium, 41, Gembloux 1976, 361–76.

——, *The Gospel according to St. John*, 2nd edition, London 1978.

Bartlet, V., 'The Historical Setting of the Second and Third Epistles of St. John', *JThS* 6 (1905) 204–16.

Becker, J., 'Aufbau, Schichtung und theologiegeschichtliche Stellung des Gebetes in Joh.17', *ZNW* 60 (1969) 56–83.

——, 'Die Abschiedsreden Jesu im Johannesevangelium', *ZNW* 61 (1970) 215–46.

Belser, J.E., *Die Briefe des Heiligen Johannes*, Freiburg 1906.

Bergmeier, R., 'Zum Verfasserproblem des II und III Johannesbriefes', *ZNW* 57 (1966) 93–100.

Beutler, J., *Martyria: Traditionsgeschichtliche Untersuchungen zum Zeugnisthema bei Johannes*, Frankfurt 1972.

Bogart, J.L., *Orthodox and Heretical Perfectionism in the Johannine Community as evident in the First Epistle of John*, SBLDS 33, Missoula 1977.

Boismard, M-É., 'L'Évolution du Thème Eschatologique dans les Traditions Johanniques', *RB* 68 (1961) 507–24.

Bonnard, P., 'La première épître de Jean est-elle johannique?', in *L'Évangile de Jean*, ed. M. de Jonge, Gembloux 1977, 301–5.

Borgen, P., *Bread from Heaven*, NT.S 10, Leiden 1965.

Boring, M.E., 'The Influence of Christian Prophecy on the Johannine Portrayal of the Paraclete and Jesus', *NTS* 25 (1978–79) 113–23.

Boyle, J.L., 'The Last Discourses (Jn. 13,31–16,33) and Prayer (Jn. 17): Some observations on their Unity and Development', *Bib.* 56 (1975) 210–22.

Braun, H., 'Literar-Analyse und theologische Schichtung im ersten Johannesbriefe', *ZThK* 48 (1951) 262–92.

Brooke, A.E., *A Critical and Exegetical Commentary on the Johannine Epistles*, International Critical Commentary, Edinburgh 1912.

Brown, R.E., 'Johannine Ecclesiology—The Community's Origins', *Interpretation* 31 (1977) 379–93.

———, ' "Other sheep not of this fold". The Johannine Perspective on Christian Diversity in the Late First Century', *JBL* 97 (1978) 5–22.

———, 'The Relationship to the Fourth Gospel shared by the author of 1 John and by his opponents', in *Text and Interpretation*, ed. E. Best and R. McL. Wilson, Cambridge 1979, 57–68.

———, *The Community of the Beloved Disciple*, New York and London 1979.

———, *The Epistles of John*, Anchor Bible 30, New York 1982.

Büchsel, F., *Der Begriff der Wahrheit in dem Evangelium und den Briefen Johannes*, Gütersloh 1911.

Bultmann, R., 'Analyse des ersten Johannesbriefes', in *Festgabe für Adolf Jülicher zum 70. Geburtstag*, Tübingen 1927, 138–58.

———, 'Johannesbriefe', *RGG*³ III, Tübingen 1959, 836–40.

———, *The Johannine Epistles*, E.T. by R.P. O'Hara et al., Hermeneia, Philadelphia 1973.

Cassem, N.H., 'A Grammatical and Contextual Inventory of the use of κόσμος in the Johannine Corpus', *NTS* 19 (1972) 81–91.

Chapman, J., 'The Historical Setting of the Second and Third Epistles of St. John', *JThS* 5 (1904) 357–68, 517–34.

Clemen, C., 'Beiträge zum geschichtlichen Verständnis der Johannesbriefe', *ZNW* 6 (1905) 271–81.

Conzelmann, H., 'Was von Anfang war', in *Neutestamentliche Studien für R. Bultmann*, ed. W. Eltester, BZNW 21, Berlin 1954, 194–201.

Corell, A., *Consummatum Est*, E.T. by the Order of the Holy Paraclete, Whitby, London 1958.

Cullmann, O., *The Johannine Circle*, E.T. by J. Bowden, London 1976.

Culpepper, R.A., *The Johannine School: An Evaluation of the Johannine-School Hypothesis based on an Investigation of the Nature of Ancient Schools*, SBLDS 26, Missoula 1975.

Dibelius, M., 'Joh.15[13]. Eine Studie zum Traditionsproblem des Johannes-Evangeliums', in *Festgabe für A. Deissmann*, Tübingen 1927, 168–86.

———, 'Johannesbriefe', *RGG*² III, Tübingen 1929, 346–9.

Dodd, C.H., 'The First Epistle of John and the Fourth Gospel', *JRLB* 21 (1937) 129–56.

———, *The Johannine Epistles*, Moffatt New Testament Commentary, London 1946.

Dölger, F.J., 'DOMINA MATER ECCLESIA und die "Herrin" im zweiten Johannesbriefe', *Antike und Christentum* V, Münster 1936, 211–17.

Donfried, K.P., 'Ecclesiastical Authority in 2–3 John', in *L'Évangile de Jean*, ed. de Jonge, 325–33.

Dunn, J., 'John VI—A Eucharistic Discourse?' *NTS* 17 (1970–71) 328–38.

Ebrard, J.H.A., *Biblical Commentary on the Epistles of St. John*, E.T. by W.B. Pope, Edinburgh 1860.

Feuillet, A., 'La recherche du Christ dans la Nouvelle Alliance d'après la Christophanie de Jo.20.11–18', in *L'homme devant Dieu*, (Mélanges offerts au H. Lubac) I, Aubier 1963, 93–112.

Funk, F.W., 'The Form and Structure of II and III John', *JBL* 86 (1967) 424–30.

Gaugler, E., 'Die Bedeutung der Kirche in den johanneischen Schriften', *IKZ* 15 (1925) 27–42.

——, *Die Johannesbriefe*, Auslegung neutestamentlicher Schriften 1, Zurich 1964.

Gibbins, H.J., 'The Second Epistle of St. John', *Exp* VI.6 (1902) 228–36.

——, 'The Problem of the Second Epistle of St. John', *Exp* VI.12 (1905) 412–24.

Gore, C., *The Epistles of St. John*, London 1920.

Grässer, E., 'Die antijüdische Polemik im Johannesevangelium', *NTS* 11 (1964–5) 74–90.

Grayston, K., *The Johannine Epistles*, New Century Bible, Grand Rapids and London 1984.

Gunther, J.J., 'The Alexandrian Gospel and Letters of John', *CBQ* 41 (1979) 581–603.

——, 'Early Identifications of the Authorship of the Johannine Writings', *JEH* 31 (1980) 407–27.

Haas, C., et al., *A Translator's Handbook on the Letters of John*, Helps for Translators 13, London 1972.

Haenchen, E., 'Neuere Literatur zu den Johannesbriefen', *ThR* 26 (1960–61) 1–43, 267–91.

——, *John*, 2 vols., E.T. by R.W. Funk, Hermeneia, Philadelphia 1984.

Hall, D., 'Fellow-workers with the Gospel', *ET* 85 (1973–74) 119–20.

Harnack, A.v., *Über den dritten Johannesbrief*, TU 15.3b, Leipzig 1897.

——, 'Zur Textkritik und Christologie der Schriften des Johannes', *SPAW* (1915) 534–73.

——, 'Das "Wir" in den johanneischen Schriften', *SPAW* (1923) 95–113.

Harris, J. Rendel, 'The Problem of the Address in the Second Epistle of John', *Exp* VI.3 (1901) 194–203.

——, 'A Study in Letter Writing', *Exp* V.8 (1898) 161–80.

Heise, J., *BLEIBEN: Menein in den johanneischen Schriften*, Hermeneut. Untersuch. zur Theologie 8, Tübingen 1967.

Héring, J., 'Y-a-t-il des Aramaïsmes dans la Première Épitre Johannique?' *RHPhR* 36 (1956) 113–21.

Hirsch, E., *Studien zum vierten Evanglium*, Tübingen 1936.

Holtzmann, H.J., 'Das Problem des ersten johanneischen Briefes in seinem Verhältnis zum Evangelium', *Jahrbücher für protestantische Theologie* 7 (1881) 690–712; 8 (1882) 128–52, 316–42, 460–85.

——, *Briefe und Offenbarung des Johannes*, Hand-Commentar zum Neuen Testament IV.2, Leipzig and Freiburg 1893.

Horvath, T., '3 Jn.11[b]. An Early Ecumenical Creed?', *ET* 85 (1973) 339–40.

Hoskyns, E.C., *The Fourth Gospel*, ed. F.N. Davey, 2nd edition, London 1947.

Houlden, J.L., *A Commentary on the Johannine Epistles*, Black's New Testament Commentaries, London 1973.

Howard, W.F., 'The Common Authorship of the Johannine Gospel and Epistles', *JThS* 48 (1947) 12–25.

Huther, J.E., *Critical and Exegetical Handbook to the General Epistles of James and John*, E.T. by P. Gloag and C.H. Irwin, Edinburgh 1882.

Johnston, G., *The Spirit-Paraclete in the Gospel of John*, SNTSMS 12, Cambridge 1970.

Jonge, M. de, 'Jewish Expectations about the "Messiah" according to the Fourth Gospel', in idem, *Stranger from Heaven*, 77–116.

——, 'The Beloved Disciple and the date of the Gospel of John', in *Text and Interpretation*, ed. E. Best and R. McL. Wilson, 99–114.

——, 'The Son of God and the Children of God', in idem, *Stranger from Heaven*, 141–68.

——, 'Variety and Development in Johannine Christology', ibid., 193–222.

——, *Jesus: Stranger from Heaven and Son of God*, Missoula 1977.

——, (ed.), *L'Évangile de Jean: Sources, rédaction, théologie*, Bibliotheca Ephemeridum Theologicarum Lovaniensium, 44, Gembloux 1977.

Käsemann, E., 'Ketzer und Zeuge', *ZThK* 48 (1951) 292–311.

——, *The Testament of Jesus*, E.T. by G. Krodel, London 1968.

Klein, G., 'Das wahre Licht scheint schon', *ZThK* 68 (1971) 261–326.

Kragerud, A., *Der Lieblingsjünger im Johannesevangelium*, Oslo 1959.

Kuhl, J., *Die Sendung Jesu und der Kirche nach dem Johannes-Evangelium*, Kaldenkirchen 1967.

Lattke, M., *Einheit im Wort*, Studien zum Alten und Neuen Testament 41, Munich 1975.

Law, R., *The Tests of Life*, Edinburgh 1909.

Leroy, H., *Rätsel und Missverständnis. Ein Beitrag zur Formgeschichte des Johannesevangeliums*, Bonner Biblische Beiträge 30, Bonn 1968.

Lieu, J.M., 'Gnosticism and the Gospel of John', *ET* 90 (1979) 233–7.

——, 'Authority to become Children of God: A Study of 1 John', *NT* 23 (1981) 210–28.

Lindars, B., *The Gospel of John*, New Century Bible, Grand Rapids and London 1972.

——, 'The Persecution of Christians in Jo 15:18–16: 4a', in *Suffering and Martyrdom in the New Testament* (for G. Styler), ed. W. Horbury and B. McNeil, Cambridge 1981, 48–69.

Loewenich W. v., *Das Johannes-Verständnis im zweiten Jahrhundert*, BZNW 13, Giessen 1932.

Lorenzen, T., *Der Lieblingsjünger im Johannesevangelium*, Stuttgarter Bibelstudien 55, Stuttgart 1971.

Lücke, F., *A Commentary on the Epistles of St.John*, E.T. by T. Gudmundson Repp, Edinburgh 1837.

Malherbe, A.J., 'The Inhospitality of Diotrephes', in *God's Christ and his People* (for N. Dahl), ed. J. Jervell and W. Meeks, Oslo 1977, 222–32.

Marshall, I.H., *The Epistles of John*, Michigan 1978.

Martyn, J.L., *History and Theology in the Fourth Gospel*, 2nd edition, New York 1979.

——, 'Glimpses into the History of the Johannine Community', in *L'Évangile de Jean*, ed. de Jonge, 149–75.

Matsunaga, K., 'Is John's Gospel Anti-Sacramental?' *NTS* 27 (1981) 516–24.

Mattill, A.J., 'Johannine Communities behind the Fourth Gospel', *TS* 38 (1977) 294–315.

Meeks, W.A., *The Prophet King*, NT.S 14, Leiden 1967.

——, 'The Man from Heaven in Johannine Sectarianism', *JBL* 91 (1972) 44–72.

——, 'Am I a Jew?', in *Christianity, Judaism and other Graeco-Roman Cults* (for M. Smith), 4 vols., ed. J. Neusner, Leiden 1975, I, 163–86.

Minear, P.S., 'The Idea of Incarnation in First John', *Interpretation* 24 (1970) 291–302.

Mingana, A., 'The Authorship of the Fourth Gospel. A New Document', *JRLB* 14 (1930) 333–39, (reprinted with additions, Manchester 1930).

Moule, C.F.D., 'A Neglected Factor in the Interpretation of Johannine Eschatology', in *Studies in John* (presented to J.N. Sevenster) 155–60.

Müller, U.B., *Die Geschichte der Christologie in der johanneischen Gemeinde*, Stuttgarter Bibelstudien 77, Stuttgart 1975.

Mussner, F., *The Historical Jesus in the Gospel of John*, E.T. by W.J. O'Hara, Quaestiones Disputatae 19, Freiburg and London 1967.

Nauck, W., *Die Tradition und der Charakter des ersten Johannesbriefes*, Wissenschaftliche Untersuchungen zum Neuen Testament 3, Tübingen 1957.

Onuki, T., *Gemeinde und Welt im Johannesevangelium*, WMANT 56, Neukirchen-Vluyn 1984.

Painter, J., 'The Farewell Discourses and the History of Johannine Christianity', *NTS* 27 (1981) 525–43.

Plummer, A., *The Epistles of St. John*, Cambridge Bible Commentary, Cambridge 1884.

Potterie, I. de la, 'L'arrière-fond du thème johannique de verité', in *Studia Evangelica* I, TU 73, Berlin 1959, 277–94.

——, 'La notion de "commencement" dans les Écrits Johanniques', in *Die Kirche des Anfangs* (für H. Schürmann zum 65 Geburtstag), ed. R. Schnackenburg et al., Leipzig 1977, 379–403.

Quispel, G., 'Het Johannesevangelie en de Gnosis', *Nederlands Theologisch Tijdschrift* 11 (1956–7) 173–203.

——, 'Love Thy Brother', *Ancient Society* 1 (1970) 83–93, reprinted in idem, *Gnostic Studies* II, Amsterdam 1975, 169–79.

——, 'Qumran, John and Jewish Christianity', in *John and Qumran*, ed. J. Charlesworth, London 1972, 137–55.

Rand, J.A. du, ed., *Studies in the Johannine Literature, Neotestamentica* 13 (1981).

Review and Expositor 69.4 (1970) was devoted to articles on the Johannine Epistles.

Richards, W.L., *The Classification of the Greek Manuscripts of the Johannine Epistles*, SBLDS 35, Missoula 1977.

Richter, G., 'Präsentische und futurische Eschatologie im 4 Evangelium', in *Gegenwart und kommendes Reich* (Festschrift A. Vögtle), ed. P. Fiedler and D. Zeller, Stuttgart 1975, 117–52.

——, 'Die Fleischwerdung des Logos im Johannesevangelium', *NT* 13 (1971) 81–126; 14 (1972) 257–76.

——, 'Zum gemeindebildenden Element in den johanneischen Schriften', in idem, *Studien zum Johannesevangelium*, ed. J. Hainz, Regensburg 1977, 383–414.

Salom, A.P., 'Some Aspects of the Grammatical Style of 1 John', *JBL* 74 (1955) 96–102.

Sanders, J.N., *The Fourth Gospel in the Early Church*, Cambridge 1943.

Schlier, H., 'Die Bruderliebe nach dem Evangelium und den Briefen Johannes', in *Mélanges Bibliques au Béda Rigaux*, ed. A. Descamps and A. de Halleux, Gembloux 1970, 235–45.

Schmiedel, P.W., *The Johannine Writings*, E.T. by M. Canney, London 1908.

Schnackenburg, R., 'Der Streit zwischen dem Verfasser von 3 Joh und Diotrephes und seiner verfassungsgeschichtliche Bedeutung', *Münchener Theologische Zeitschrift* 4 (1953) 18–26.

——, 'Zum Begriff der "Wahrheit" in den beiden kleinen Johannesbriefen', *BZ* 11 (1967) 253–7.

——, *The Gospel according to St. John*, 3 vols., E.T. by K. Smyth et al., New York 1968–82.

——, *Die Johannesbriefe*, 1st edition, Freiburg 1953; 6th edition, Freiburg 1979. Unless otherwise stated the 6th edition is cited.

Schunack, G., *Die Briefe des Johannes*, Zürcher Bibelkommentare, Zurich 1982.

Schwartz, E., *Über den Tod der Söhne Zebedaei*, AGWG.PH 7.5, Berlin 1904.

Schweizer, E., 'The Concept of the Church in the Gospel and Epistles of St. John', in *New Testament Essays* (Studies in Memory of T.W. Manson), ed. A.J.B. Higgins, Manchester 1959, 230–45.

——, 'Jesus der Zeuge Gottes', in *Studies in John* (presented to J.N. Sevenster) 161–8.

Segovia, F., 'Love and Hatred of Jesus and Johannine Sectarianism', *CBQ* 42 (1981) 258–72.

(Sevenster, J.N.), *Studies in John* (presented to J.N. Sevenster), NT.S 24, Leiden 1970.

Smalley, S.S., *1, 2, 3 John*, Word Biblical Commentary 51, Waco Texas 1984.

Smith, D.M., 'Johannine Christianity: Some Reflections on its Character and Delineation', *NTS* 21 (1974–5) 222–48.

Snyder, G.F., 'John 13:16 and the Anti-Petrinism of the Johannine Tradition', *BR* 16 (1971) 5–15.

Strecker, G., 'Die Anfänge der johanneischen Schule', *NTS* 32 (1986) 31–47.

Thiele, W., *Wortschatzuntersuchungen zu den lateinischen Texten der Johannesbriefe*, Vetus Latina. Aus der Geschichte der lateinischen Bibel 2, Freiburg 1958.

Thyen, H., 'Johannes 13 und die "kirchliche Redaktion" des vierten Evangeliums', in *Tradition und Glaube* (Festgabe für K.G. Kuhn), ed. G. Jeremias et al., Göttingen 1971, 343–56.

———, 'Entwicklungen innerhalb der johanneischen Theologie und Kirche im Spiegel von Joh 21 und der Lieblingsjüngertexte des Evangeliums', in *L'Évangile de Jean*, ed. de Jonge, 259–99.

Thüsing, W., *Die Johannesbriefe*, Düsseldorf 1970.

Weiss, B., *Die Katholischen Briefe. Textkritische Untersuchungen und Textherstellung*, TU 8.3, Leipzig 1892.

———, *Die drei Briefe des Apostel Johannes*, Göttingen 1899.

Weiss, K., 'Orthodoxie und Heterodoxie im 1 Johannesbrief', *ZNW* 58 (1967) 247–55.

Wendt, H.H., 'Der "Anfang" am Beginne des 1 Johannesbriefes', *ZNW* 21 (1922) 38–42.

———, 'Die Beziehung unseres 1 Johannesbriefes auf den zweiten', *ZNW* 21 (1922) 140–6.

———, 'Zum ersten Johannesbrief', *ZNW* 22 (1923) 57–79.

———, 'Zum zweiten und dritten Johannesbriefe', *ZNW* 23 (1924) 18–27.

———, *Die Johannesbriefe und das johanneische Christentum*, Halle 1925.

Westcott, B.F., *The Epistles of St. John*, London 1883.

Whitacre, R., *Johannine Polemic*, SBLDS 67, Chico 1982.

Williams, R.R., *The Letters of John and James*, Cambridge Bible Commentary on the New English Bible, Cambridge 1965.

Wilson, W.G., 'An Examination of the Linguistic Evidence adduced against the Unity of Authorship of the First Epistle of John and the Fourth Gospel', *JThS* 49 (1948) 147–56.

Windisch, H., *Die Katholischen Briefe*, 3rd edition by H. Preisker, Handbuch zum Neuen Testament, Tübingen 1951.

Woll, D.B., *Johannine Christianity in Conflict*, SBLDS 60, Chico 1981.

B. Other Literature

Aland, K., *The Problem of the New Testament Canon*, London 1962.

Bacon, B.W., 'Date and Habitat of the Elders of Papias', *ZNW* 12 (1911) 176–87.

——, 'The Elder John in Jerusalem', *ZNW* 26 (1927) 187–202.

Bagnani, G., 'Peregrinus Proteus and the Christians', *Historia* 4 (1955) 107–112.

Bardy, G., 'Sévérien de Gabala', *Dictionnaire de Théologie Catholique* 14, 2, Paris 1941, 2000–6.

Barrett, C.K., 'Jews and Judaisers in the Epistles of Ignatius', in *Jews, Greeks and Christians* (Essays in Honor of W.D. Davies), ed. R. Hamerton-Kelly and R. Scroggs, Leiden 1976, 220–44.

Bauer, W., *Orthodoxy and Heresy in Earliest Christianity*, E.T. ed. by R. Kraft and G. Krodel, Philadelphia 1971.

Berger, K., 'Apostelbrief und apostolische Rede: Zum Formular frühchristlicher Briefe', *ZNW* 65 (1974) 190–231.

Best, E., 'Scripture, Tradition and the Canon of the New Testament', *JRLB* 61 (1978–9) 258–89.

——, and R. McL. Wilson, ed., *Text and Interpretation* (Studies presented to M. Black), Cambridge 1979.

Betz, H.D., 'Lukian von Samosata und das Christentum', *NT* 3 (1959) 226–37.

Bornkamm, G., 'πρέσβυς', *TDNT* VI, 651–80.

Bousset, W., *The Antichrist Legend*, E.T. by A.H. Keane, London 1896.

——, *Kyrios Christos*, E.T. by J. Steely, Nashville 1970.

Brown, R. and Meier, J., *Antioch and Rome*, London 1983.

Bruns, J.E., 'Biblical Citations and the Agraphon in Pseudo-Cyprian's Liber De Montibus Sina et Sion', *VigChr* 26 (1972) 112–6.

Buchanon, E.S., 'The Codex Muratorianus', *JThS* 8 (1907) 537–45.

Bultmann, R., *Theology of the New Testament*, 2 volumes, E.T. by K. Grobel, London 1952, 55.

——, 'ἀλήθεια' D, *TDNT* I, 241–7.

Campenhausen, H.v., *Polycarp von Smyrna und die Pastoralbriefe*, SHAW.PH, Heidelberg 1951.

——, *Ecclesiastical Authority and Spiritual Power in the church of the first three centuries*, E.T. by J. Baker, London 1969.

Chadwick, H., 'Justification by Faith and Hospitality', *Studia Patristica* IV, TU 79, Berlin 1961, 281–5.

Conzelmann, H., *An Outline of the Theology of the New Testament*, E.T. by J. Bowden, London 1969.

Corssen, P., *Monarchianische Prologe zur den vier Evangelien*, TU 15.1, Leipzig 1896.

Cramer, J.A., *Catenae Graecorum Patrum in Novum Testamentum*, vol. 8, *In Epistolas Catholicas et Apocalypsin*, Oxford 1884.

Dahl, N.A., *Das Volk Gottes*, Oslo 1941.

Danielou, J., *The Theology of Jewish Christianity*, The Development of Christian Doctrine before the Council of Nicaea I, E.T. by J.A. Baker, London 1964.

Deissmann, A., *Bible Studies*, E.T. by A. Grieve, Edinburgh 1901.

——, *Licht vom Osten*, 4th edition, Tübingen 1923.

Delling, G., 'Zur Taufe von "Hausern" im Urchristentum', *NT* 7 (1965) 105–12.

Denzinger, H., *Enchiridion Symbolorum*, 33rd edition, Freiburg 1965.

Dix, G., 'The Use and Abuse of Papias on the Fourth Gospel', *Theol.* 24 (1932) 8–20.

Donovan, J., 'The Elder John and Other Johns', *IER* 31 (1928) 337–50.

Doty, W.G., *Letters in Primitive Christianity*, Philadelphia 1973.

Ehrhardt, A., *The Apostolic Succession*, London 1953.

——, 'Christianity before the Apostles' Creed', *HThR* 55 (1962) 74–119.

——, 'The Gospels in the Muratorian Fragment', in idem, *The Framework of the New Testament Stories*, Cambridge 1964, 11–36.

Evans, C.F., 'I will go before you to Galilee', *JThS* NS 5 (1954) 3–18.

Exler, F.X.J., *The Form of the Ancient Greek Letter*, Washington 1923.

Filson, F.V., 'The Significance of the Early House Churches', *JBL* 58 (1939) 105–12.

Fischer, B., 'Das Neue Testament in lateinischer Sprache', in *Die Alten Übersetzungen des Neuen Testaments, die Kirchenväterzitate und Lektionare*, ed. K. Aland, Arbeiten zur neutestamentlichen Textforschung V, Berlin and New York 1972, 1–92.

——, 'Ein neuer Zeuge zum westlichen Text der Apostelgeschichte', in *Biblical and Patristic Studies* (for R.P. Casey), ed. J.N. Birdsall and R.W. Thomson, Freiburg 1963, 33–64.

Fitzmyer, J.A., 'Some Notes on Aramaic Epistolography', in *Studies in Ancient Letter Writing*, Semeia 22, ed. J.L. White, Chico 1981, 25–58; (revised from *JBL* 93 (1974) 201–25).

Frankemölle, H., 'Amtskritik im Matthäus-Evangelium?', *Bib.* 54 (1973) 247–62.

Funk, F.W., 'The Apostolic Parousia', in *Christian History and*

Interpretation (Studies presented to J. Knox), ed. W. Farmer et al., Cambridge 1967, 249–68.

Furnish, V., *The Love Command in the New Testament*, London 1973.

Gamble, H., *The Textual History of the Letter to the Romans*, Studies and Documents 42, Michigan 1977.

Goguel, M., *L'Église Primitive*, Paris 1947.

Grant, R.M., 'Notes on Gnosis', *VigChr* 11 (1957) 145–51.

Greeven, H., 'Propheten, Lehrer, Vorsteher bei Paulus', *ZNW* 44 (1952–3) 1–43.

Grundmann, W., 'ἀγαθοποιεῖν' *TDNT* I, 17–8.

Gustafsson, A., 'Eusebius' Principles in handling his sources as found in his Church History Books I–VII', *Studia Patristica* IV, TU 79, Berlin 1961, 428–41.

Hahn, F., *Mission in the New Testament*, E.T. by F. Clarke, London 1965.

Hanse, H., 'ἔχειν', *TDNT* II, 816–27.

Hanson, R.P.C., *Tradition in the Early Church*, London 1962.

Harnack, A.v., *Lehre der zwölf Apostel*, 2 parts, TU 2.1,2, Leipzig 1886.

——, *The Expansion of Christianity in the first three centuries*, 2 volumes, E.T. by J. Moffatt, London 1904–5.

——, *Zur Revision der Prinzipien der neutestamentlichen Textkritik*, Beiträge zur Einleitung in das Neue Testament VII, Leipzig 1916.

Harrisville, R.A., 'The Concept of Newness in the New Testament', *JBL* 74 (1955) 69–79.

Harvey, A.E., 'Elders', *JThS* NS 25 (1974) 318–32.

Hauschildt H., πρεσβύτεροι in Agypten im I–III Jahrhundert n. Chr.', *ZNW* 4 (1903) 235–42.

Hesse, F.H., *Das Muratori'sche Fragment*, Giessen 1873.

Hill, D., *New Testament Prophecy*, London 1979.

Hock, R., *The Social Context of Paul's Ministry*, Philadelphia 1980.

Holmberg, B., *Paul and Power*, Coniectanea Biblica N.T. Series 11, Lund 1978.

Hornschuh, M., 'Das Leben des Origenes und die Entstehung der alexandrinischen Schule', *ZKG* 71 (1960) 1–25, 193–214.

Howorth, H., 'The Origin and Authority of the Biblical Canon according to the Continental Reformers', *JThS* 8 (1906–7) 321–65; 9 (1908) 188–230.

Hyldahl, N., 'A Supposed Synagogue Inscription', *NTS* 25 (1978–9) 396–8.

Judge, E.A., *The Conversion of Rome*, Sydney 1980.

Käsemann, E., *Exegetische Versuche und Besinnungen* II, Göttingen 1964.
——, *New Testament Questions of Today*, E.T. by W.J. Montague, London 1969.
——, (ed.), *Das Neue Testament als Kanon*, Göttingen 1970.
Katz, P., 'The Johannine Epistles in the Muratorian Canon', *JThS* NS 8 (1957) 273–4.
Kelly, J.N.D., *Jerome*, London 1975.
Kihn, H., *Theodor von Mopsuestia und Junilius Africanus als Exegeten*, Freiburg 1880.
Kim, C-H., *Form and Structure of the Familiar Greek Letter of Recommendation*, SBLDS 4, Missoula 1972.
Kimelman, R., '*Birkat Ha-Minim* and the Lack of Evidence for an Anti-Christian Jewish Prayer in Late Antiquity', in *Jewish and Christian Self-Definition*, ed. Sanders et al., II, 226–44.
Klijn, A.F.J. and Reinink, G.J., *Patristic Evidence for Jewish-Christian Sects*, NT.S 36, Leiden 1973.
Kötting, B., *Peregrinatio Religiosa*, Münster 1950.
Koschkorke, K., *Die Polemik der Gnostiker gegen das kirchliche Christentum*, N.H. Studies 12, Leiden 1978.
Koskenniemi, H., *Studien zur Idee und Phraseologie des griechischen Briefes bis 400 n. Chr.*, Annales Academicae Scientiarum Fennicae, Helsinki 1956.
Kretschmar, G., 'Ein Beitrag zur Frage nach dem Ursprung frühchristlicher Askese', *ZThK* 61 (1964) 27–67.
——, 'Christliches Passa im 2 Jahrhundert', *RSR* 60 (1972) 287–323.
Kummel, W.G., *The New Testament. The History of the Investigation of its Problems*, E.T. by S.M. Gilmour and H.C. Kee, London 1973.
Lagrange, M-J., 'Le Canon d'Hippolyte et le Fragment de Muratori', *RB* 42 (1933) 161–86.
Lake, K., 'De Strijd tusschen het oudste Christendom en de Bedriegers', *Theologisch Tijdschrift* 42 (1908) 395–411.
Langdon, S., 'History of the Use of ἐάν for ἄν in Relative Clauses', *American Journal of Philology* 24 (1903) 447–51.
Larfeld, W., 'Das Zeugnis des Papias über die beiden Johannes von Ephesus', *NKZ* 33 (1922) 490–512.
Leipoldt, J., *Geschichte des neutestamentlichen Kanons*, 2 volumes, Leipzig 1907–8.
Lewis, A.S., *Catalogue of the Syriac MSS in the Convent of S. Catherine on Mount Sinai*, Studia Sinaitica I, London 1894.

Lieu, J.M., ' "Grace to you and peace": The Apostolic Greeting', *JRLB* 68 (1985) 161–78.

Lightfoot, J.B., *Essays on the Work entitled 'Supernatural Religion'*, London 1880.

——, *St. Paul's Epistle to the Philippians*, London 1908.

McHugh, J., *The Mother of Jesus in the New Testament*, London 1975.

Maclean, A.J., *East Syrian Daily Offices*, London 1894.

Manson, T.W., 'Entry into membership of the Early Church', *JThS* 48 (1947) 25–33.

Mayser, E., *Grammatik der griechischen Papyri aus der Ptolemäerzeit*, II.1, Berlin 1926.

Meecham, H., *Light from Ancient Letters*, London 1923.

——, 'The Present Participle of Antecedent Action—Some New Testament Instances', *ET* 64 (1953) 285–6.

Ménard, J.E., 'Les Élucubrations de l'Evangelium Veritatis sur le "Nom" ', *Studia Montis Regii* V, Montreal 1962, 185–214.

Metzger, B.M., *The Early Versions of the New Testament*, Oxford 1977.

Michel, O., 'οἶκος' etc., *TDNT* V, 119–34.

Moffatt, J., *Introduction to the New Testament*, 3rd edition, London 1918.

Moule, C.F.D., *The Birth of the New Testament*, London 1962.

Moulton, J.H., *A Grammar of New Testament Greek*, 4 vols., Edinburgh 1906–76.

——, and Howard, W.F., *Accidence and Word Formation*, ibid. vol. II.

——, and Milligan, G., *The Vocabulary of the Greek Testament illustrated from the Papyri and other non-literary Sources*, London 1914–29.

Müller, M., 'Die Überlieferung des Eusebius in seiner Kirchengeschichte über die Schriften des N.T. und deren Verfasser', *ThStKr* 105 (1933) 425–55.

Munck, J., 'Presbyters and Disciples of the Lord in Papias', *HThR* 52 (1959) 223–43.

Oepke, A., 'παῖς', *TDNT* V, 636–54.

Pagels, E., ' "The Demiurge and His Archons"—A Gnostic View of Bishops and Presbyters?', *HThR* 69 (1976) 301–24.

Pape, D., *God and Women*, London 1976.

Plumpe, J.C., *Mater Ecclesia*, Washington 1943; see also the review by C. Mohrmann, *VigChr* 2 (1948) 57–8.

Poland, F., *Geschichte des griechischen Vereinswesens*, Leipzig 1909.

Regul, J., *Die Antimarcionitischen Evangelienprologe*, Vetus Latina. Aus der Geschichte der lateinischen Bibel 6, Freiburg 1969.

Reiling, J., *Hermas and Christian Prophecy*, NT.S 37, Leiden 1973.

Robert, L., *Hellenica* 13 (1965).

Robinson, J.A., *St. Paul's Epistle to the Ephesians*, London 1903.

Robinson, J.M., 'Die Hodaiot-Formel in Gebet und Hymnus des Frühchristentums', in *Apophoreta: Festschrift E. Haenchen*, ed. W. Eltester and F.H. Kettler, BZNW 30, Berlin 1964, 194–235.

——, and Koester, H., *Trajectories through Early Christianity*, Philadelphia 1971.

Roller, O., *Das Formular der Paulinischen Briefe*, Beiträge zur Wissenschaft vom Alten und Neuen Testament IV.6, Stuttgart 1933.

Ruwet, J., 'Les "Antilegomena" dans les oeuvres d'Origène', *Bib.* 23 (1942) 18–42.

——, 'Clément d'Alexandrie: Canon des Écritures et Apocryphes', *Bib.* 29 (1948) 77–99, 240–68, 391–408.

Sanday, W., 'The Cheltenham List of the Canonical Books of the Old and New Testament and of the Writings of Cyprian', in *Studia Biblica* III, ed. S.R. Driver et al., Oxford 1891, 216–325.

Sanders, E.P., et al., *Jewish and Christian Self-Definition*, 3 vols., London 1980–2.

Schepens, P., ' "Johannes in epistula sua" (Saint Cyprien, *passim*)', *RSR* 11 (1921) 87–9.

Schoedel, W., 'Theological Norms and Social Perspectives in Ignatius of Antioch', in *Jewish and Christian Self-Definition*, ed. Sanders, I, 30–56.

Schottroff, L., *Der Glaubende und die feindliche Welt*, Wissenschaftliche Monographien zum Alten und Neuen Testament 37, Neukirchen-Vluyn 1970.

Schubert, P., *The Form and Function of the Pauline Thanksgivings*, BZNW 20, Berlin 1939.

Schulz, A., *Nachfolgen und Nachahmen. Studien über das Verhältnis der neutestamentlichen Jüngerschaft zur urchristlichen Vorbildethik*, Studien zum Alten und Neuen Testament 6, Munich 1962.

Schweizer, E., 'Diodor von Tarsus als Exeget', *ZNW* 40 (1941) 33–75.

——, *Church Order in the New Testament*, E.T. by F. Clarke, London 1961.

——, 'Law Observance and Charisma in Matthew', *NTS* 16 (1969–70) 213–30.

——, 'The Matthaean Church', *NTS* 20 (1973–4) 215.

——, *The Good News according to Matthew*, E.T. by D.E. Green, London 1976.

Scroggs, R., 'The Sociological Interpretation of the New Testament: the Present State of Research', *NTS* 26 (1980) 164–79.

Selwyn, E.C., *The Christian Prophets and the Prophetic Apocalypse*, London 1900.

Sherk, R.K., *Roman Documents from the Greek East*, Maryland 1969.

Soden, H.F.v., *Das lateinische Neue Testament im Afrika zur Zeit Cyprians*, TU 33, Leipzig 1909.

Souter, A., 'The New Testament Text of Irenaeus', in *Novum Testamentum Sancti Irenaei Episcopi Lugdunensis*, ed. W. Sanday and C.H. Turner, Old Latin Biblical Texts 7, Oxford 1923, cxii–clxix.

Staab, K., 'Die griechischen Katenkommentare zu den katholischen Briefen', *Bib.* 5 (1924) 296–353.

Stählin, G., 'προκόπτειν', *TDNT* VI, 703–19.

Stanton, G., '5 Ezra and Matthaean Christianity in the Second Century', *JThS* NS 28 (1977) 67–83.

Steen, H.A., 'Les clichés épistolaires dans les lettres sur papyrus grecs', *Classica et Mediaevalia* 1 (1938) 119–76.

Stendahl, K., 'The Apocalypse of John and the Epistles of Paul in the Muratorian Fragment', in *Current Issues in New Testament Interpretation* (Essays in Honour of O. Piper), ed. W. Klassen and G. Snyder, London 1962, 239–45.

Stenzel, M., 'Der Bibelkanon des Rufin von Aquileja', *Bib.* 23 (1942) 43–61.

Strathmann, H., 'μαρτύς', *TDNT* IV, 474–515.

Stuhlmacher, P., *Der Brief an Philemon*, Zurich 1975.

Sundberg, A.C., 'Canon Muratori: A Fourth Century List', *HThR* 66 (1973) 1–41.

Swete, H.B., 'John of Ephesus', *JThS* 17 (1916) 375–8.

Theissen, G., 'Legitimation and Subsistence: An Essay on the Sociology of Early Christian Missionaries', in idem, *The Social Setting of Pauline Christianity*, E.T. by J.H. Schutz, Edinburgh 1982, 27–67.

——, ' "Wir haben alles verlassen" (Mc.X.28). Nachfolge und soziale Entwurzelung in der jüdisch-palästinischen Gesellschaft des 1 Jahrhunderts n. Chr.', *NT* 19 (1977) 161–96.

——, *The First Followers of Jesus*, E.T. by J. Bowden, London 1978.

Treu, K., 'Christliche Empfehlungs-Schemabriefe auf Papyrus', in *Zetesis* (for E. de Strycker), Antwerp 1973, 629–36.

Trites, A., *The New Testament Concept of Witness*, SNTSMS 31, Cambridge 1977.

Turner, C.H., 'Documents. An Exegetical Fragment of the Third Century', *JThS* 5 (1904) 218–41.

Turner, N., *Syntax, Grammar of New Testament Greek*, ed. Moulton, Vol. III.

——, *Style*, ibid., Vol. IV.

Vallée, G., 'Theological Norms and Non-Theological Motives in Irenaeus's Refutation of the Gnostics', in *Jewish and Christian Self-Definition*, ed. Sanders, Vol. 1, 174–85.

Vassall-Phillips, O.R., *The Works of St. Optatus Against the Donatists*, London 1917.

Vermes, G., 'The Targumic Versions of Genesis 4:3–16', in idem, *Post-Biblical Jewish Studies*, Leiden 1975.

Westcott, B.F., *A General Survey of the History of the Canon of the New Testament*, 2nd edition, London 1866; 7th edition, London 1896. The 7th edition is cited unless otherwise stated.

White, J.L., 'Introductory Formulae in the Body of the Pauline Letter', *JBL* 90 (1971) 91–7.

——, *The Form and Function of the Body of the Greek Letter*, SBLDS 2, Missoula 1972.

——, *The Form and Structure of the Official Petition*, SBLDS 5, Missoula 1972.

——, 'St. Paul and the Apostolic Letter Tradition', *CBQ* 45 (1983) 433–44.

Wilamowitz-Möllendorf,. U.v., 'Lesefruchte', *Hermes* 33 (1898) 529–31.

Wilson, B.R., *Patterns of Sectarianism*, London 1967.

Wilson, R. McL. 'The New Testament in the Nag Hammadi Gospel of Philip', *NTS* 9 (1962–3) 291–4.

Wilcox, M., 'On investigating the use of the Old Testament in the New Testament', in *Text and Interpretation*, ed. Best & McL. Wilson, 231–43.

Wisse, F., 'The Epistle of Jude in the History of Heresiology', in *Essays on the Nag Hammadi Texts in Honour of A. Böhlig*, ed. M. Krause, N.H. Studies 3, Leiden 1972, 133–43.

——, 'Prolegomena to the Study of the New Testament and Gnosis', in *The New Testament and Gnosis* (for R. McL. Wilson), ed. A. Logan and A. Wedderburn, Edinburgh 1983, 138–45.

Zahn, T., *Forschungen zur Geschichte des neutestamentlichen Kanons*, 10 volumes, 1–3 Erlangen, 4–5 Erlangen and Leipzig, 6–10 Leipzig 1881–1929.

——, *Geschichte des neutestamentlichen Kanons*, 2 volumes, Erlangen 1888–92.

——, 'Das Neue Testament Theodore von Mopsuestia und der ursprüngliche Kanon der Syrer', *NKZ* 11 (1900) 788–806.

Ziemann, F., *De Epistularum Graecarum formulis sollemnibus Quaestiones Selectae*, Dissertatio Halis 1910.

Zimmermann, A., *Die urchristlichen Lehrer*, Tübingen 1984.

Indexes

Biblical References (including Apocrypha)

Leviticus
19.18   73

Numbers
10.32   117

Judges
17.13   117

Ruth
2.12   88

Isaiah
43.20   67
54   66-7

Daniel
3.31 (LXX) 46

Zephaniah
1.12   117

2 Esdras
9-10   66

Wisdom of Solomon
               22-3

Baruch
4-5   66-7

1 Maccabees
10.1   113

Matthew
               126
5.38f.   127
5.47   108
6.7   108
6.25-32   127
7.19   130
8.20f.   127

10.11f.   97
10.23   127
10.40-2   126
16.21   53
18.17   108
19.17   78
21.23   53
22.39   73
23.6-10   134
24.11   80
26.3   53
27.63   217

Mark
               62
3.4   117
6.7   109
7.5   78
9.37f.   126
10.29   127
12.31   73
13.20, 22,
  27   67
13.22   80
13.23   88

Luke
               21
6.9, 33, 35   117
10.16   126
10.27   73
23.8   220

John
1.1   173
1.5ff.   199
1.7-9   185
1.10-11   185
1.11   179
1.12   68
1.12-13   195
1.14   137, 173, 208, 212

1.14-17	47, 217, 221	6.27ff.	89
1.15	214	6.37	194, 195, 201, 218
1.18	116, 138	6.39f.	197
1.19-34	188	6.40	185
1.30	214	6.44	145, 195
1.34	67, 217	6.46	116
1.35-40	139	6.47	194, 196
1.41	178	6.48-58	215
1.45	178	6.51	185, 201
1.46	117, 219	6.51b-58	208, 212
2.11	178	6.54	197, 201
2.15	218	6.56	93, 199, 202
2.17	178	6.60ff.	137, 212
2.22	177	6.60-71	196
3.3f.	186-7	6.65	213
3.3-8	195	6.66	212-14
3.11	120, 187	6.67	137
3.16	74, 183, 185	6.68f.	187
3.16-21	145, 194, 196	6.69	213
3.19	185, 199	6.70	67, 196, 213
3.19-21	194-5	6.70f.	137
3.20	202	7.7	185
3.21	69, 72	7.12	117, 219
3.29	41, 99, 219, 226	7.16f.	217
3.31	86, 186	7.19-24	189
3.35	204	7.34f.	187
3.36	196	7.37	185
4.4-42	214	7.39	177
4.20-24	170	8.9	220
4.23	218	8.12	72, 185, 199
4.26	185	8.19	201
4.36	217	8.21	187
4.38	185	8.22f.	186
5.17-18	202	8.23	185-6
5.20	205	8.31	93, 137, 178, 202-3
5.24f.	194	8.31ff.	197-8, 212
5.26	197	8.32	68-9, 224
5.26-29	215	8.35	206
5.28f.	208	8.37	104
5.29	117, 219	8.39	68
5.33	104	8.43-47	194
5.33ff.	188	8.44	75, 188, 197-8
5.39	188-89	8.47	116, 194-5
5.45	220	8.51f.	178-9
5.45-47	189	8.55	179
5.46f.	188	8.56	188
6.14	86, 185	8.58	189
6.17-65	187	9	214

9.16	218	14.7-9	201
9.22	187, 214	14.9	136
9.34f.	218	14.12	189
9.41	146, 197	14.15	178, 205
10.3	194	14.16	137, 140
10.4	218	14.17	175, 185
10.14	194	14.19	202-3
10.15	201	14.20	201-2
10.17f.	201	14.21	137, 142, 178, 205
10.18	72, 77, 216, 224	14.21-24	205
10.26, 28	194	14.23	178-9, 202-3, 205
10.30	202	14.24	178-9
11.9-10	72	14.26	140, 177, 189, 219
11.11	219	14.27	220
11.27	86, 185	14.28	202, 205
11.48	108	14.30	188
11.50	201	14.31	205, 211
11.50-52	108	15-17	215
11.52	68	15	211
12.16	177	15.1-10	170, 201-2
12.25	185	15.1-17	75, 93, 179, 215
12.31	185, 188, 218	15.3	215
12.34	206	15.4-7	93, 199
12.35	72	15.4-10	178
12.42	187	15.7	215
12.44	201	15.8	137
12.46	185	15.10	74, 178-9
12.48	197	15.11	41, 99, 226
12.48-50	179	15.12	73-4, 205
13-17	74, 137, 210-1, 222	15.13f.	74, 205, 219
13.1	185, 194, 205	15.14	137
13.5	137	15.15	123
13.12-17	156-7, 215	15.16	67, 195
13.16	138	15.17	73, 205
13.18	67, 195	15.18	74, 185-6
13.20	126, 157	15.18f.	145
13.20-26	215	15.18-16.4a	120, 185-6
13.22	137	15.18-16.15	211, 215
13.23	138-9	15.19	67
13.28	139	15.19b-20a	215
13.33	68	15.20	178
13.34	73-5, 205, 209, 225	15.21	76
13.34f.	205, 211, 215	15.22, 24	146, 197
13.35	137	15.26	140, 175, 177, 189
13.36-14.3	203	15.26f.	176
14.3	84	15.27	75, 137
14.6	201	16.2	137, 187
14.7	178, 189, 194, 199	16.7	177

16.8	198, 202
16.8-11	140, 185
16.10	198
16.11	185, 188
16.12-13	177
16.13	140, 175, 177
16.14	140, 178
16.16-33	215
16.17	137
16.18	84
16.21-22	99
16.24	41, 99, 226
16.25	177
16.27	205
16.28	185
16.29	137
16.32	196
16.33	185, 206, 220
17	73, 148, 178-9, 186, 197, 202, 204, 210-12
17.2	185
17.3	199, 215
17.4	186
17.6	179, 195
17.6f.	189, 194
17.9	145
17.12	136
17.12b	215
17.13	41, 99, 226
17.14f.	145
17.16	215
17.18	186
17.18f.	185
17.20	137
17.20f.	215
17.21	204
17.22	194
17.23-26	74, 204
17.24	203
18.4	84
18.15f.	138-9
18.17	138
18.19	217
18.23	117, 219
18.25ff.	138
18.30	117, 219
18.35	108
18.36	185

18.37	69, 72, 185, 194
19.12	219
19.26f.	138
19.29	220
19.34-35	211
19.35	120-1, 127
19.38	137
20-21	170
20.3-8	138
20.9	139, 177
20.11-18	66
20.19-21	211
20.19, 21, 26	48, 122, 220
20.21	185
20.24	137
20.28	139
21	139, 141, 211, 215
21.5	68
21.7	138
21.15-19	138
21.19-22	203
21.20-22	138
21.23	64
21.24	112, 120-1, 123, 138, 144, 216, 229
21.24f.	140, 176

Acts

	21
5.40f.	108
5.41	107
6.3	118
9.16	107-8
10.22	118
14.22	94
15.3	106
15.23-9	45, 220
15.29	48
16.15, 34	132
20.17	53
20.38	106
21.5	106
21.13	107
22.12	118
23.26-30	45

Romans

	9
1.5	108
6.4	71
8.28-30	196
8.29	199
15.24	106
16.1	127
16.1-2	119, 130
16.2	107
16.3, 9, 21	107
16.3-16, 21-23	41
16.13	217
16.23	101, 132

1 Corinthians

1.4-9	39
1.11	126
1.14	101
1.16	132
1.18	195
3.1f.	192
3.9	107
4.14, 17	69
4.16	117
5.1	132
5.2	114
5.11	33
9.18	133
11.11	117
12.12	130
12.28	128
14.19	105
16.6, 11	106

2 Corinthians

1.16	106
1.24	107
3.3	220
4.2	71
6.8	217
8.23	107
10-13	158
11.2	66
11.7f.	133
12.13	133

Galatians

1.9	130
4.19	68
4.21-31	66-7
6.16	48

Ephesians

4.1	107
4.11	127
5.1	117
5.2	71
5.25f.	66
6.23	48

Philippians

1.3	39
1.27	107
2.9	108
2.25	107, 126
4.3	107
4.10	40
4.18	126

Colossians

1.10	107
1.25	94
4.10-15	41
4.11	107
4.12	126

1 Thessalonians

1.2	44
1.6	117
2.12	107, 219
2.14	117
3.2	107
5.21	130

2 Thessalonians

2.8-12	80
3.6	132
3.7	117, 219
3.9	219
3.11	132

1 Timothy

	50, 172
1.2	46, 47, 68, 217

1.10   165
2.15   94
3.2   132
3.4   133
4.1   217
5.10   118, 132
5.13   219
6.14   78

2 Timothy
    50, 172
1.2   46-7, 68, 102, 217
2.7   33
2.14   114
2.17   9
3.13   91-2
3.14   94
4.3   165

Titus
    50, 172
1.9   132, 165
1.13   132
2.1   165
3.10-11   9
3.13   106

Philemon
    31, 50, 181
1, 24   107

Hebrews
    11, 182
5.12-14   192
6.4-6   191
6.12   117
11   182
11.2   118
11.4   181
13.2   126
13.7   117, 219
13.24   220
13.25   48

James
    11, 12, 14-19
1.1   45-6, 220
2.7   108

5.13   17

1 Peter
    6, 8-9, 12, 14, 16-20, 23, 27
1.2   46
1.3ff.   40
2.9   67
2.14f.   117
3.6, 17   117
4.9   126
4.19   117
5.3   54
5.13   29, 66, 99, 220
5.14   48, 122

2 Peter
    8, 12, 14-15, 17, 27
1.2   46

1 John
1.1   75, 112, 179
1.1f.   7, 13, 21, 158, 173-4
1.1-4   143, 209
1.3   174, 198
1.4   41, 99, 226
1.5   174, 199
1.6   69, 72, 198
1.6ff.   90
1.6-10   143
1.7   72, 200
1.7-2.2   193
1.8   69, 146
1.8f.   192-3
2.1   68, 143-4, 175, 200
2.2   183, 200
2.2-3   143
2.3   179
2.3-4   198
2.3-6   199
2.3-8   179
2.3-11   75
2.4   69, 179, 193
2.5   179
2.6   93, 200
2.7   75-6, 94, 174
2.7-8   74, 143, 209, 225
2.8   182-3, 192
2.9f.   75, 193

2.11	72	3.23	76
2.12	68	3.23f.	175, 179, 199
2.12-14	143	3.23-4.5	174
2.13f.	75	3.24	179
2.14	68	4.1	69, 79, 140, 142, 146, 148, 225
2.15	205		
2.15-17	146, 183	4.1-3	79, 172, 179
2.17	183, 192, 206	4.1-6	90, 175
2.18	68, 80, 182, 218	4.2	7-8, 28, 31-2, 81-2, 84-6, 116, 172-3
2.18-22	78-82		
2.19	9, 80, 148, 164, 184	4.2f.	84, 225
2.20	174	4.3	218, 225
2.20f.	98, 146	4.4	68, 90, 98, 199, 206
2.21	68-9, 143, 224	4.4-6	183
2.22	82, 171, 173, 218, 225	4.5	80, 146, 148
2.22-23	90-1, 199	4.6	69, 80, 116, 199
2.23	95, 226	4.6-8	198
2.24	75, 93-4, 173-4, 225	4.7	192, 198, 225
2.26	90, 143	4.7-5.2	205
2.27	90, 93-4, 98, 142, 144, 146, 159, 174-5	4.8	205
		4.9	183
2.27-28	199	4.11-16	199
2.28	68, 192	4.12	116, 199
2.28-3.3	193	4.12-16	144
2.29	192, 198-9	4.13	175, 199
3	193	4.14	174, 183
3.1	68, 183, 192, 198-9	4.15	82, 173, 199
3.2	68, 182, 192, 198	4.16	183, 199, 205
3.2-3	193, 199	4.17	192-3, 196, 200
3.3, 5	200	4.20	116
3.6	198-9	4.20-5.2	205
3.6-10	116, 229	4.21	199
3.7	68, 198, 200	5.1	82, 173, 192, 198-9
3.8	75	5.1f.	183
3.8-10	197	5.2	68, 198
3.9	192, 195, 198	5.2-3	179, 199
3.10	68, 116, 198-9	5.3	76-7, 179, 225
3.11	75, 225	5.4	192, 198, 206
3.11-18	205	5.5	82, 173, 199, 206
3.12	181	5.6	19, 175
3.13	146, 183	5.6f.	211
3.14	192	5.7-8	26
3.15	198	5.10	182
3.16	183, 200	5.10-13	199
3.18	68-9	5.12	90, 192
3.19	69, 72	5.13	143
3.22	179	5.18	192, 198-9
3.22-24	199	5.19	98, 146, 183, 199

5.20	198	3–8	103–110
5.21	68	4	17, 47, 63, 67, 71–2, 102, 104,
			217, 224
2 John		5	26, 40, 105–6
I	12–3, 28–9, 31, 42, 49, 51, 52–	5–8	96
	64, 65–8, 147, 227	6	26, 70, 104–5, 106–7, 111,
I–3	39, 47–8, 64–70		118–9
I–4	224	6–10	228
2	68, 70	7	27, 107–8
3	26, 46, 51, 68–70, 104, 158	8	16, 106, 109, 156, 181
4	39, 63, 69, 71–2, 104, 198,	9	40, 109–113
	216, 227	9–10	103, 105, 110–15
4–6	71–78	10	112–5
5	40, 49, 76–7	11	40, 107, 161, 198
5–6	87, 89, 94, 148, 172	11–12	115–21
5–8	225	11–15	229
6	26, 76–7	12	26, 41, 70, 109, 112, 115,
7	7, 8, 28, 31–2, 69, 78–87, 91,		117–21, 216
	94, 148, 172, 198, 216, 218	13–14	41, 122, 226
8	16, 25, 87–90	13–15	121–3
8–9	87–95	15	39, 42, 48–9, 50–1, 122, 226
9	17, 33–4, 83, 90–95, 171, 178,		
	198	*Jude*	
9–11	32–4		9, 12, 14, 15, 17, 19–20, 23,
9–13	226		27, 30, 80, 97, 172
10	33–4, 83, 93, 131	2	46, 217
10–11	9, 15, 27, 28, 95–8, 109, 114,	3	165
	131, 149, 159, 161, 181	11	181
11	19, 88, 97		
12	41, 99, 122	*Revelation*	
12–13	98–100, 229		8, 11, 13, 15, 21, 23, 30, 59,
13	48, 54, 65–7, 99–100		61, 78, 86, 117, 153, 222
		1.1, 4	11
3 John		1–3	94
I	12–3, 26, 28, 31, 39, 46, 47,	2.2	96, 130, 132
	50–1, 52–64, 224	3.8, 10	78
I–2	101–2	12.17	78
I–5	227	14.12	78
2	26, 39, 40, 42–4	19.20	80
3	26, 39, 70, 102, 103–4, 107,	21.1	66
	109, 118–9, 224	22.7, 9	78
3f.	39	22.21	48

Ancient Authors and Sources

Aeschines, 120
Alexander of Alexandria, 15, 33
Ambrose, 8, 21, 33
'Ambrosiaster', 15, 32, 101
Amphilocius of Iconium, 15
Apostolic Constitutions, 101
Aristotle, 92
Athanasius, 15, 54
Augustine, 8, 28, 33
Ps. Augustine, *Speculum*, 28-9, 32-3, 88
Aurelius of Chullabi, 9, 27, 33

Barnabas, Epistle of, 19, 85
Beatus of Liebana, 32, 34
Bede, 1, 3, 4, 5, 14, 30, 32, 34

Cajetan, 36
Calvin, 36
Cassiodorus, 8, 19-20, 28, 31, 32
Cheltenham List (*Canon Mommsensiensis*),
    14
Chrysostom, 15-6
Ps. Chrysostom, *De Pseudoprophetis*, 16
Clement of Alexandria, 7, 8, 18-20, 29,
    31, 32, 56, 62-3, 66, 92
1 Clement, 118, 134, 165
2 Clement, 92, 117
Ps. Clement, *Homilies*, 109
Ps. Clement, *Recognitions*, 131
Cosmas Indicopleustes, 1, 3, 4, 15, 18, 35-
    6
Cyprian, 8-9, 32
Ps. Cyprian, *De Montibus Sina et Sion*, 9-
    10
Cyril of Jerusalem, 15

Decretum Damasi, 14, 35
Demetrius, *De Elocutione*, 37-8
Demosthenes, 92
Didache, 80, 96, 126-32, 134, 149
Diodore of Tarsus, 16
Diognetus, Epistle of, 117
Dionysius of Alexandria, 11, 33, 61

Ephraem, 17
Epictetus, 126

Epiphanius, 8
Erasmus, 36
Eusebius, 2, 6, 12-13, 18-20, 55-63, 66
Euthalius, 31, 32, 35
Eutychius, 54

Filastrius, 15
Firmilian, 9, 33
Ps. Fulgentius, *Pro Fide*, 34

Gregory the Great, 34
Gregory of Nazianzus, 15
Grotius, 14

Hermas, 66-7, 108, 117, 126, 130, 134-5
Ps. Hilary of Arles, 31, 34
Hippolytus, 92

Ignatius, 50-1, 97, 108, 126, 129-30, 132-4,
    146, 158, 162
Irenaeus, 7, 18-19, 32-3, 55-60, 85, 169
Isho'dad of Merv, 16-17
Isidore of Pelusium, 16
Isidore of Seville, 14

Jerome, 12-13, 16, 28, 31, 34-5, 56, 61
Josephus, 106
Junilius Africanus, 16-17

Karlstadt, 36
Bar Kochba Letters, 45, 48

Leontius of Byzantium, 16
Lucian of Samosata, 108, 129
Lucifer of Calaris, 27-8, 32-4

Muratorian Canon, 7, 20-3

Nag Hammadi Codices:
    Apocalypse of Peter, 134
    Discourse on the Eighth and the Ninth, 92
    Gospel of the Egyptians, 92
    Gospel of Philip, 10
    Gospel of Thomas, 73
    Gospel of Truth, 10, 194
    Interpretation of Knowledge, 92, 133

Odes of Solomon, 66
Oecumenius, 14, 31, 32, 85
O.G.I.S., 92
Optatus, 33
Origen, 11-12, 129, 134

Palladius, 16
Papyri Editions:
  BGU, 38-41, 43-4
  P. Fay., 47, 70
  P. Lond., 93
  P. Mich., 42-3
  P. Oslo, 40, 119
  P. Oxy., 43, 119
Papias, 5, 6, 12-13, 55-64, 150-3
'Paul', *3 Corinthians*, 98
Peter, Apocalypse of, 19, 80
Photius, 19-20
Plutarch, 111

Polycarp, 6, 7, 54, 60, 79, 81, 106
Priscillian, 28, 32

Qumran Literature, 73

Rufinus, 11-12, 15, 20

Seneca, 37, 43
Severian, (Ps. Chrysostom, *De qua potestate*), 15, 35
Strabo, 31
Suidas, 16

Tertullian, 8, 22, 32, 85
Theodore of Mopsuestia, 16
Theodoret of Cyr, 17

Ps. Vigilius, *C. Varimardum*, 34
Vincent of Lerins, 33

Modern Authors

Abbott, E. A., 86
Aland, K., 2, 24

Bacon, B. W., 60-61
Bagnani, G., 129
Bardy, G., 15
Barrett, C. K., 18, 48, 133, 179, 197, 202-3
Bartlet, V., 101
Bauer, W., 155
Becker, J., 75, 93, 179, 210-2, 215
Belser, J. E., 150
Benner, A. R. & Fobes, F. H., 46
Berger, K., 47, 51, 102
Bergmeier, R., 70, 171-2
Best, E., 2
Betz, H. D., 129
Beutler, J., 118
Bogart, J. L., 192, 198, 208
Boismard, M-E., 208
Bonnard, P., 190
Borgen, P., 189
Boring, M. E., 141, 202
Bornkamm, G,. 53, 58-61, 128, 152
Bousset, W., 79, 91, 123, 142
Boyle, J. L., 210-1
Braun, H., 81, 82, 200
Brooke, A. E., 10, 29, 83, 85, 105, 119, 121, 152, 169
Brown, R. E., 4, 63, 68, 70, 77, 83, 85, 89, 94, 109, 111, 112, 139, 141, 143, 147, 153, 164, 190, 208, 213-5
Brown, R. E. & Meier, J., 134
Bruns, J. E., 10
Buchanon, E. S., 20
Büchsel, F., 69, 109
Bultmann, R., 69, 71, 75, 81, 85, 86, 89, 91, 94, 116, 151, 155, 164, 178, 189, 195, 196

Campenhausen, H. v., 7, 98, 136, 142, 152, 154, 157
Cassem, N. H., 80
Chadwick, H., 134
Chapman, J., 72, 101, 107, 150
Conzelmann, H., 75, 94, 171-2, 196
Corell, A., 190

Corssen, P., 8
Cramer, J. A., 16
Cullmann, O., 182
Culpepper, R. A., 63

Dahl, N. A., 178
Danielou, J., 108
Deissmann, A., 38, 49, 53, 107, 118
Delling, G., 132
Denzinger, H., 36
Dibelius, M., 204
Dix, G., 61
Dodd, C. H., 55, 71, 77, 85, 115, 151, 169-71, 174-5, 192
Dölger, F. J., 65
Donfried, K. P., 54, 152-3, 210
Donovan, J., 61
Doty, W. G., 37
Dunn, J., 212

Ebrard, J. H. A., 65, 108
Ehrhardt, A., 8, 21, 58, 113, 131, 134, 159
Evans, C. F., 93
Exler, F. X. J., 42, 44-6

Feuillet, A., 66
Filson, F. V., 132
Fischer, B., 25, 26
Fitzmyer, J. A., 45-6, 48
Frankemölle, H., 134
Funk, F. W., 40, 41, 44
Furnish, V., 75

Gamble, H., 48-9
Gaugler, E., 65, 91, 152, 193
Gibbins, H. J., 66
Goguel, M., 114, 151
Gore, C., 81, 84
Grässer, E., 186
Grant, R. M., 66
Grayston, K., 89, 110, 153, 167, 209
Greeven, H., 128
Grundmann, W., 117
Gunther, J. J., 11, 19, 59
Gustafsson, A., 59
Gwynn, J., 17

Haenchen, E., 54, 67, 89, 109, 114, 119, 150, 152, 169, 213-4
Hahn, F., 80, 186
Hall, D., 109
Hanse, H., 91
Hanson, R. P. C., 9, 60
Harnack, A. v., 14, 26, 56, 89, 95, 97-8, 104, 106-7, 110, 112, 123, 125, 127, 143-4, 150-4
Harris, J. R., 42, 44, 65, 88
Harrisville, R. A., 73, 75
Harvey, A. E., 53
Hauschildt, H., 53
Heise, J., 155, 164
Hercher, R., 46
Héring, J., 174
Hesse, F. H., 22
Hill, D., 142
Hirsch, E., 46
Hock, R., 126
Holmberg, B., 133
Holtzmann, H. J., 81, 85, 89, 169
Hornschuh, M., 63
Horvath, T., 115
Hoskyns, E. C., 7, 73, 137
Houlden, J. L., 50, 54, 116, 151-2, 155, 175, 193, 208
Howard, W. F., 169-70
Howorth, H., 36
Hyldahl, N., 65

Johnston, G., 140-1, 172
Jonge, M. de, 168, 185, 189-90, 199, 211
Judge, E. A., 126

Käsemann, E., 2, 4, 53, 113, 153-5, 178, 204-5
Katz, P., 23
Kelly, J. N. D., 14, 31
Kihn, H., 17
Kim, C-H., 37, 41, 119
Kimelman, R., 187
Klein, G., 182, 211
Klijn, A. F. J. & Reinink, G., 82
Kötting, B., 13
Koschkorke, K., 133
Koskenniemi, H., 42-5, 48

Kragerud, A., 63, 128, 138-9, 141, 151, 172
Kretschmar, G., 127-9, 141, 151
Kuhl, J., 185
Kummel, W. G., 14, 36

Lagrange, M-J., 23
Lake, K., 129-30
Langdon, S., 105
Larfeld, W., 61
Lattke, M., 204
Law, R., 169, 199
Leipoldt, J., 17, 20, 36
Leroy, H., 187-8
Lewis, A. S., 17
Lieu, J. M., 45-7, 51, 81-2, 90, 193-4, 199, 209
Lightfoot, J. B., 57, 58
Lindars, B., 120, 137, 188
Loewenich, W. v., 165
Lorenzen, T., 138
Lücke, F., 65, 108

McHugh, J., 66
Maclean, A. J., 17
Malherbe, A. J., 119, 157
Manson, T. W., 26
Marshall, I. H., 85
Martyn, J. L., 187, 214
Matsunaga, K., 213
Mattill, A. J., 208
Mayser, E., 112
Meecham, H., 42, 84
Meeks, W., 79, 142-3, 145, 147, 162, 186-7, 214
Ménard, J. E., 108
Metzger, B. M., 17
Michel, O., 97
Mingana, A., 61
Moffatt, J., 97, 169, 175, 199
Moule, C. F. D., 23, 192
Moulton, J. H., 105
Moulton, J. H. & Milligan, G., 42
Müller, M., 18
Müller, U. B., 208, 212
Munck, J., 57, 62
Mussner, F., 139, 203

Nauck, W., 75, 175, 192

Oepke, A., 67
Onuki, T., 186

Pagels, E., 134
Painter, J., 211
Pape, D., 65
Pardee, D., 48
Plummer, A., 85
Plumpe, J. C., 65
Poland, F., 53, 111
Potterie, I. de la, 75, 109

Quispel, G., 73, 108

Rand, J. A. du, 223
Regul, J., 59
Reiling, J., 128, 134
Resseguie, J. L., 214
Richards, W. L., 24-5
Richter, G., 162, 205, 212, 215
Robert, L., 118
Robinson, J. A., 44
Robinson, J. M., 40, 163
Roller, O., 37-8
Rordorf, W., 126, 129
Ruwet, J., 11, 20

Salom, A. P., 169
Sanday, W., 14, 20
Sanders, E. P., 1, 163
Sanders, J. N., 165
Schepens, P., 9
Schlier, H., 75
Schnackenburg, R., 38, 46, 50, 57, 70, 71, 79, 85, 89, 94, 114, 119, 136, 143, 150, 174-5
Schoedel, W., 133, 159
Schottroff, L., 183
Schubert, P., 40
Schulz, A., 203
Schunack, G., 99, 164
Schwartz, E., 52, 84
Schweizer, E., 16, 54, 105, 126, 165, 178, 201
Scroggs, R., 147
Segovia, F., 179, 186

Selwyn, E. C., 53, 86
Sherk, R. K., 50
Smalley, S. S., 85, 208
Smith, D. M., 136, 141, 161
Snyder, G., 138
Soden, H. F. v., 9, 89
Souter, A., 32
Staab, K., 16
Stählin, G., 91
Stanton, G., 129
Steen, H. A., 40
Stendahl, K., 23
Stenzel, M., 11, 12
Strathmann, H., 118
Strecker, G., 85, 110, 155
Stuhlmacher, P., 97, 132
Sundberg, A. C., 21
Swete, H. B., 59

Tarelli, C., 170
Theissen, G., 125, 127-8, 131, 133, 142
Thiele, W., 24-30
Thüsing, W., 85
Thyen, H., 110, 141, 157, 210-1, 215
Tregelles, S. P., 20, 22-3
Treu, K., 119
Trites, A., 118
Turner, C. H., 14, 85
Turner, N., 44, 68, 93

Vallée, G., 58
Vassal-Phillips, O. R., 33
Vermes, G., 181

Weiss, B., 106, 108
Weiss, K., 144
Wendt, H. H., 75, 93, 155
Westcott, B. F., 3, 15, 20-3, 32, 36, 71, 77, 81, 84, 89, 94, 121, 150
Whitacre, R., 168
White, J. L., 37, 40-1, 49
Wilamowitz-Möllendorf, U. v., 102
Wilcox, M., 181
Williams, R. R., 85
Wilson, B., 147-8
Wilson, R. Mcl., 10
Wilson, W. G., 169

Windisch, H., 85, 89, 91
Wisse, F., 80, 97, 167
Woll, D. B., 176

Zahn, T., 10-11, 15, 17, 22-3, 28-9, 57
Ziemann, F., 44
Zimmermann, A., 125, 128

Subjects

For all references to ancient authors and sources and also to Biblical books, excluding general references to the Johannine literature, see the appropriate indexes. See also the references given for particular words and themes in Appendix I.

Abiding, 93-4, 171-3, 178, 198-9, 201-2 (*see* 2 Jn 9)
Alogi, 8
Antichrist, 7, 78-80, 87, 90, 97, 107, 146 (*see* 1 Jn 2.18, 22; 4.3; 2 Jn 7)
Antidocetism, 81-2, 85, 86-7, 200, 204, 208, 210-11
Apostles, 96, 126-7, 130, 133, 151-2 (*see* prophet-teachers); in John, 137, 213
Asia Minor, 65, 96, 118, 131; Elders in, 55-7, 60, 151; John the Apostle in, 55-6
Authority, in early church, 127-8, 133-5; 'patriarchal', 150, 152-3; in Johannine thought, 140-5, 154, 156-7; claimed by Diotrephes, 111-12, 115, 135, 150-5, 158; claimed by the Elder, 55, 70, 99f., 111-13, 115, 123, 135, 150-4, 157-8, 163
Authorship of Johannine writings, 1, 11-14, 29, 30-1, 35, 57, 124, 148, 155, 168-70

Beginning, from the, 75-7, 93-4, 143-4, 172-6, 180-1, 189, 208-9
Belief, 82, 168, 173, 191 (*see* confession)
Beloved Disciple, 137-41, 157, 211, 215
Brethren, 96, 103-9, 111-14, 121, 128, 135, 154-6, 158-60, 165 (*see* 3 Jn 3, 5f.)

Canon, 2 and 3 John in, 5-36 *passim*; significance of, 2-3, 35-6, 165, 216
Catholic (canonical) Epistles, in the canon, 11, 12, 14, 15-18, 19, 20, 23-4, 27-8, 31; as Epistles, 40, 99; and prophet-teachers, 127
Charismatics; charismatic gifts, 56, 60, 125, 127, 130, 134, 154 (*see* prophet-teachers)
'Children', 63, 67-8, 71-2, 89, 99, 102, 104, 144, 158 (*see* 2 Jn 1, 4; 3 Jn 4); of God, 68, 183, 192-3, 198-9
Church, in Johannine thought, 63, 66, 136ff., 181-90, 191-4, 204, 207; in 2 John, 51, 67, 147; in 3 John, 105, 110f., 114, 135 (*see* 3 Jn 6, 9)
Command, 72-8, 87, 96, 137, 143, 146, 167, 172-4, 178-80, 193, 198, 209, 211
Confession, 96, 173, 176, 191, 200; in 1 Jn 4.2, 81-3; in 2 Jn 7, 84-7 (*see* 2 Jn 7)

Demetrius, 115, 117-21, 160, 163 (*see* 3 Jn 12)
Diotrephes, 103, 105, 111-15, 123, 149-60, 162-3 (*see* 3 Jn 9)
Disciples in John, 74, 136-7, 139, 142, 176-8, 185-6, 189, 195-7, 202-3, 213
Dualism, 69, 73, 84, 87, 145, 175, 184, 194, 212

Egypt, 11, 44, 54, 96, 161
Elder, The, 30-1, 52-64, 99, 110-15, 123, 141, 149-60, 163 (*see* 2 Jn 1; 3 Jn 1; John the Elder)
Elders, in Jewish and Graeco-Roman world, 53; in local church, 53-4, 152; as 'disciples of the Apostles', 55; in Papias, 55-7, 60-1, 150-3; in Irenaeus and Clement, 55-6, 58-60, 62-3, 152; authority of, 56, 60, 151-3 (*see* John the Elder)
'Elect Lady', 31, 42, 51-2, 65-7, 100, 147 (*see* 2 Jn 1)
Ephesus, Gospel of John in, 161; home of 'John', 56, 59, 62, 99; tomb of 'John' at, 5, 13, 61 (*see* Asia Minor)

Eschatology, in John, 188, 194, 196-7, 205-7; in 1 John, 192-3, 208-9, 211; in 2 John, 88; and appearance of false teachers, 80, 90, 97, 142, 182

Exclusivism, 98, 145, 147, 159-60, 162, 181, 184, 205

Falsehood, 69, 83

False prophets, 79-80, 83, 88, 140, 142, 172 (see 1 Jn 4.1; 2 Jn 7)

False teachers, in Johannine Epistles, 8off., 89-90, 91, 97f., 100, 146, 191, 207-9; in 2 John, 83-7, 93, 95-7, 100, 149; in Ignatius, 97, 130, 159; in Pastoral Epistles, 132; in early church, 130-1

Fellowship, 97, 99, 109, 114

Gaius, 42, 54, 101-3, 106, 110-11, 123, 163-4 (see 3 Jn 1)

Gnosticism, and John, 155, 188, 194; as heresy behind 1 and 2 John, 81-2, 87, 91; use of 1 John, 10; as an elite within the church, 133-4; progress in, 91-2

God, in 3 John, 107, 116, 123, 198; 'of God', 76, 90, 98, 116, 146, 160, 188, 191, 194-5

Hospitality, 117, 119, 126, 129, 131-2, 135; denial of, 34, 97, 131f.; in 2 John, 95, 97, 100, 114, 135, 149, 181; in 3 John, 105, 112-14, 135

Household churches, 3, 65, 97, 132-4, 162-3

Individualism in Johannine thought, 73, 142, 146, 207

Jesus, in John, 177-9, 186-90, 194-7, 201-5, 206-7, 212; in 1 John, 82, 175-6, 199-200, 208-9, 212; in 2 John, 70, 77, 84-5, 94, 198; in 3 John, 198; in false teachers, 81-2, 84-6, 207-8

Jews in John, 168, 185-7, 188-9, 212-13

Johannine Christianity, 72, 87, 100, 104, 119, 139-40, 147, 149, 153, 161, 166, 205; isolation of, 73, 145-7, 161-2, 165, 184, 187, 190, 205, 207; as a sect, 147

Johannine community(ies), 69, 73-7, 99f., 123f., 138, 153-4, 166, 181, 207; history of, 165, 166-8, 187, 196-7, 203, 207-8, 212-14

Johannine school, 6, 63, 141

Johannine tradition, 3-4, 63, 100, 125, 135, 149, 153, 162, 166, 210-12; in 2 John, 47, 70, 74-6, 86-7, 90-1, 99, 157, 164, 216; in 3 John, 102, 116f., 120-1, 123, 155-7, 160, 164, 216

John the Apostle, as author of Gospel, 8, 11, 13, 19, 21, 169-70; as author of 1 John, 8, 11-14, 21, 27; as author of 1 and 2 John, 9, 27-9, 33; as author of 2 and 3 John, 1, 5, 11-12, 14-15, 19, 150, 153; as author of Revelation, 8, 11-12, 170; in Asia, 56, 59, 61 (see John the Elder)

John the Elder, in Papias, 12-13, 55-7, 61-2, 64; as disciple of Apostle John, 61; confused with Apostle John, 56-7; as teacher of Papias, 6, 58-9; as author of Revelation, 13, 61; as author of 2 and 3 John, 5, 12-14, 35-6, 56, 61, 151

Latin version, 23-8, 31-2, 34, 88, 97

Letters, opening greetings in, 38, 44-48, 50, 102; health wish in, 39, 43-4, 50, 102; thanksgivings in, 39-40; exchange of greetings in, 39, 41; farewell in, 38, 48; conventions in, 40, 42, 65, 70, 99, 102, 122; style in, 112

Letters, literary, 46-7; of recommendation, 41, 119, 130; contrasted with Epistles, 49

Love, 26, 47, 68-70, 72-7, 103-4, 137, 139, 183, 193, 204 (see command)

Mission, in Johannine thought, 163, 182, 184-6, 206; in 3 John, 106-7, 109, 113, 117, 128, 156, 181; by false teachers, 80, 83-4, 107, 146, 183; and the Elder, 123, 151-2, 154

Name, the, 107-8

Old Testament, 181-2, 188-9

Parthians, Epistle to the, 28-9
Paul, letters of, 21-2, 31, 34, 37, 39-41, 47, 49-50, 100, 132
Peter, 137-40, 157, 196, 203
Presbyter(s), *see* Elder(s)
Prophet-teachers, 50, 60, 96, 125f., 134, 141-2, 151, 154, 156; in *Didache*, 96, 126-31; in Origen, 129; authority of, 127-9, 134, 151; problems caused by, 129-30; testing of, 96, 130-2 (*see* Apostles; charismatics)
Prophetic ministry in Johannine church, 140-2, 151, 154
Proteus Peregrinus, 129

Rebaptism, appeal to 2 John for, 9, 33
Redaction theories (John), 75, 93, 179-80, 208, 210-13, 215

Schism in Johannine community, 80, 83, 95, 148, 153-4, 157, 168, 184, 190, 196, 207f., 212
Sin, 146, 183, 192-3, 197, 200, 202, 207, 209-10
Spirit, in Johannine thought, 137, 139-43, 154-5, 172, 174-80, 185, 189, 195, 200, 202-3, 206, 208-9; absence in 2 and 3 John, 83-4, 141-2, 154, 172; testing, 79, 82-3, 90, 94, 130, 148, 172; spirit of error, 80, 82, 84, 172, 175
Synagogue, *see* Jews
Syria, christianity in, 96, 131
Syriac church, Johannine Epistles in, 10, 17-18, 24

Teaching, 83, 93-4, 96, 142, 171, 174, 198 (*see* 2 Jn 9)
Tradition, in Johannine thought, 70, 72, 74-7, 90, 94-5, 98, 143-6, 148-9, 171-80, 181, 191, 206; in early church, 58, 98, 165, 172
Truth, 47, 68-72, 102-4, 109, 117, 119-20, 160-1, 172, 175, 189, 194, 201, 212

'We', in Johannine tradition, 112, 120, 144, 157, 187; in 1 John, 143-4, 174, 182; in 3 John, 112-13, 120-1, 123
Witness, 21, 26, 104, 118-21, 137, 143-5, 156-8, 174, 176, 180, 182, 189, 211
Word, 93, 143-4, 173-4, 178-9, 189, 202-3, 206, 209
World, 74, 83-4, 86, 90, 98, 145-6, 148, 182-90, 191-2, 194, 206, 210